Amelia Cole and the IMPOSSIBLE FATE

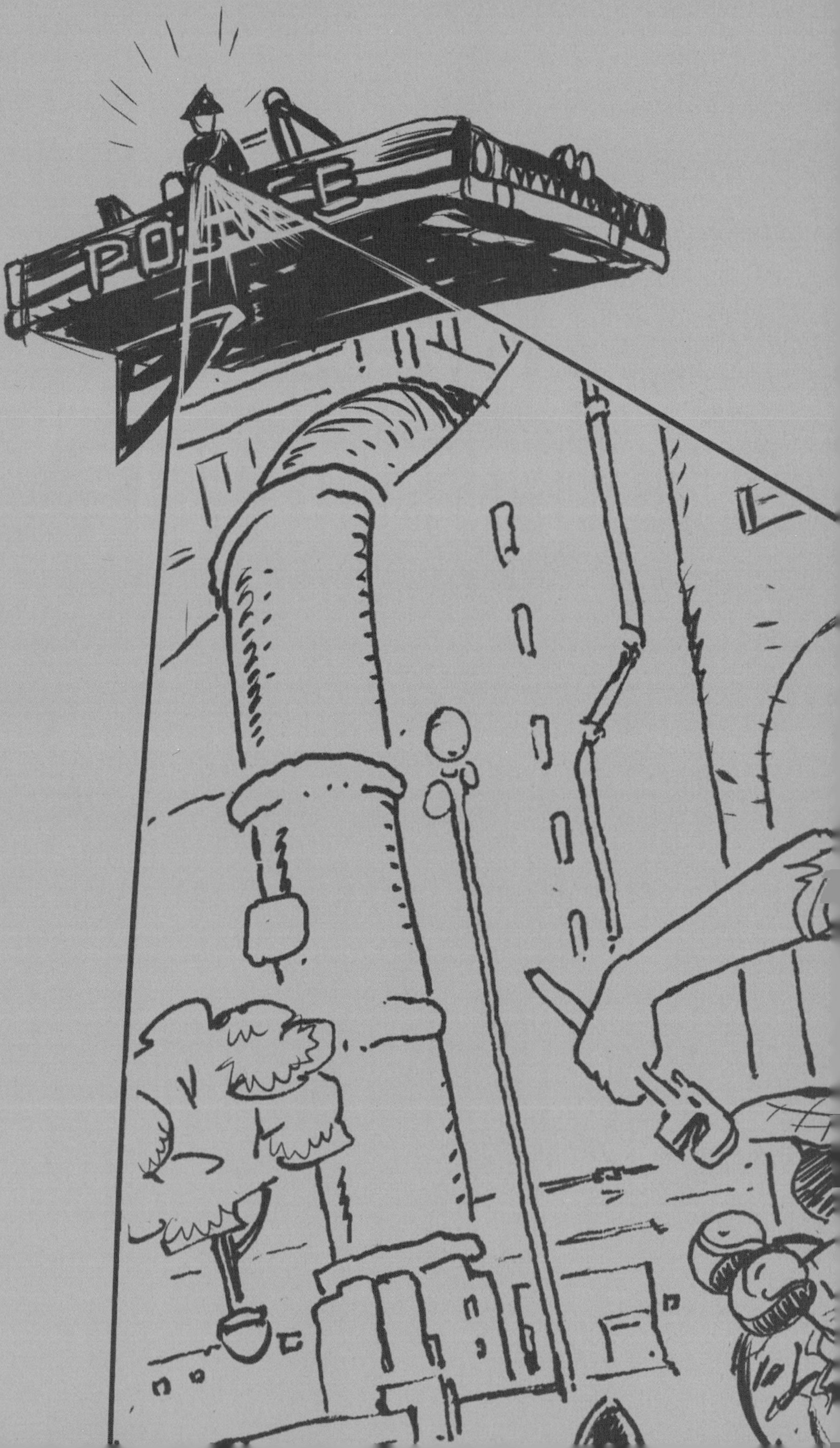

WRITERS
ADAM P. KNAVE & D.J. KIRKBRIDE

ARTIST + COLORIST
NICK BROKENSHIRE

LETTERER
RACHEL DEERING

LETTERER—ISSUE 24
FRANK CVETKOVIC

TRADE DESIGNER
DYLAN TODD

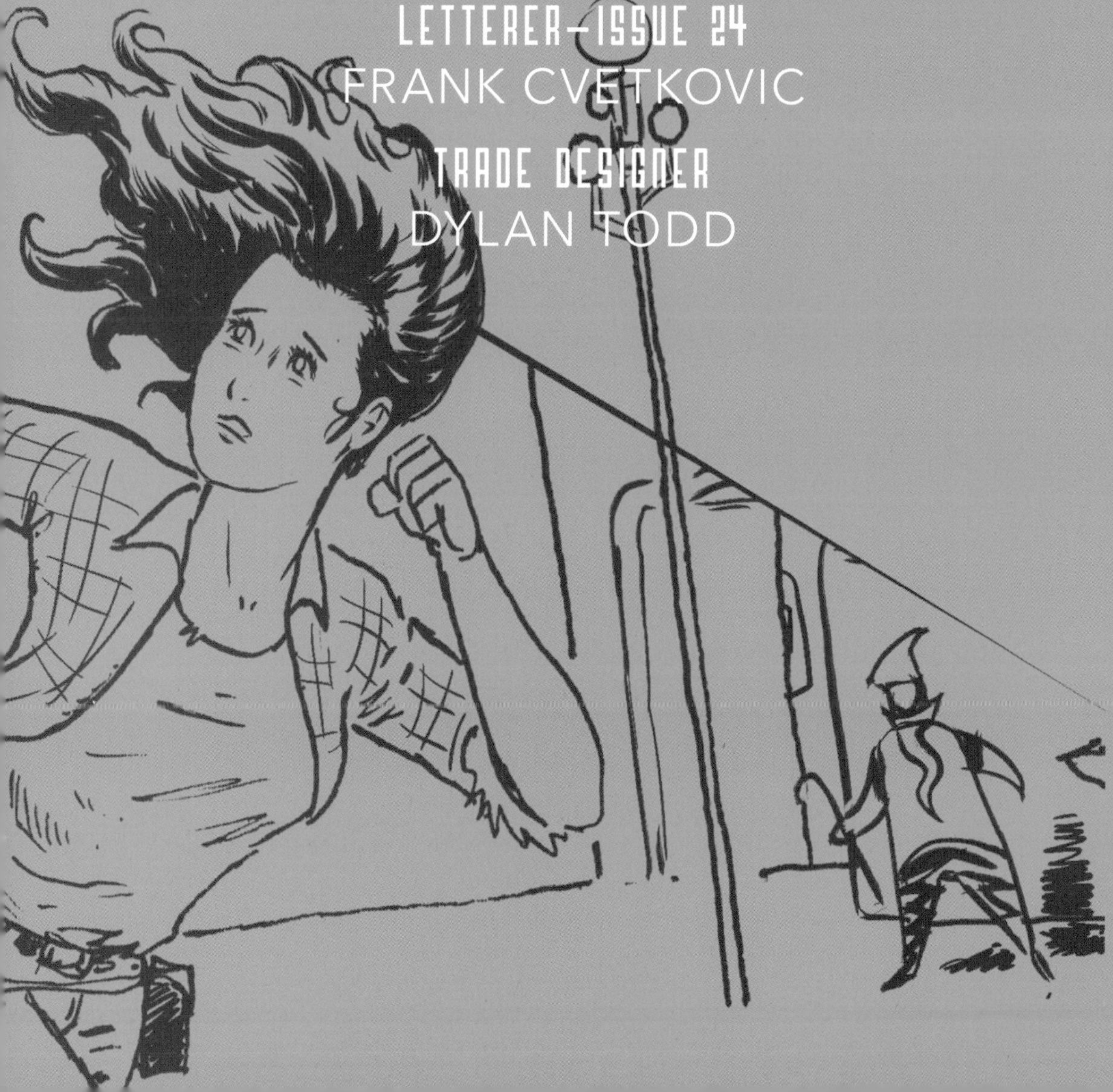

GET ALL THE ADVENTURES OF AMELIA COLE

VOLUME 1 *AMELIA COLE AND THE UNKNOWN WORLD*

VOLUME 2 *AMELIA COLE AND THE HIDDEN WAR*

VOLUME 3 *AMELIA COLE AND THE ENEMY UNLEASHED*

VOLUME 4 *AMELIA COLE AND THE IMPOSSIBLE FATE*

...AND MORE TO COME!

ISBN: 978-1-63140-422-1

18 17 16 15   1 2 3 4

IDW

www.IDWPUBLISHING.com
IDW founded by Ted Adams, Alex Garner, Kris Oprisko, and Robbie Robbins

Ted Adams, CEO & Publisher
Greg Goldstein, President & COO
Robbie Robbins, EVP/Sr. Graphic Artist
Chris Ryall, Chief Creative Officer/Editor-in-Chief
Matthew Ruzicka, CPA, Chief Financial Officer
Alan Payne, VP of Sales
Dirk Wood, VP of Marketing
Lorelei Bunjes, VP of Digital Services
Jeff Webber, VP of Digital Publishing & Business Development

Facebook: facebook.com/idwpublishing
Twitter: @idwpublishing
YouTube: youtube.com/idwpublishing
Tumblr: tumblr.idwpublishing.com
Instagram: instagram.com/idwpublishing

Originally published digitally by Monkeybrain Comics as AMELIA COLE issues #19–24.

INTRODUCTION

When I was a kid, there were no comic retailers near me, and digital comics… well… the very idea of something like that was pure science fiction. Issues of *Fantastic Four* or *Batman* were purchased at newsstands, where you hoped you'd find the follow-up issue the next month, so you'd know how the story concluded. In some cases, I had to wait years to find out how a story ended. That's what it was like in the good old days, when the sight of "still only 35 cents" filled you with a sense of dread, because it meant the price of comic books was about to go up.

There was no Internet back in those days, and comic book journalism/criticism largely consisted of talking to the one other kid you knew who read comics—that fellow nerd, who kept their comic-loving identity on the down-low, for fear of getting a wedgie on the playground. Seriously, there was a time when an open love for comics meant you either got wedgies, or you learned to fight. And yet the love of comics endured, and it was shared with the handful of other people that thrilled to the larger-than-life adventures that graced the pages of whatever comic you could get your hands on.

With the price of comics lower in those days, and options limited to whatever was on the stands, you were apt to take more chances and try titles you'd never heard of, or never read before. Sometimes you had 35 cents burning a hole in your pocket, and you just had to have a comic book, and there was only one title available on the stand. Seriously, this happened to me once, and it's how I discovered one of my favorite comics of all time, *Skull the Slayer.* Or maybe that friend who read comics would tell you about something cool they'd bought, and you'd rush to the newsstand, hoping there was another copy (this is how I discovered *X-Men*).

When I first started reading *Amelia Cole*, it reminded me of my old days of collecting comics, when I might take a chance for whatever reason, and stumble across something that turned out to be truly great. That's what happened, when I got my iPad, and went shopping for digital comics for the first time. Now, in all fairness, I'd already met *Amelia Cole* co-writer D.J. Kirkbride at that point, and I also knew the folks at Monkeybrain Comics, so my first digital purchases were all Monkeybrain titles. At that time, I had no idea what titles I would like, nor could I imagine that twenty-something issues later, I'd still be reading *Amelia Cole.* My only real complaint was that the series was digital, so I couldn't simply hand a copy to my friends (sending links simply isn't as personal). That did not, however, stop me from singing the praises of Adam, D.J. and Nick's incredible work.

Something about those first issues of *Amelia Cole and the Unknown World* pulled me, and kept me coming back for more. Since you're reading this introduction, I'm going to assume that you are already familiar with the adventures of Amelia Cole. Maybe that's being a bit presumptuous— maybe this is your introduction to *Amelia Cole*, even though it is the fourth trade paperback collection. Maybe you're the sort of person that likes to start with something more recent, and work your way backward. And if that's the case, hey, more power to you, and I apologize for jumping to the conclusion that you're already a fan of this series. But trust me, even if this is your first foray into the world of *Amelia Cole*, you're going to love it here.

Whether you discovered this series in its original digital format, picked up one of the earlier trade paperback collections, or are just now embarking on an incredible journey, I applaud you for taking a chance and venturing away from the mainstream realm of superhero comics. Within these pages is the sense of discovery that makes for the best comic book reading.

DAVID F. WALKER

David F. Walker is a writer. His credits include Cyborg *for DC Comics,* Number 13 *for Dark Horse Comics, and* Shaft *for Dynamite Entertainment. He is a Sagittarius.*

PREVIOUSLY

Things look bleak for our hero Amelia Cole. She started out tossed into an unknown world, and then found her way into an all-out war. Worse yet, it's a war she seems to have lost. Along with her one-time foe, Hector, she's been tossed into the space between worlds by the evil Council!

Now she and Hector must figure out where they each are and how to rejoin the battle. Meanwhile, Omega Company and Amelia's pal Lemmy are all that's left to defend Amelia's new home against insurmountable odds.

Can these far-flung heroes hope to survive their impossible fate?

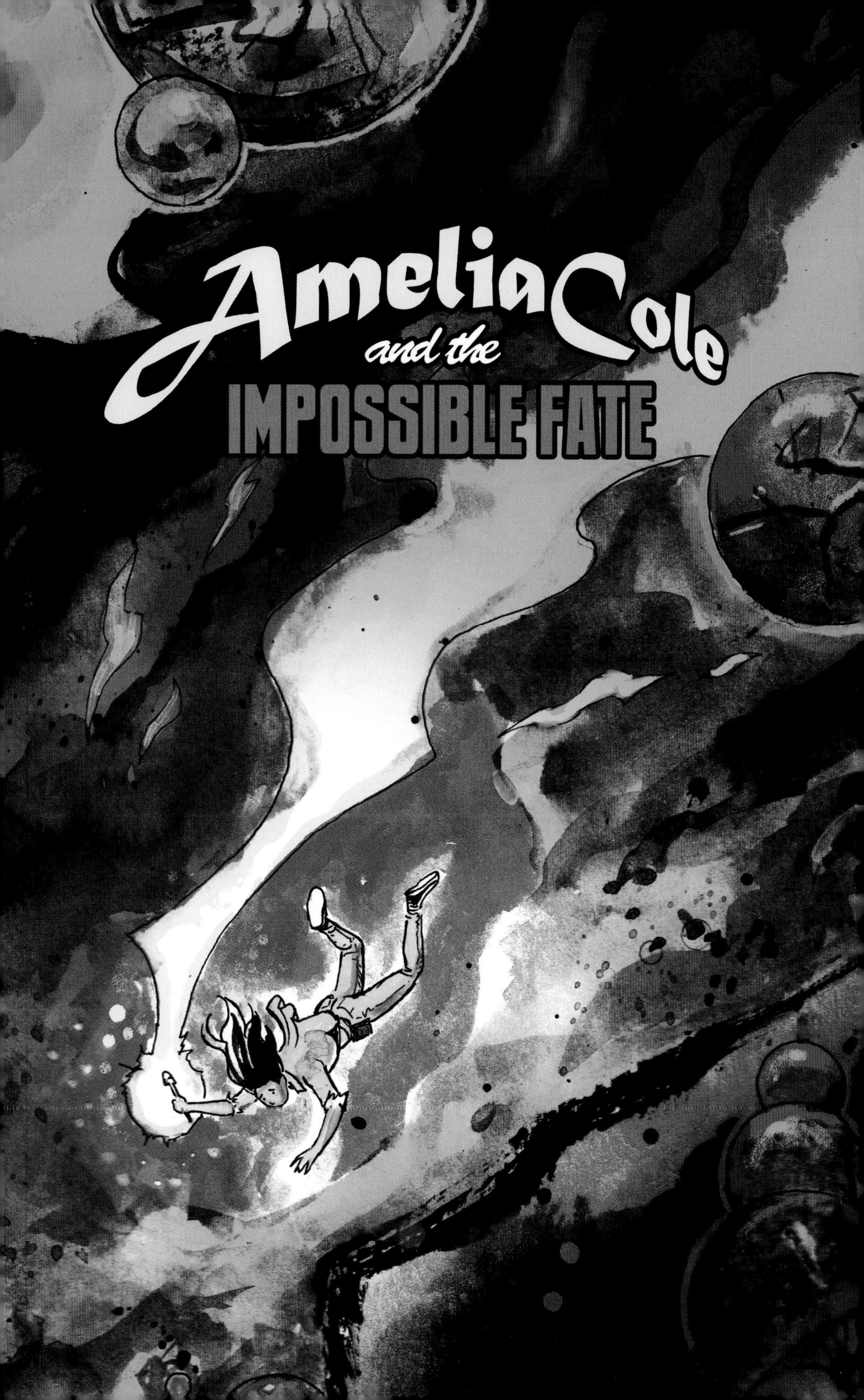
Amelia Cole
and the
IMPOSSIBLE FATE

CHAPTER 1

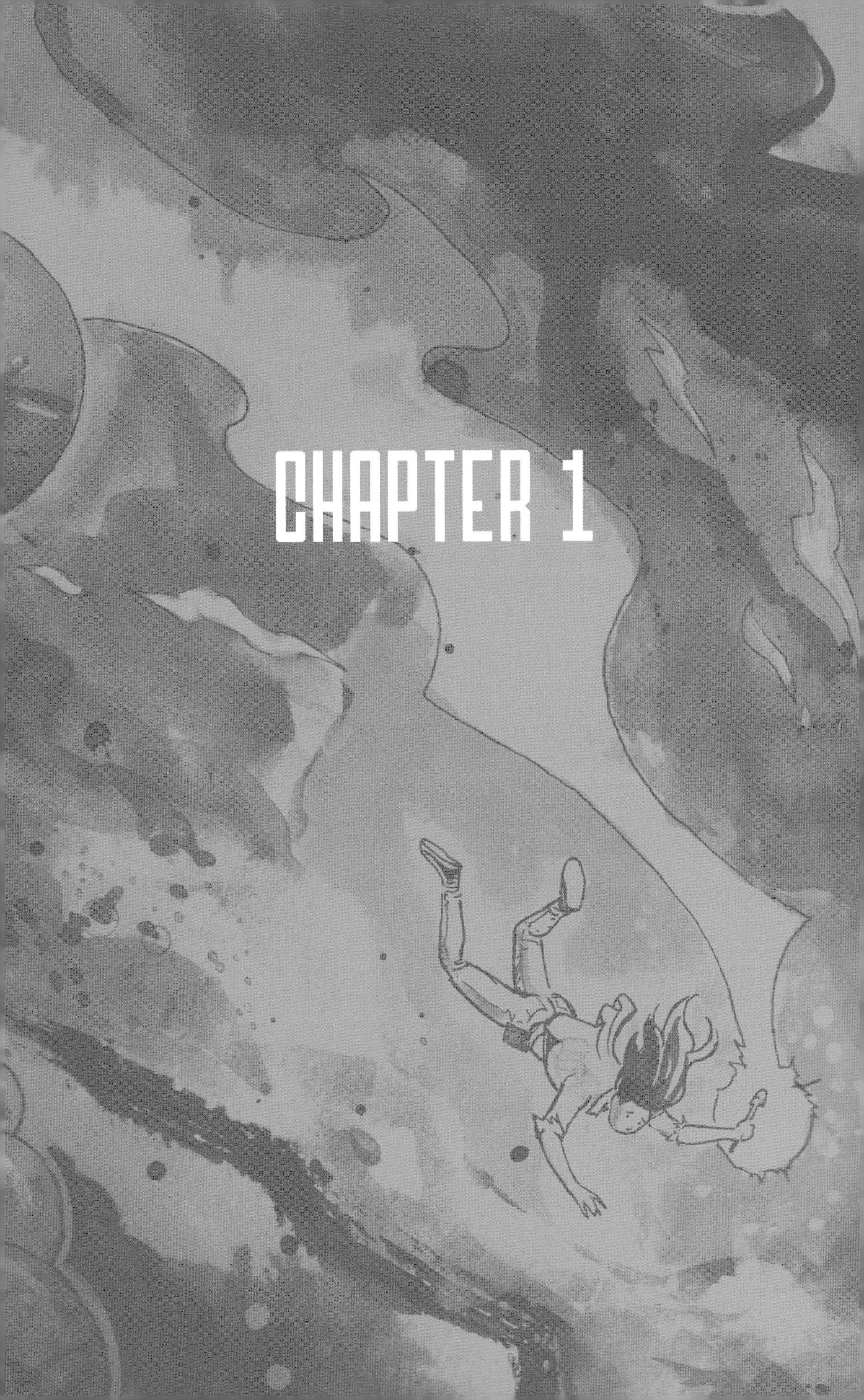

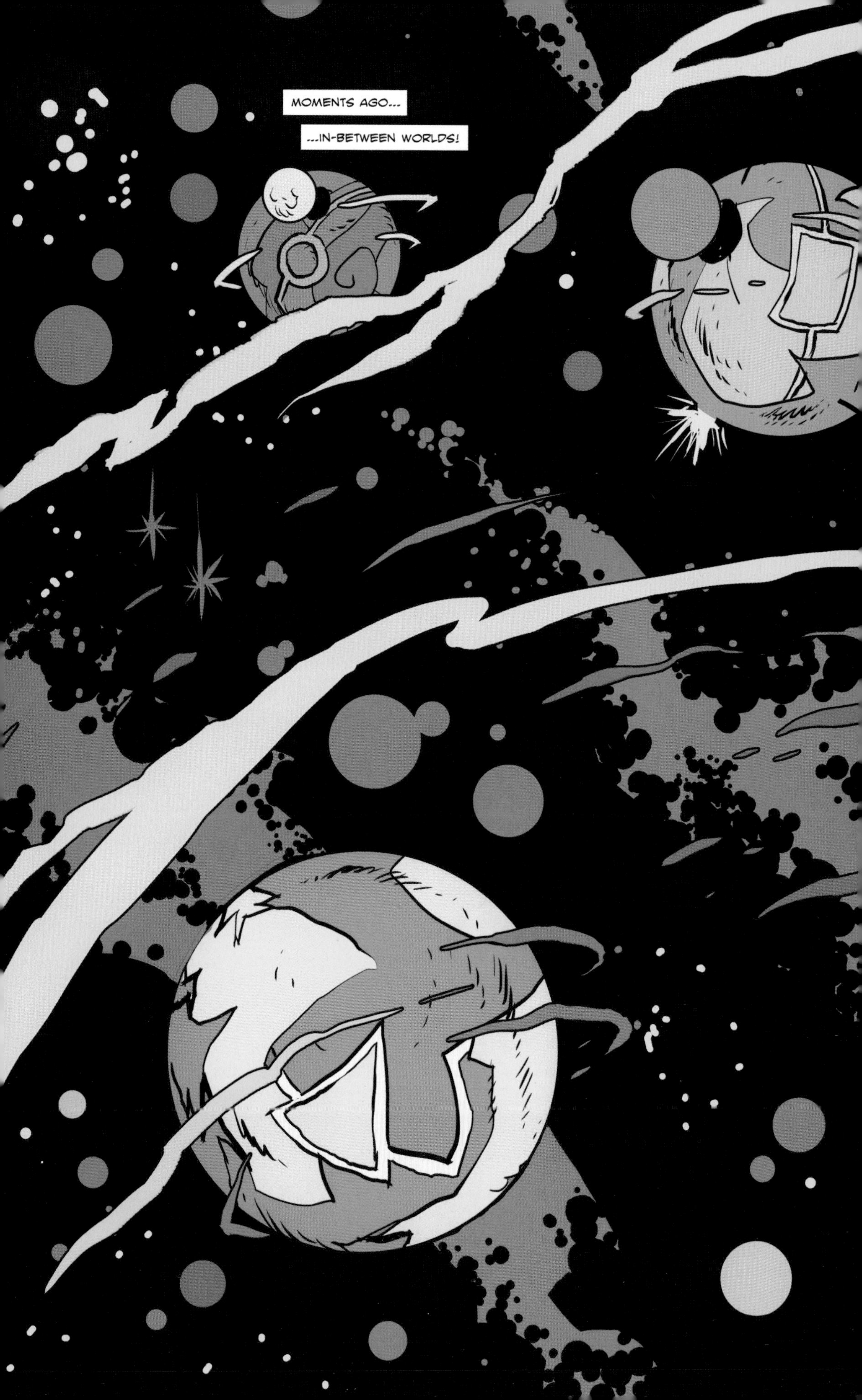
MOMENTS AGO...
...IN-BETWEEN WORLDS!

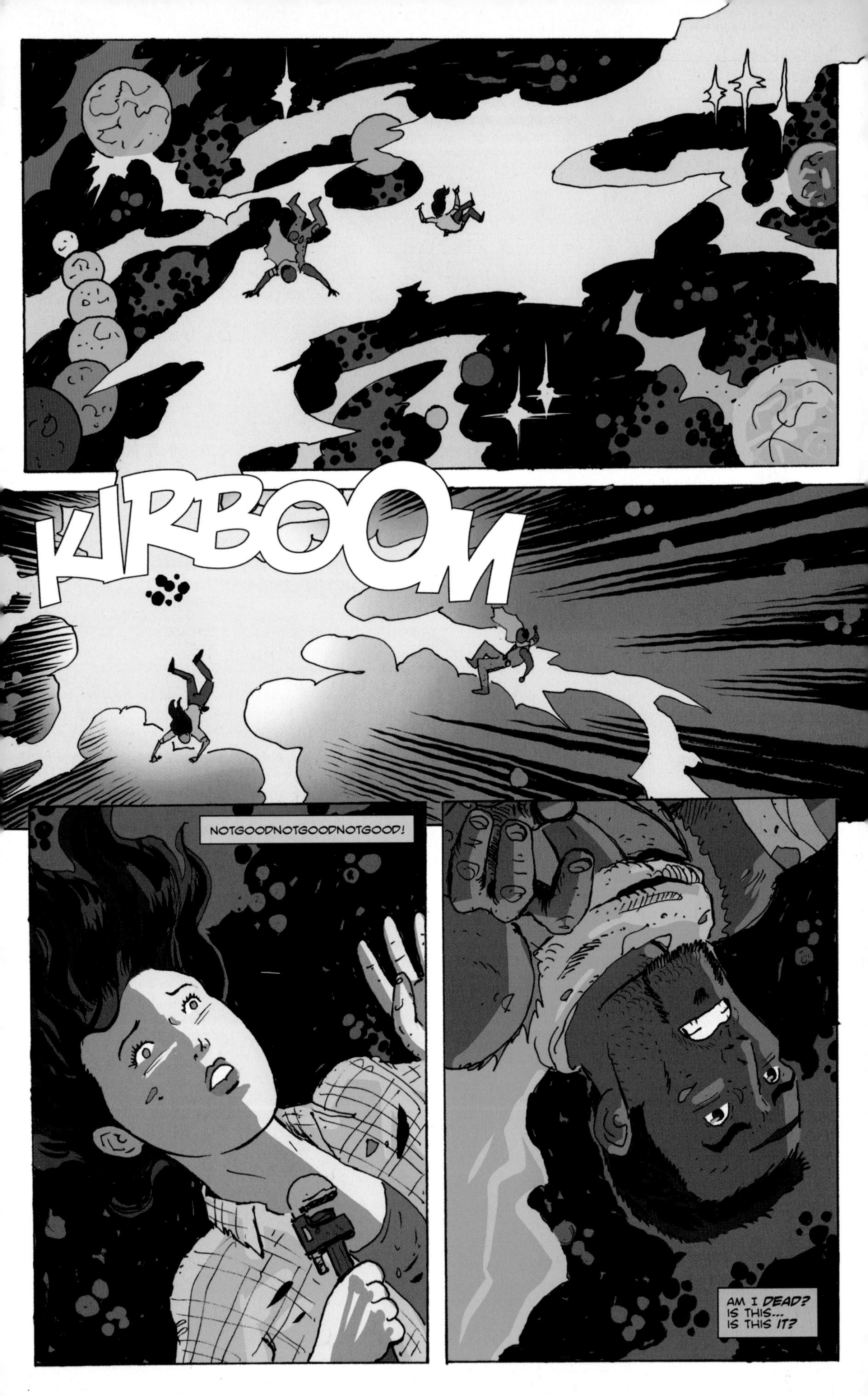
KIRBOOM
NOTGOODNOTGOODNOTGOOD!
AM I DEAD? IS THIS... IS THIS IT?

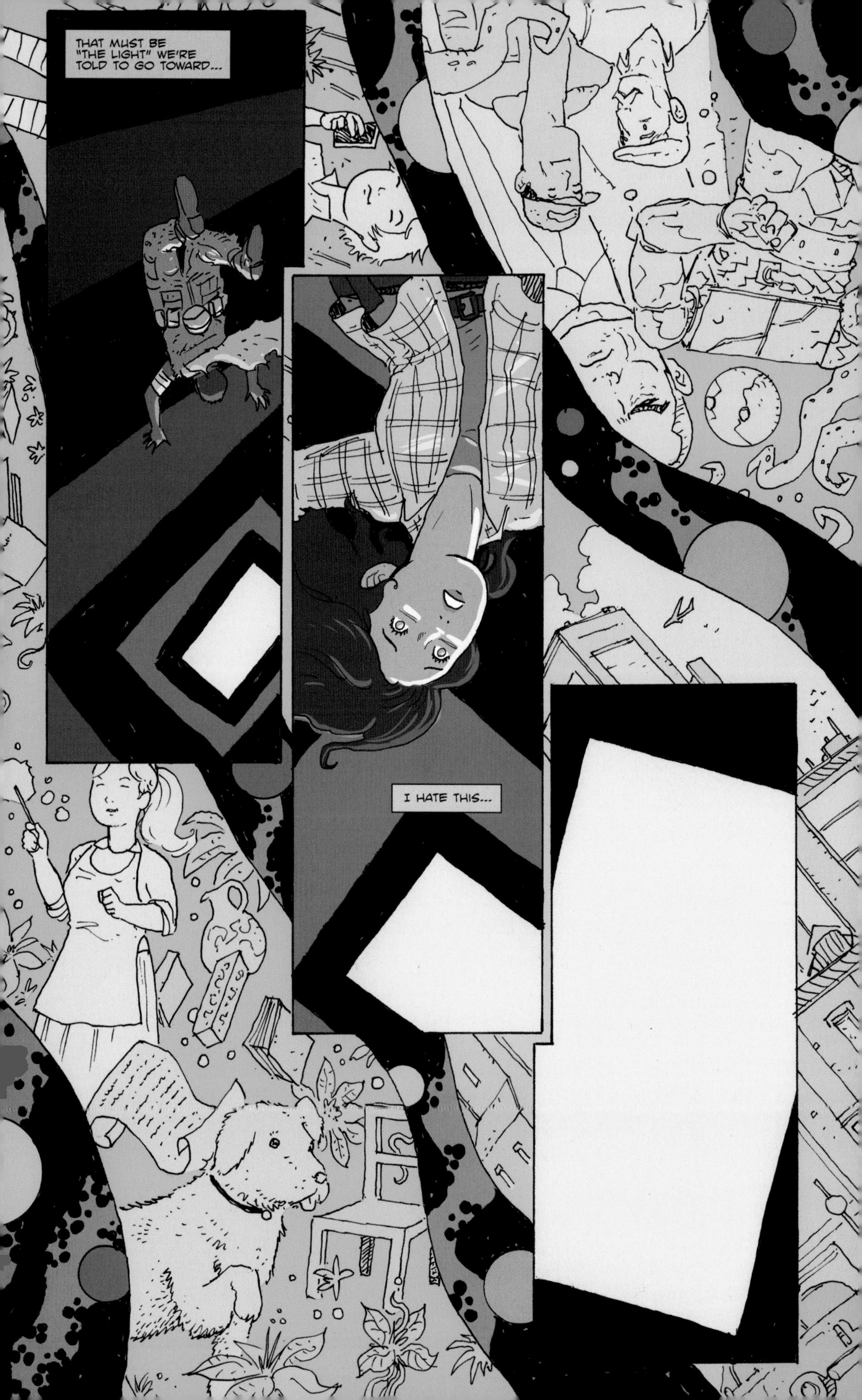
THAT MUST BE "THE LIGHT" WE'RE TOLD TO GO TOWARD...
I HATE THIS...

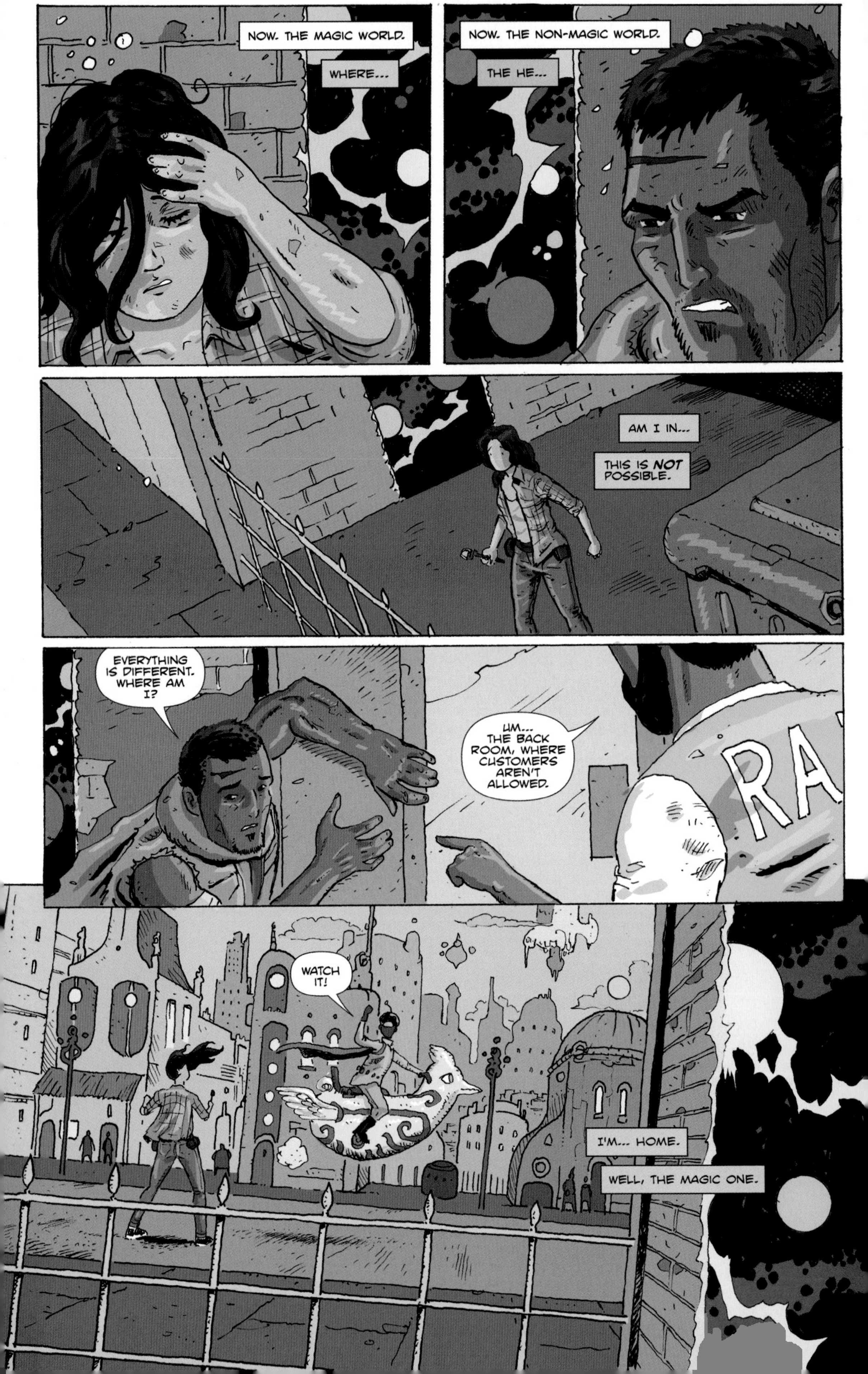
NOW. THE MAGIC WORLD.
WHERE...
NOW. THE NON-MAGIC WORLD.
THE HE...
AM I IN...
THIS IS **NOT** POSSIBLE.
EVERYTHING IS DIFFERENT. WHERE AM I?
UM... THE BACK ROOM, WHERE CUSTOMERS AREN'T ALLOWED.
RA
WATCH IT!
I'M... HOME.
WELL, THE MAGIC ONE.

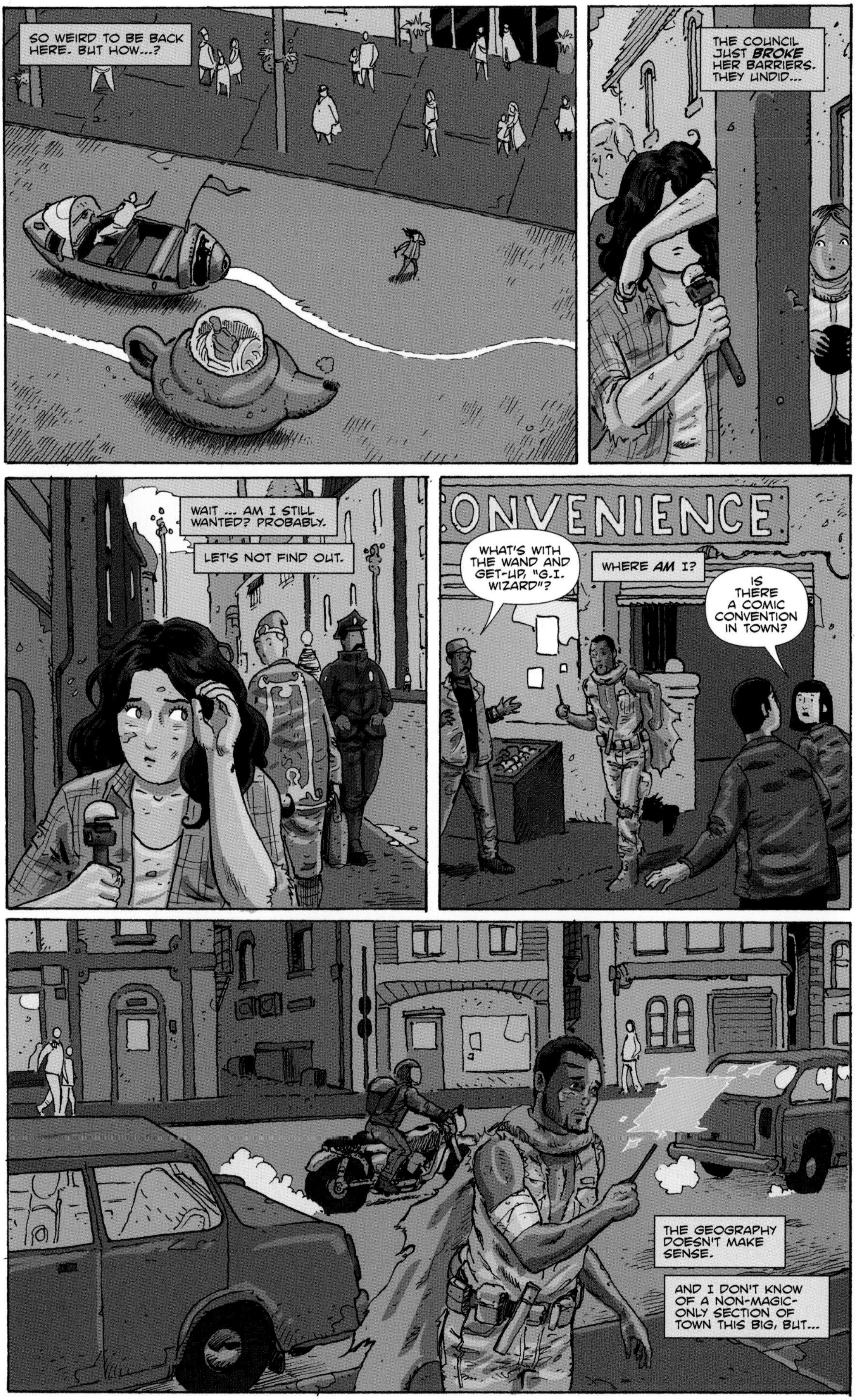
SO WEIRD TO BE BACK HERE. BUT HOW...?
THE COUNCIL JUST BROKE HER BARRIERS. THEY UNDID...
WAIT ... AM I STILL WANTED? PROBABLY.
LET'S NOT FIND OUT.
CONVENIENCE
WHAT'S WITH THE WAND AND GET-UP, "G.I. WIZARD"?
WHERE AM I?
IS THERE A COMIC CONVENTION IN TOWN?
THE GEOGRAPHY DOESN'T MAKE SENSE.
AND I DON'T KNOW OF A NON-MAGIC-ONLY SECTION OF TOWN THIS BIG, BUT...

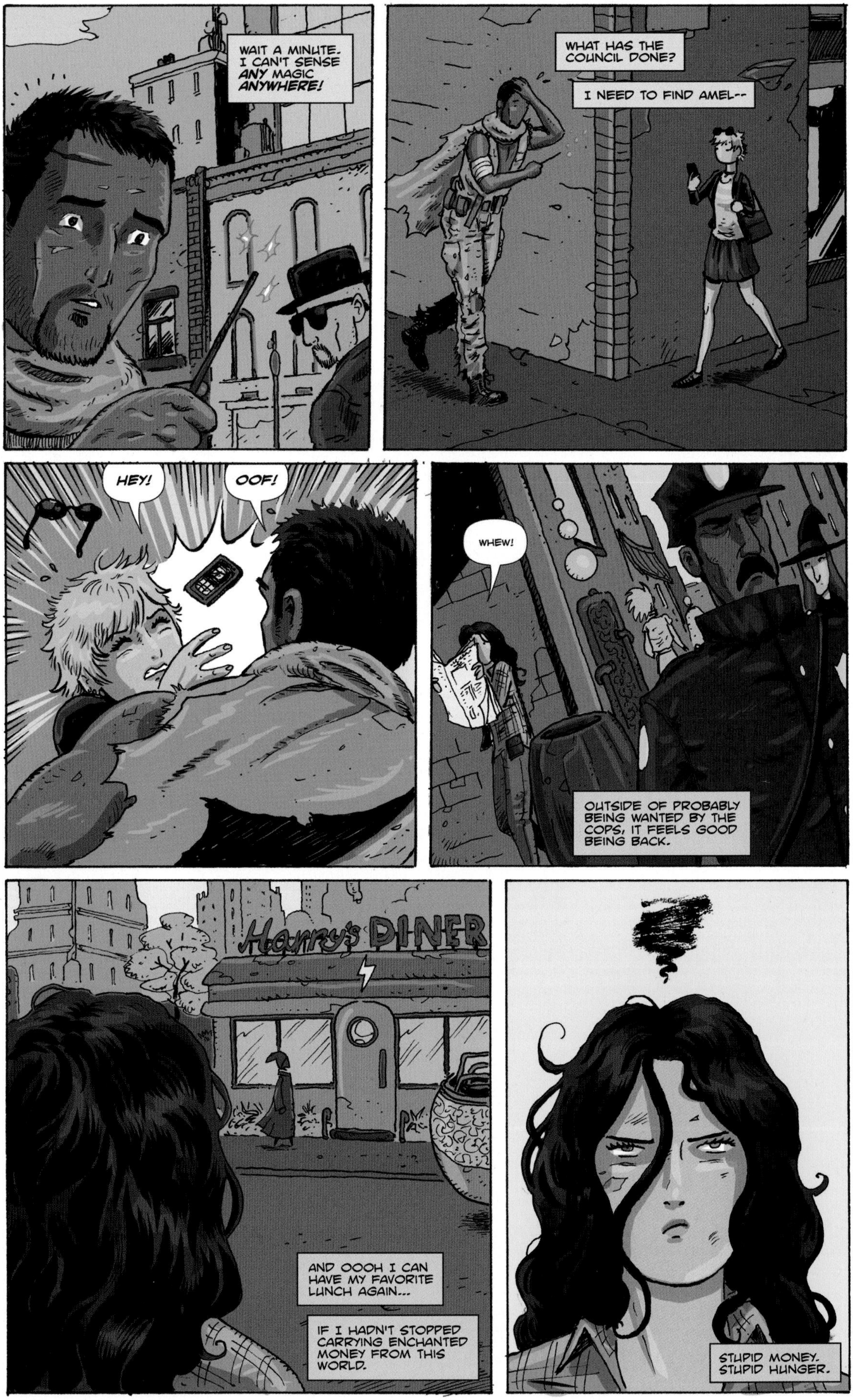

WAIT A MINUTE. I CAN'T SENSE ANY MAGIC ANYWHERE!
WHAT HAS THE COUNCIL DONE?
I NEED TO FIND AMEL--
HEY!
OOF!
WHEW!
OUTSIDE OF PROBABLY BEING WANTED BY THE COPS, IT FEELS GOOD BEING BACK.
Harry's DINER
AND OOOH I CAN HAVE MY FAVORITE LUNCH AGAIN...
IF I HADN'T STOPPED CARRYING ENCHANTED MONEY FROM THIS WORLD.
STUPID MONEY. STUPID HUNGER.

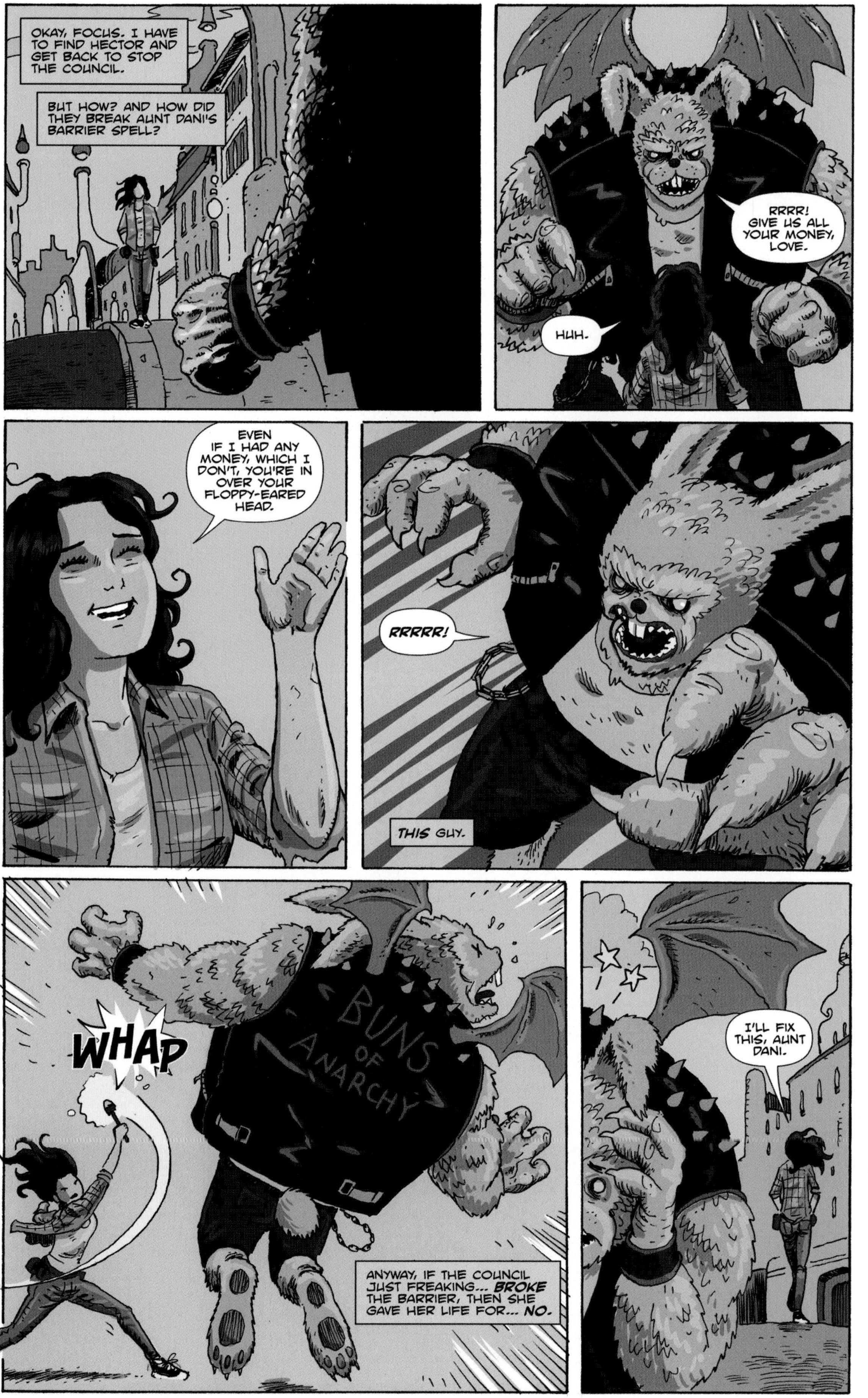

OKAY, FOCUS. I HAVE TO FIND HECTOR AND GET BACK TO STOP THE COUNCIL.
BUT HOW? AND HOW DID THEY BREAK AUNT DANI'S BARRIER SPELL?
RRRR! GIVE US ALL YOUR MONEY, LOVE.
HUH.
EVEN IF I HAD ANY MONEY, WHICH I DON'T, YOU'RE IN OVER YOUR FLOPPY-EARED HEAD.
RRRRR!
THIS GUY.
WHAP
BUNS OF ANARCHY
ANYWAY, IF THE COUNCIL JUST FREAKING... BROKE THE BARRIER, THEN SHE GAVE HER LIFE FOR... NO.
I'LL FIX THIS, AUNT DANI.

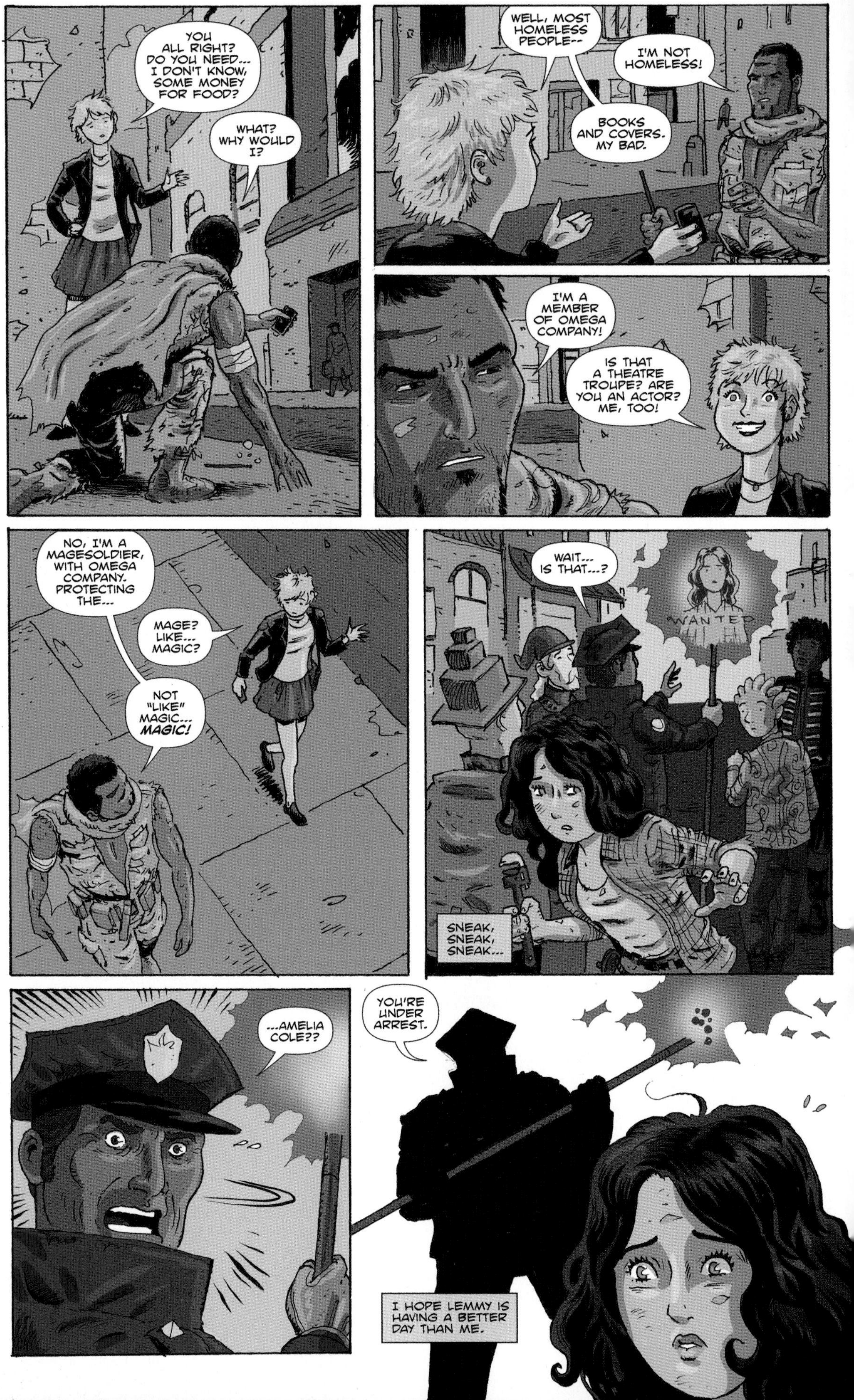

YOU ALL RIGHT? DO YOU NEED... I DON'T KNOW, SOME MONEY FOR FOOD?
WHAT? WHY WOULD I?
WELL, MOST HOMELESS PEOPLE--
I'M NOT HOMELESS!
BOOKS AND COVERS. MY BAD.
I'M A MEMBER OF OMEGA COMPANY!
IS THAT A THEATRE TROUPE? ARE YOU AN ACTOR? ME, TOO!
NO, I'M A MAGESOLDIER, WITH OMEGA COMPANY. PROTECTING THE...
MAGE? LIKE... MAGIC?
NOT "LIKE" MAGIC... MAGIC!
WAIT... IS THAT...?
WANTED
SNEAK, SNEAK, SNEAK...
...AMELIA COLE??
YOU'RE UNDER ARREST.
I HOPE LEMMY IS HAVING A BETTER DAY THAN ME.

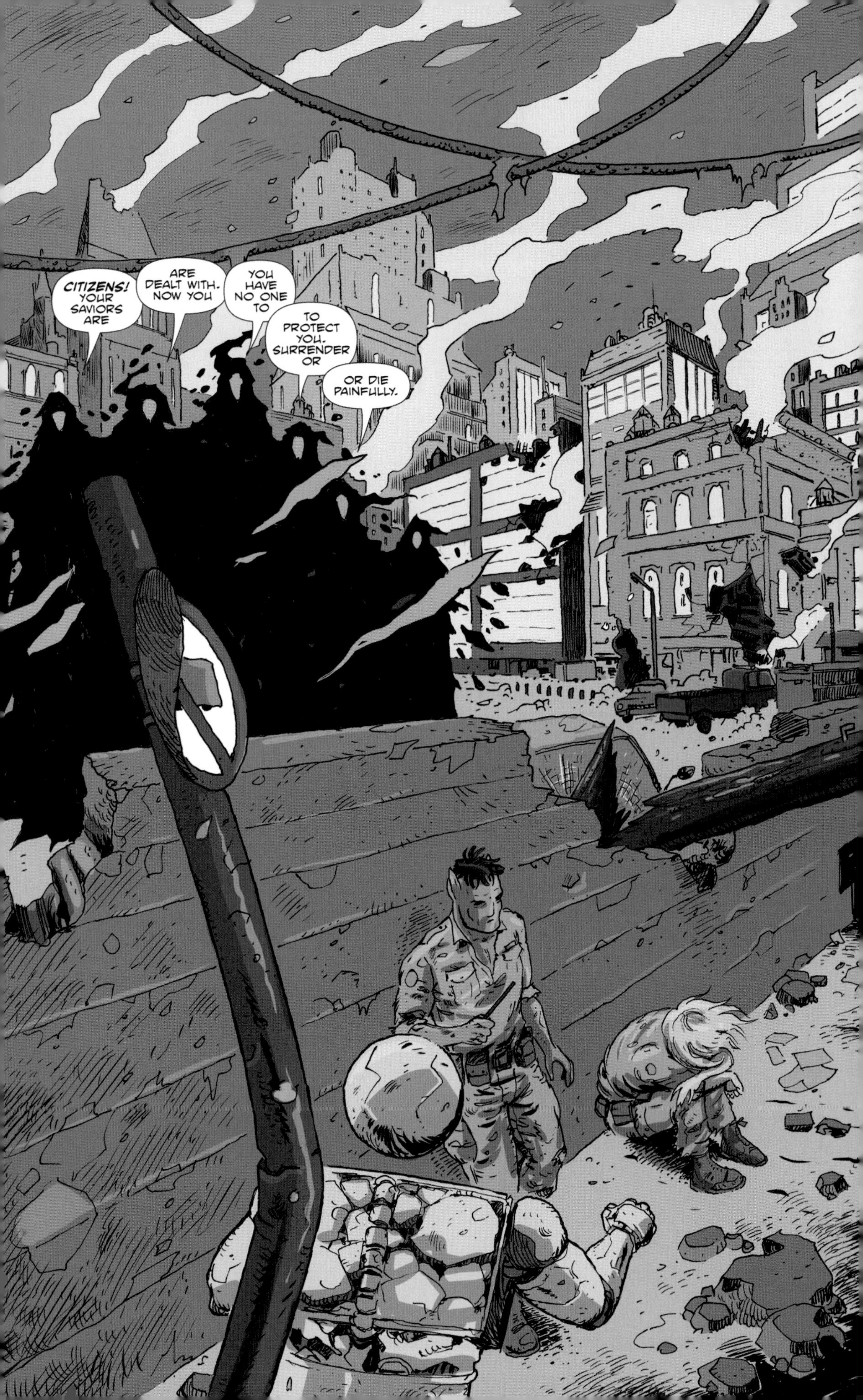
CITIZENS! YOUR SAVIORS ARE
ARE DEALT WITH. NOW YOU
YOU HAVE NO ONE TO
TO PROTECT YOU. SURRENDER OR
OR DIE PAINFULLY.

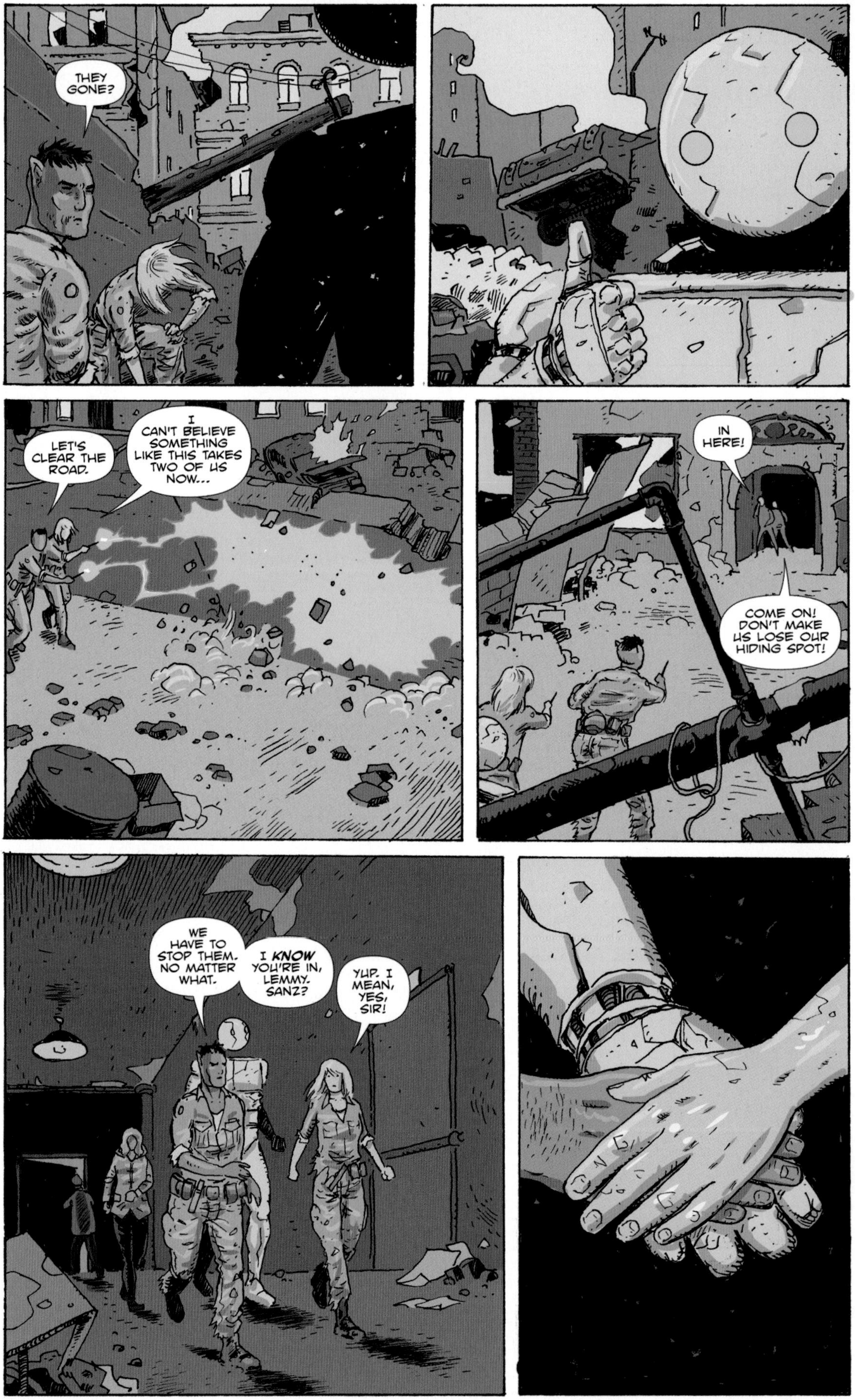
THEY GONE?
LET'S CLEAR THE ROAD.
I CAN'T BELIEVE SOMETHING LIKE THIS TAKES TWO OF US NOW...
IN HERE!
COME ON! DON'T MAKE US LOSE OUR HIDING SPOT!
WE HAVE TO STOP THEM. NO MATTER WHAT.
I KNOW YOU'RE IN, LEMMY. SANZ?
YUP. I MEAN, YES, SIR!

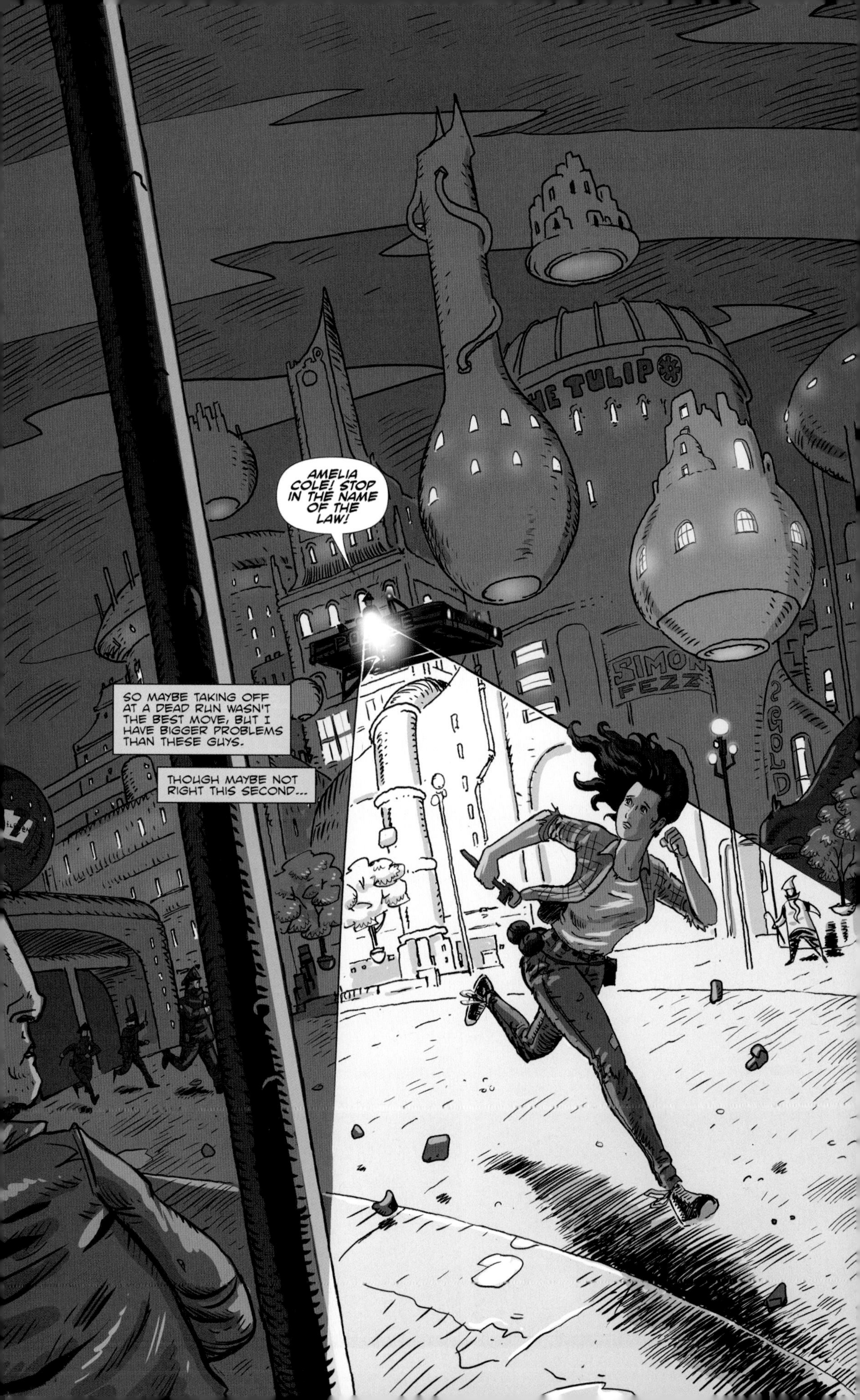
AMELIA COLE! STOP IN THE NAME OF THE LAW!
SO MAYBE TAKING OFF AT A DEAD RUN WASN'T THE BEST MOVE, BUT I HAVE BIGGER PROBLEMS THAN THESE GUYS.
THOUGH MAYBE NOT RIGHT THIS SECOND...
THE TULIP
SIMON FEZZ
GOLD

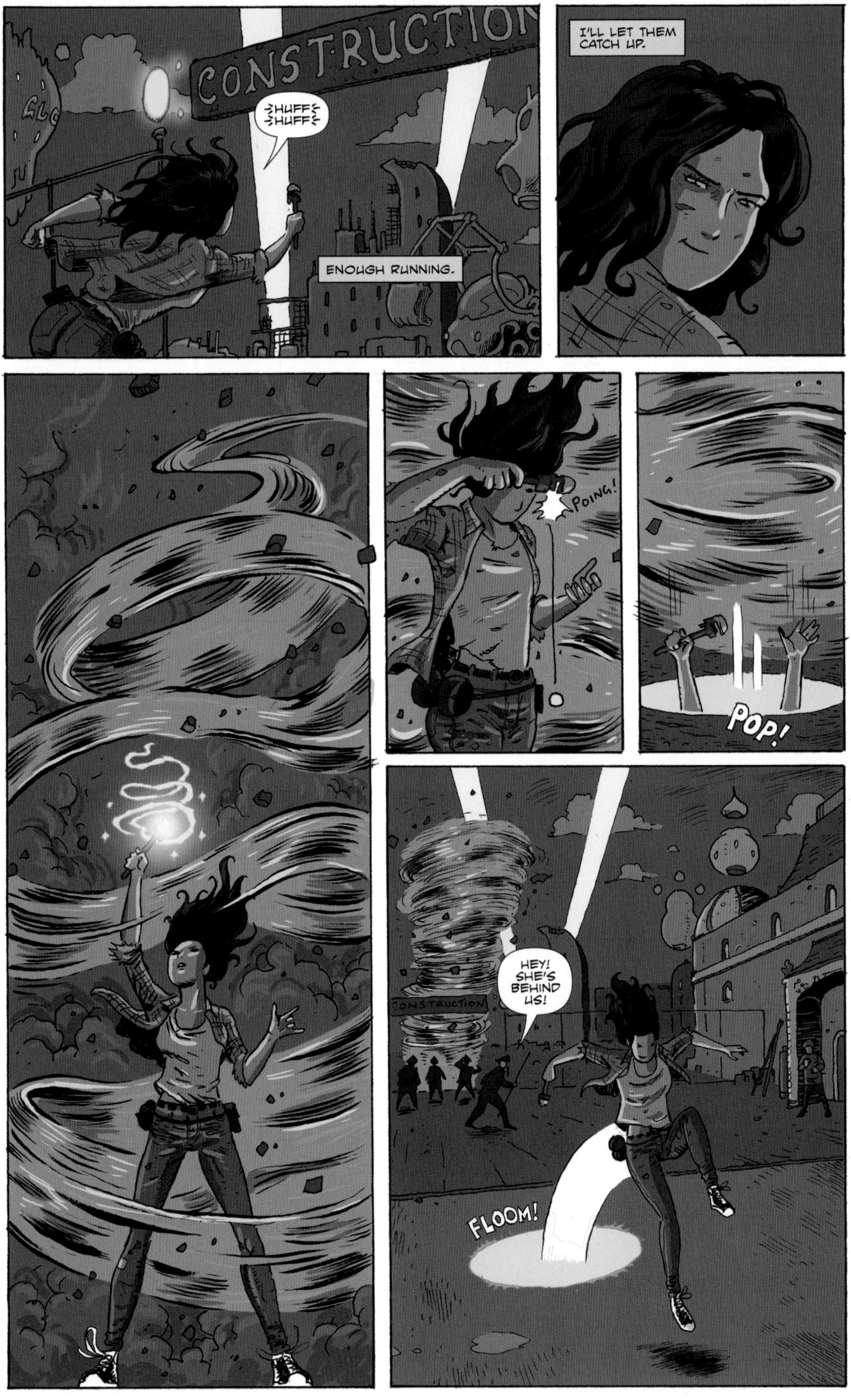
CONSTRUCTION
HUFF HUFF
ENOUGH RUNNING.
I'LL LET THEM CATCH UP.
POING!
POP!
HEY! SHE'S BEHIND US!
FLOOM!

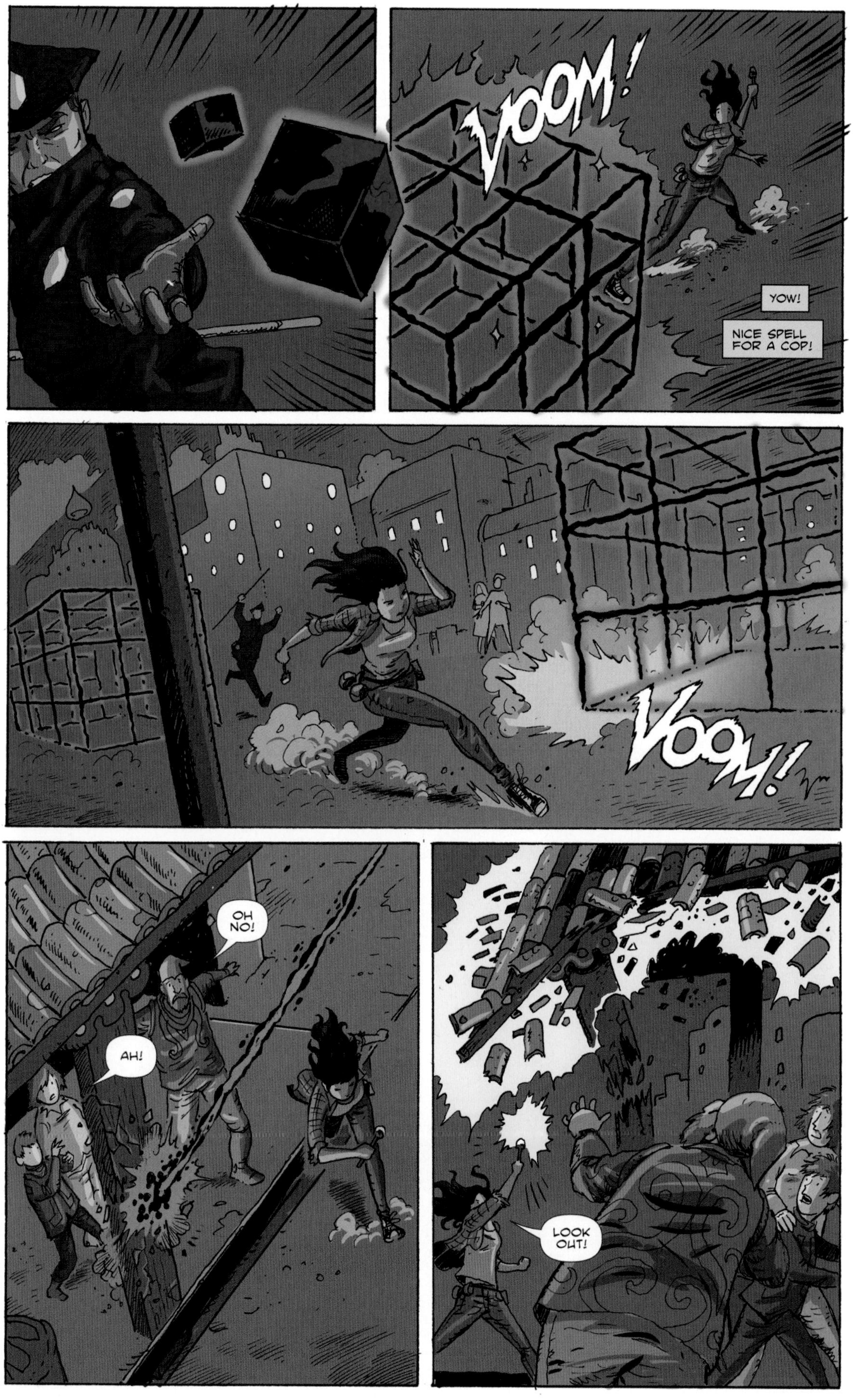
VOOM!
YOW!
NICE SPELL FOR A COP!
VOOM!
OH NO!
AH!
LOOK OUT!

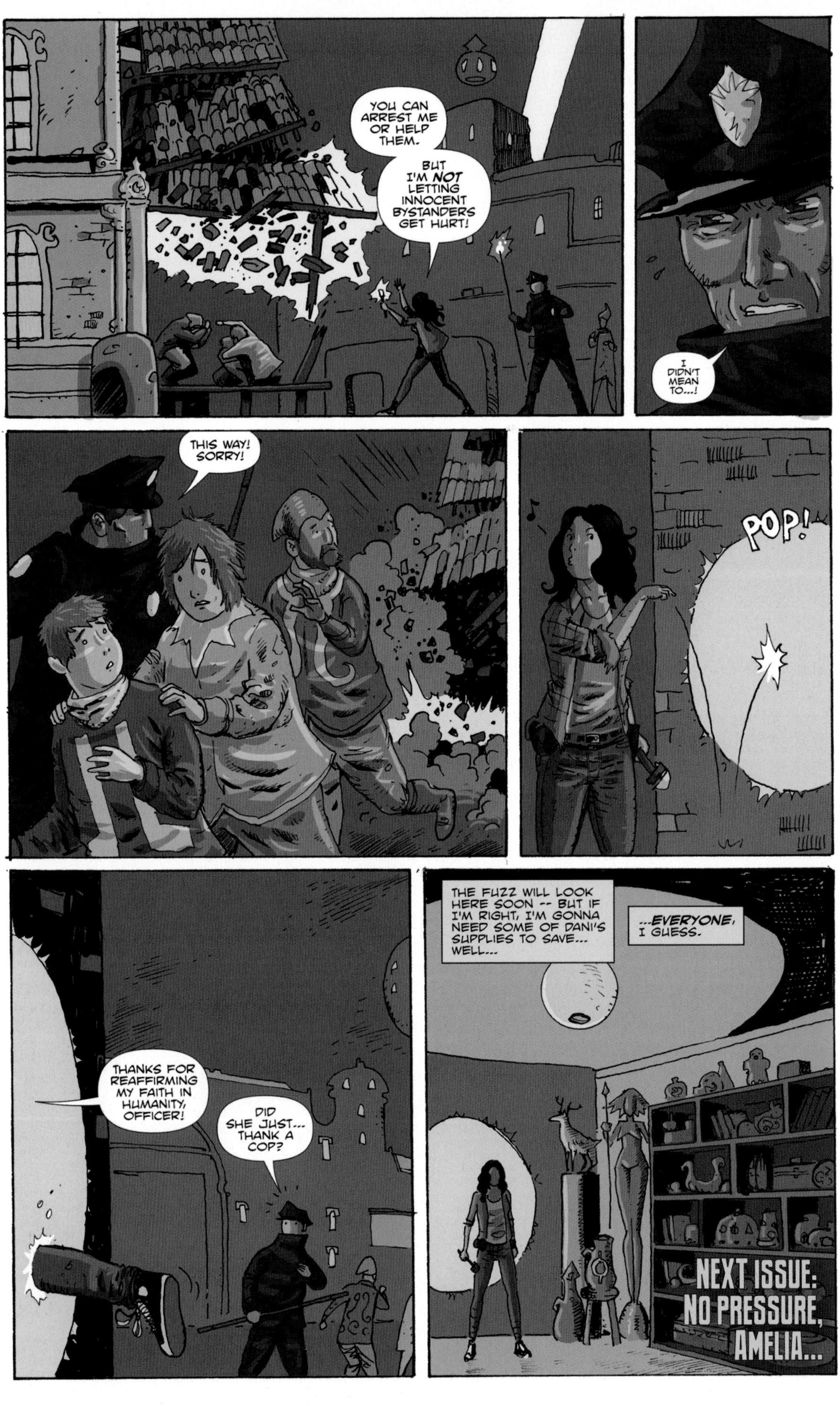
YOU CAN ARREST ME OR HELP THEM.
BUT I'M **NOT** LETTING INNOCENT BYSTANDERS GET HURT!
I DIDN'T MEAN TO...!
THIS WAY! SORRY!
POP!
THANKS FOR REAFFIRMING MY FAITH IN HUMANITY, OFFICER!
DID SHE JUST... THANK A COP?
THE FUZZ WILL LOOK HERE SOON -- BUT IF I'M RIGHT, I'M GONNA NEED SOME OF DANI'S SUPPLIES TO SAVE... WELL...
...***EVERYONE***, I GUESS.
NEXT ISSUE: NO PRESSURE, AMELIA...

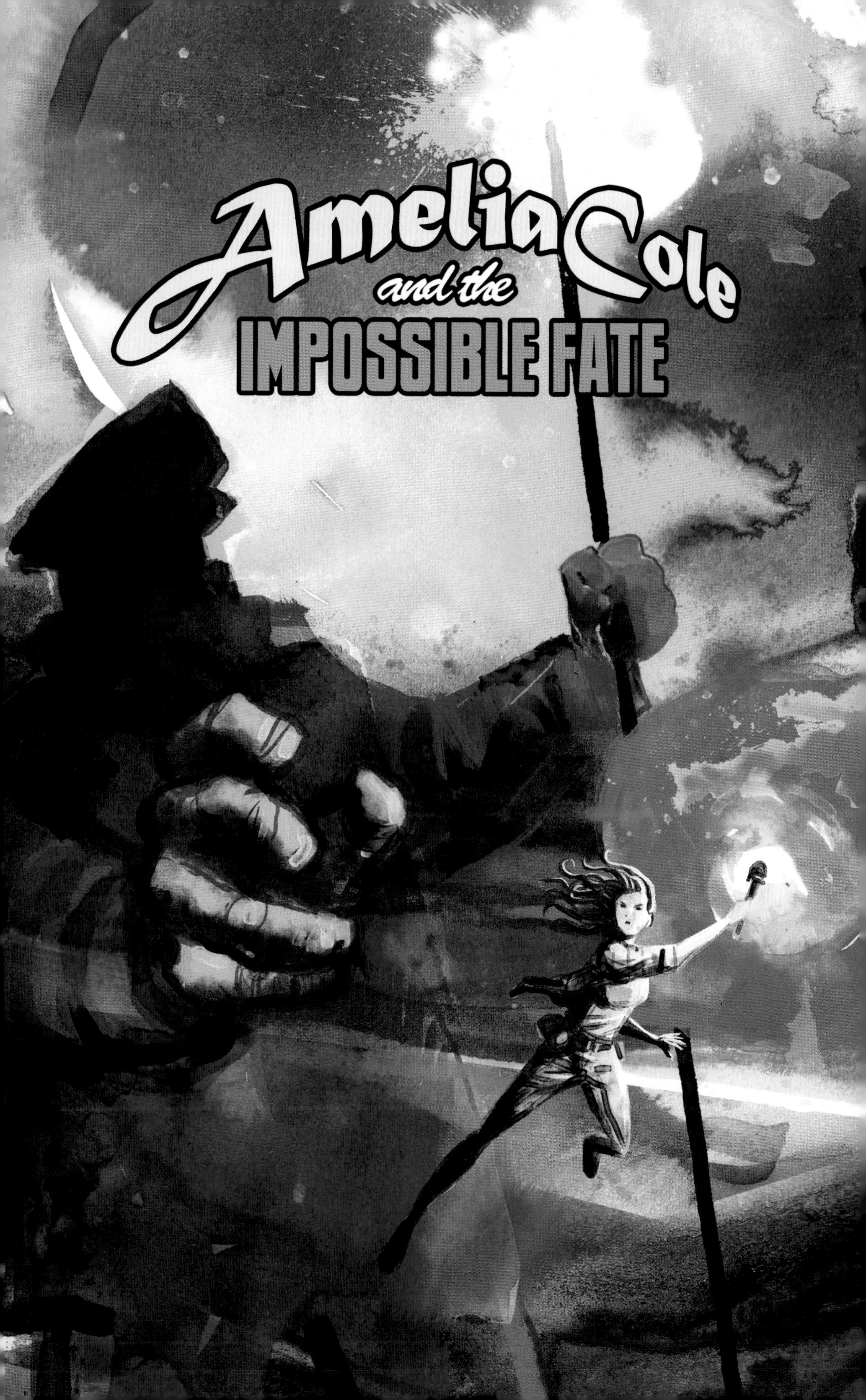
Amelia Cole
and the
IMPOSSIBLE FATE

CHAPTER 2

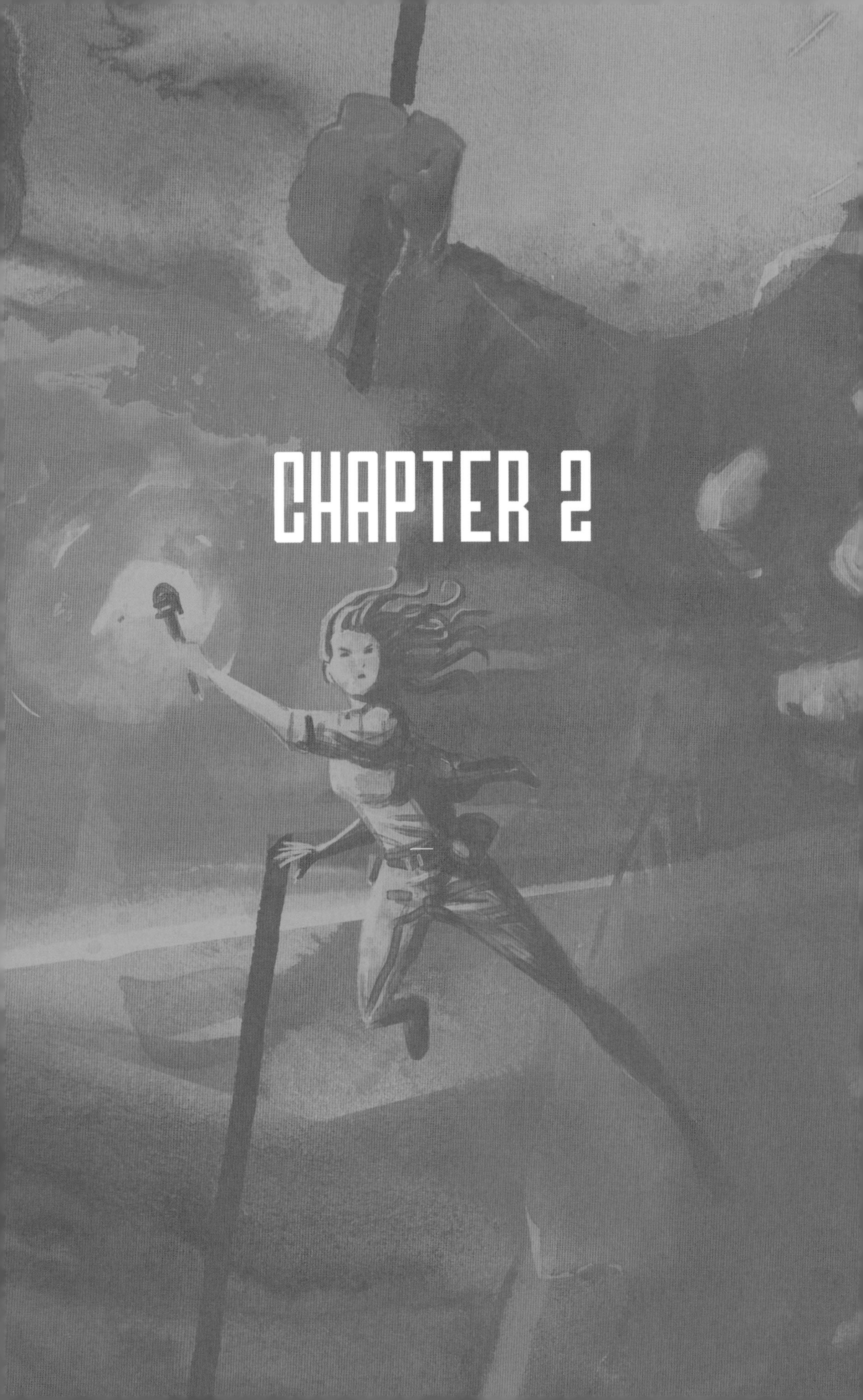

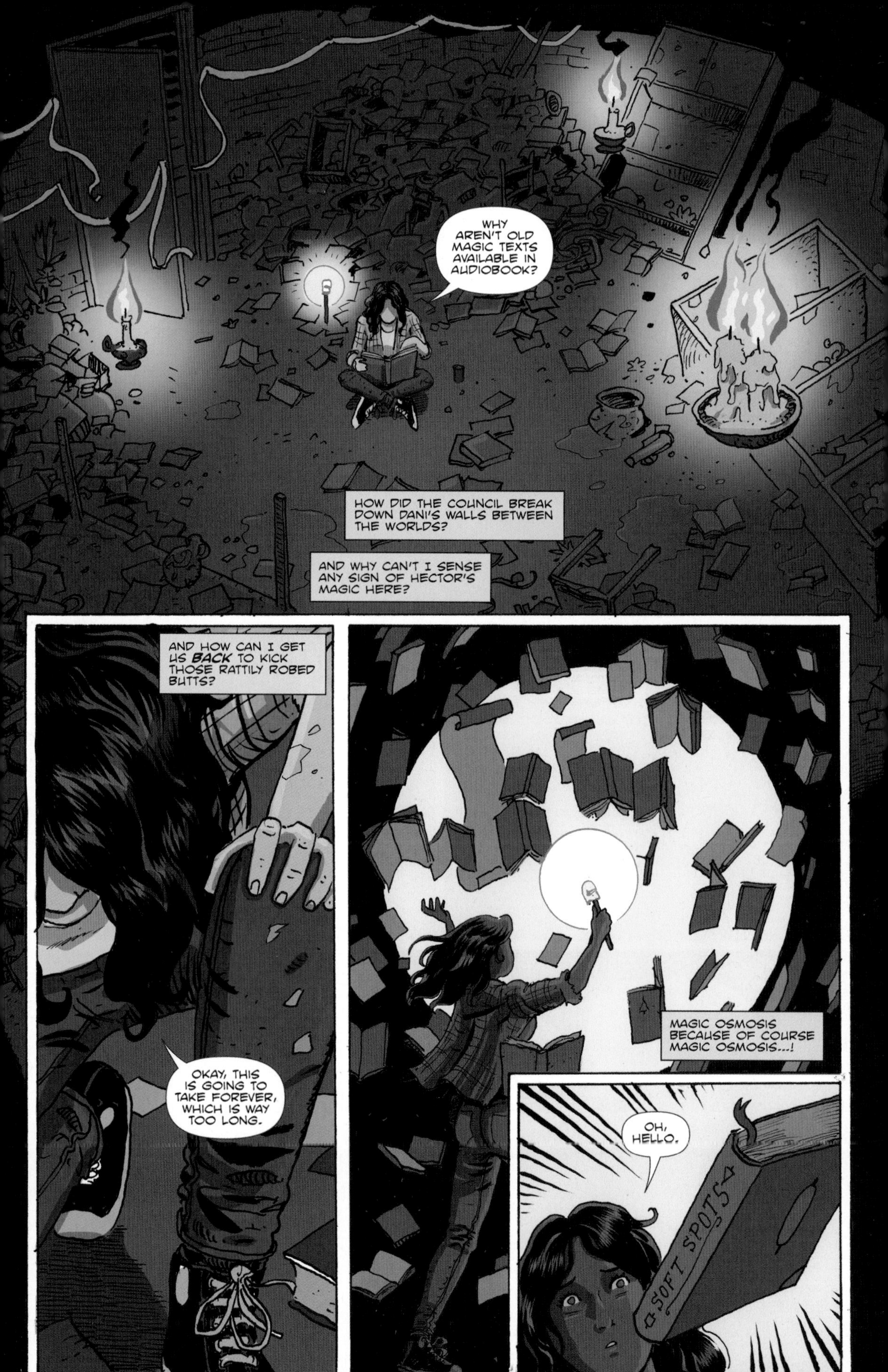
WHY AREN'T OLD MAGIC TEXTS AVAILABLE IN AUDIOBOOK?
HOW DID THE COUNCIL BREAK DOWN DANI'S WALLS BETWEEN THE WORLDS?
AND WHY CAN'T I SENSE ANY SIGN OF HECTOR'S MAGIC HERE?
AND HOW CAN I GET US *BACK* TO KICK THOSE RATTILY ROBED BUTTS?
OKAY, THIS IS GOING TO TAKE FOREVER, WHICH IS WAY TOO LONG.
MAGIC OSMOSIS BECAUSE OF COURSE MAGIC OSMOSIS...!
OH, HELLO.
SOFT SPOTS

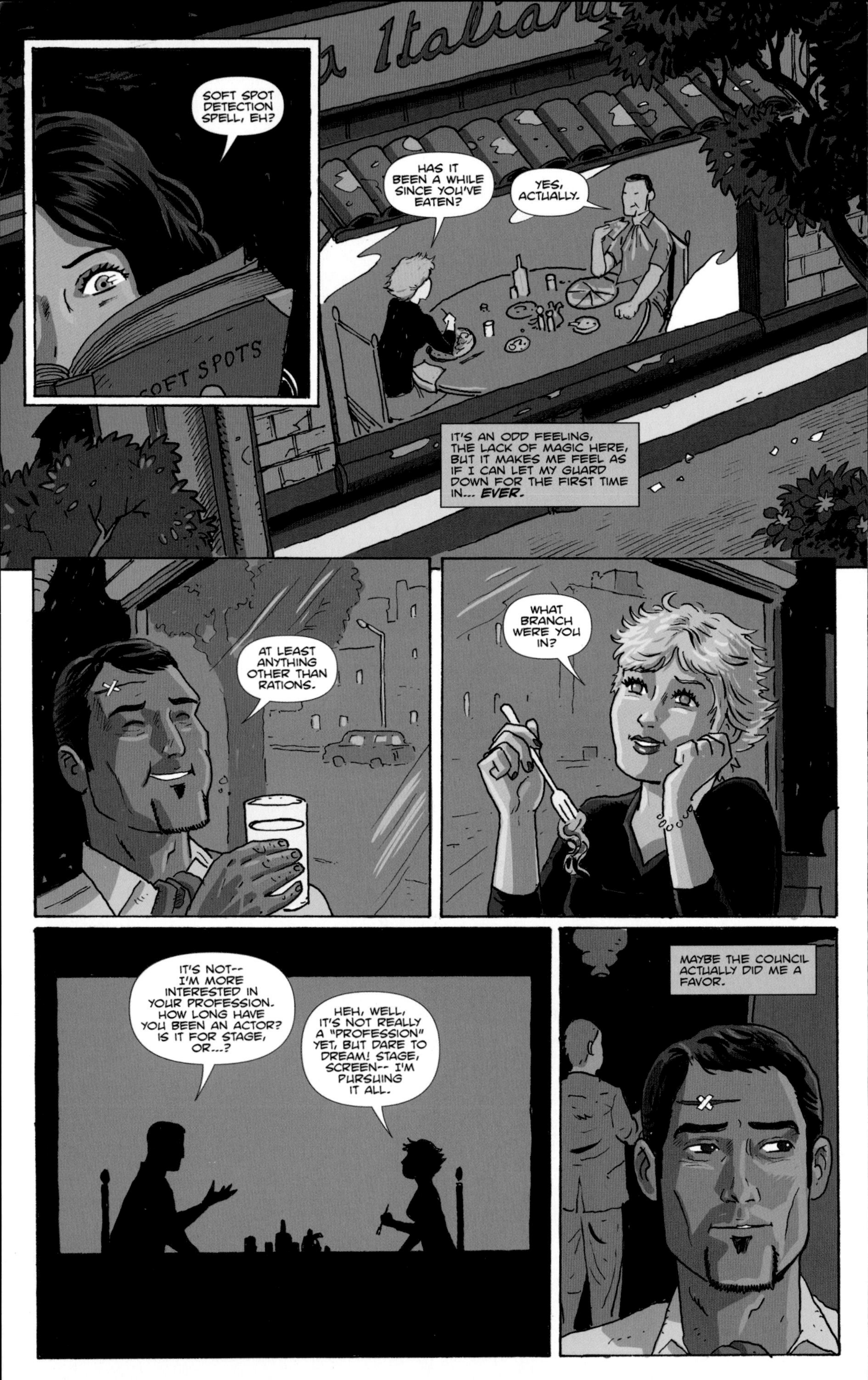

SOFT SPOT DETECTION SPELL, EH?
SOFT SPOTS
HAS IT BEEN A WHILE SINCE YOU'VE EATEN?
YES, ACTUALLY.
IT'S AN ODD FEELING, THE LACK OF MAGIC HERE, BUT IT MAKES ME FEEL AS IF I CAN LET MY GUARD DOWN FOR THE FIRST TIME IN... *EVER.*
AT LEAST ANYTHING OTHER THAN RATIONS.
WHAT BRANCH WERE YOU IN?
IT'S NOT-- I'M MORE INTERESTED IN YOUR PROFESSION. HOW LONG HAVE YOU BEEN AN ACTOR? IS IT FOR STAGE, OR...?
HEH, WELL, IT'S NOT REALLY A "PROFESSION" YET, BUT DARE TO DREAM! STAGE, SCREEN-- I'M PURSUING IT ALL.
MAYBE THE COUNCIL ACTUALLY DID ME A FAVOR.

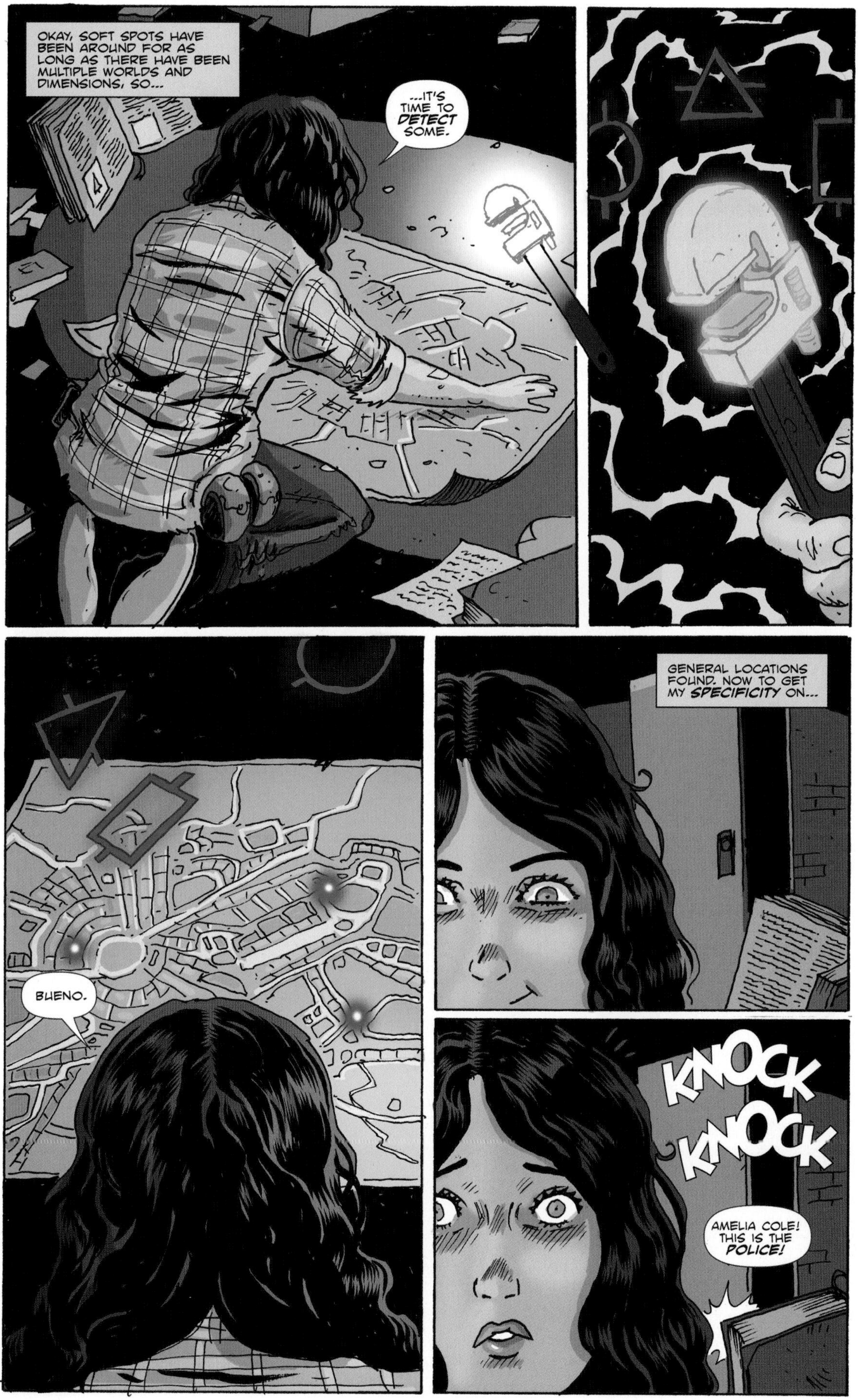

OKAY, SOFT SPOTS HAVE BEEN AROUND FOR AS LONG AS THERE HAVE BEEN MULTIPLE WORLDS AND DIMENSIONS, SO...
...IT'S TIME TO DETECT SOME.
BUENO.
GENERAL LOCATIONS FOUND. NOW TO GET MY SPECIFICITY ON...
KNOCK KNOCK
AMELIA COLE! THIS IS THE POLICE!

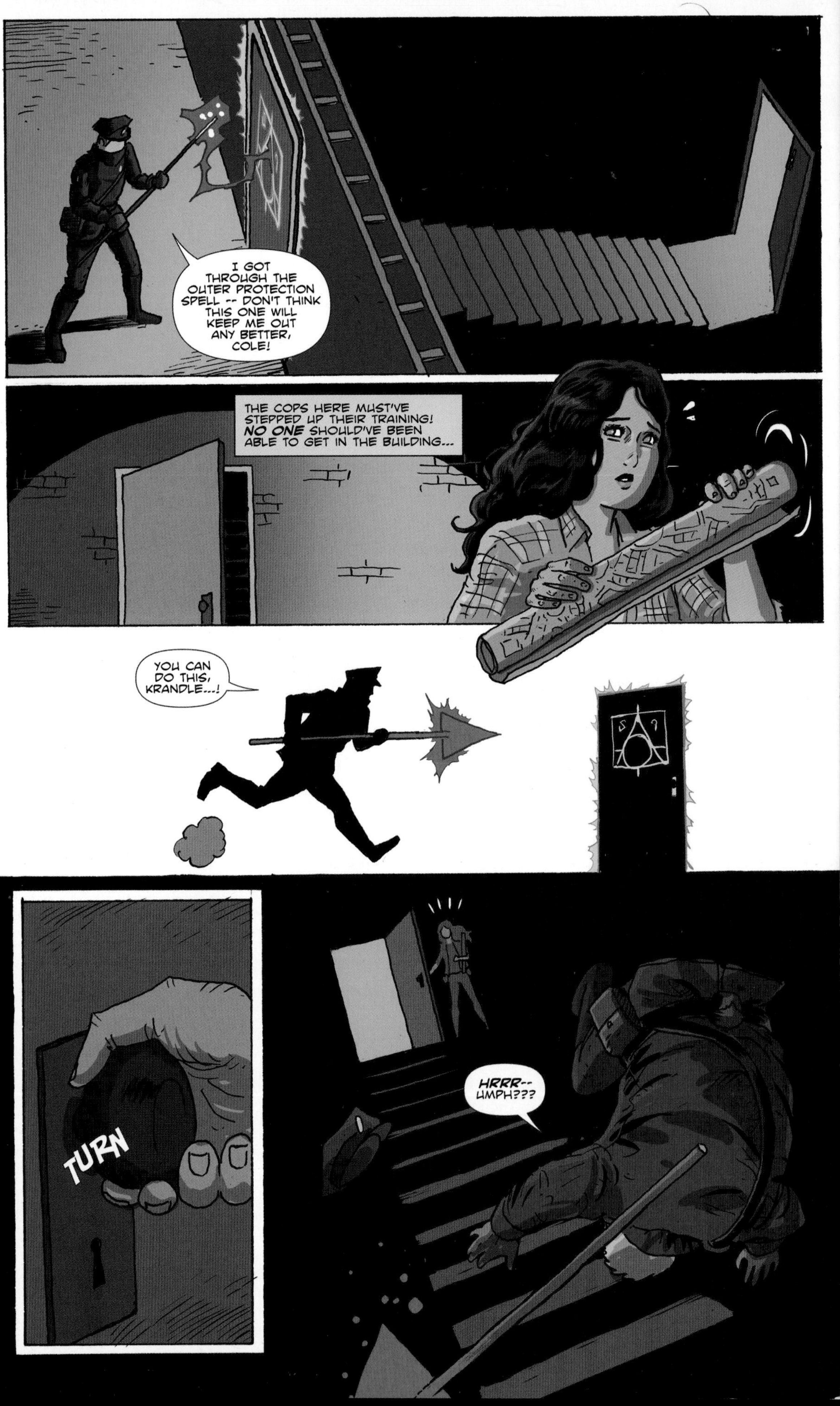
I GOT THROUGH THE OUTER PROTECTION SPELL -- DON'T THINK THIS ONE WILL KEEP ME OUT ANY BETTER, COLE!
THE COPS HERE MUST'VE STEPPED UP THEIR TRAINING! NO ONE SHOULD'VE BEEN ABLE TO GET IN THE BUILDING...
YOU CAN DO THIS, KRANDLE...!
TURN
HRRR-- UMPH???

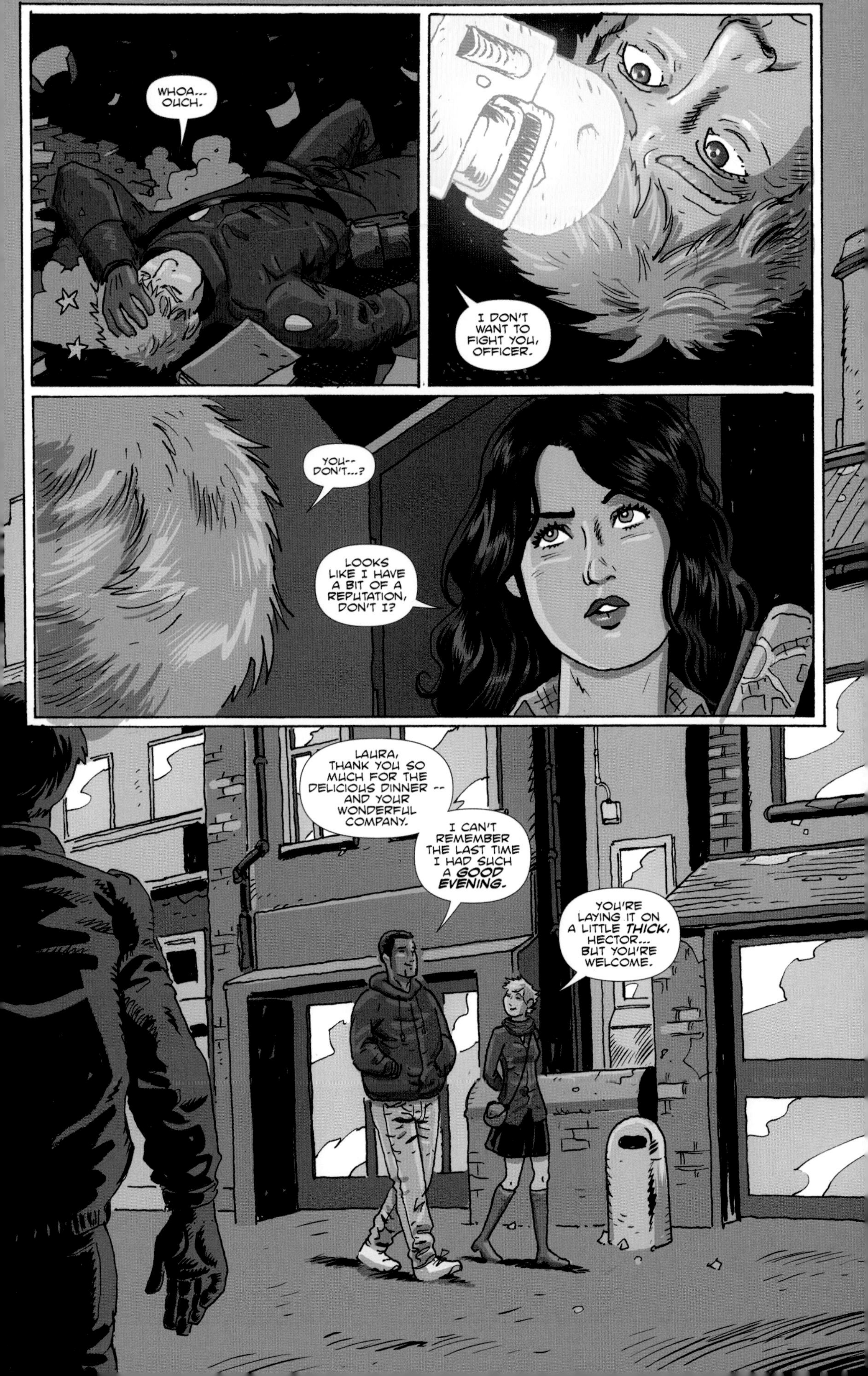
WHOA... OUCH.
I DON'T WANT TO FIGHT YOU, OFFICER.
YOU-- DON'T...?
LOOKS LIKE I HAVE A BIT OF A REPUTATION, DON'T I?
LAURA, THANK YOU SO MUCH FOR THE DELICIOUS DINNER -- AND YOUR WONDERFUL COMPANY.
I CAN'T REMEMBER THE LAST TIME I HAD SUCH A GOOD EVENING.
YOU'RE LAYING IT ON A LITTLE THICK, HECTOR... BUT YOU'RE WELCOME.

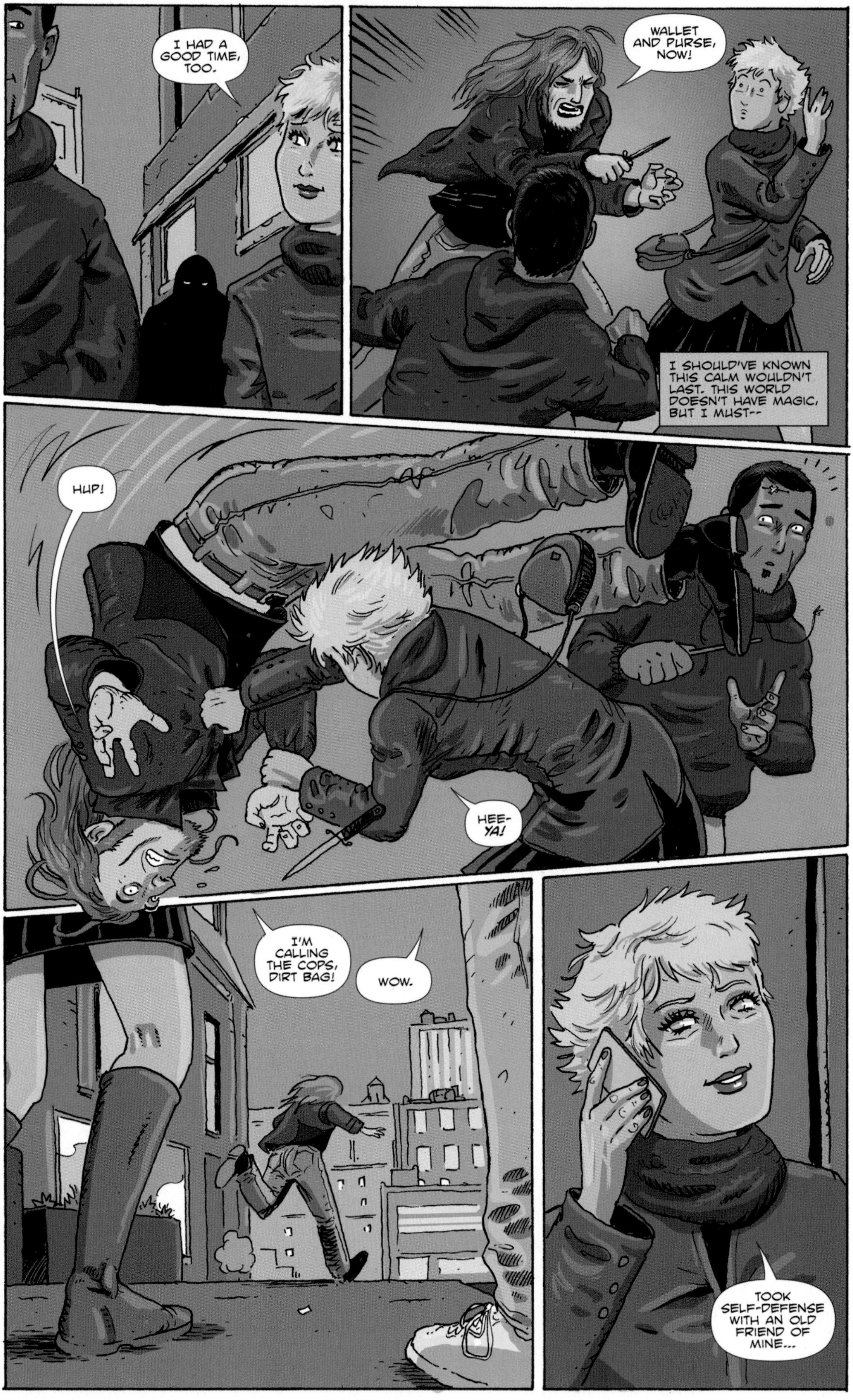
I HAD A GOOD TIME, TOO.
WALLET AND PURSE, NOW!
I SHOULD'VE KNOWN THIS CALM WOULDN'T LAST. THIS WORLD DOESN'T HAVE MAGIC, BUT I MUST--
HUP!
HEE-YA!
I'M CALLING THE COPS, DIRT BAG!
WOW.
TOOK SELF-DEFENSE WITH AN OLD FRIEND OF MINE...

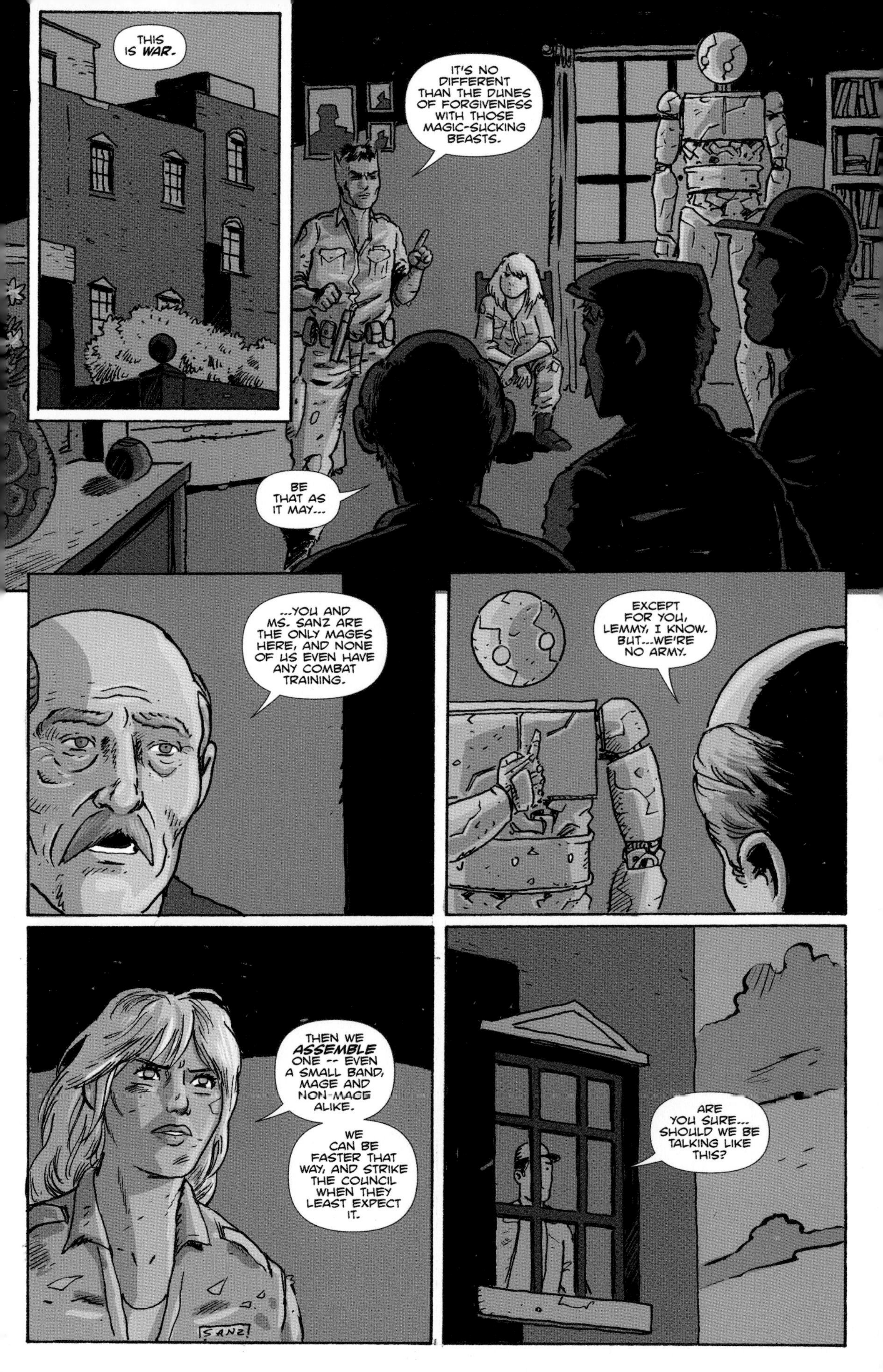
THIS IS WAR.
IT'S NO DIFFERENT THAN THE DUNES OF FORGIVENESS WITH THOSE MAGIC-SUCKING BEASTS.
BE THAT AS IT MAY...
...YOU AND MS. SANZ ARE THE ONLY MAGES HERE, AND NONE OF US EVEN HAVE ANY COMBAT TRAINING.
EXCEPT FOR YOU, LEMMY, I KNOW. BUT...WE'RE NO ARMY.
THEN WE ASSEMBLE ONE -- EVEN A SMALL BAND, MAGE AND NON-MAGE ALIKE.
WE CAN BE FASTER THAT WAY, AND STRIKE THE COUNCIL WHEN THEY LEAST EXPECT IT.
SANZ!
ARE YOU SURE... SHOULD WE BE TALKING LIKE THIS?

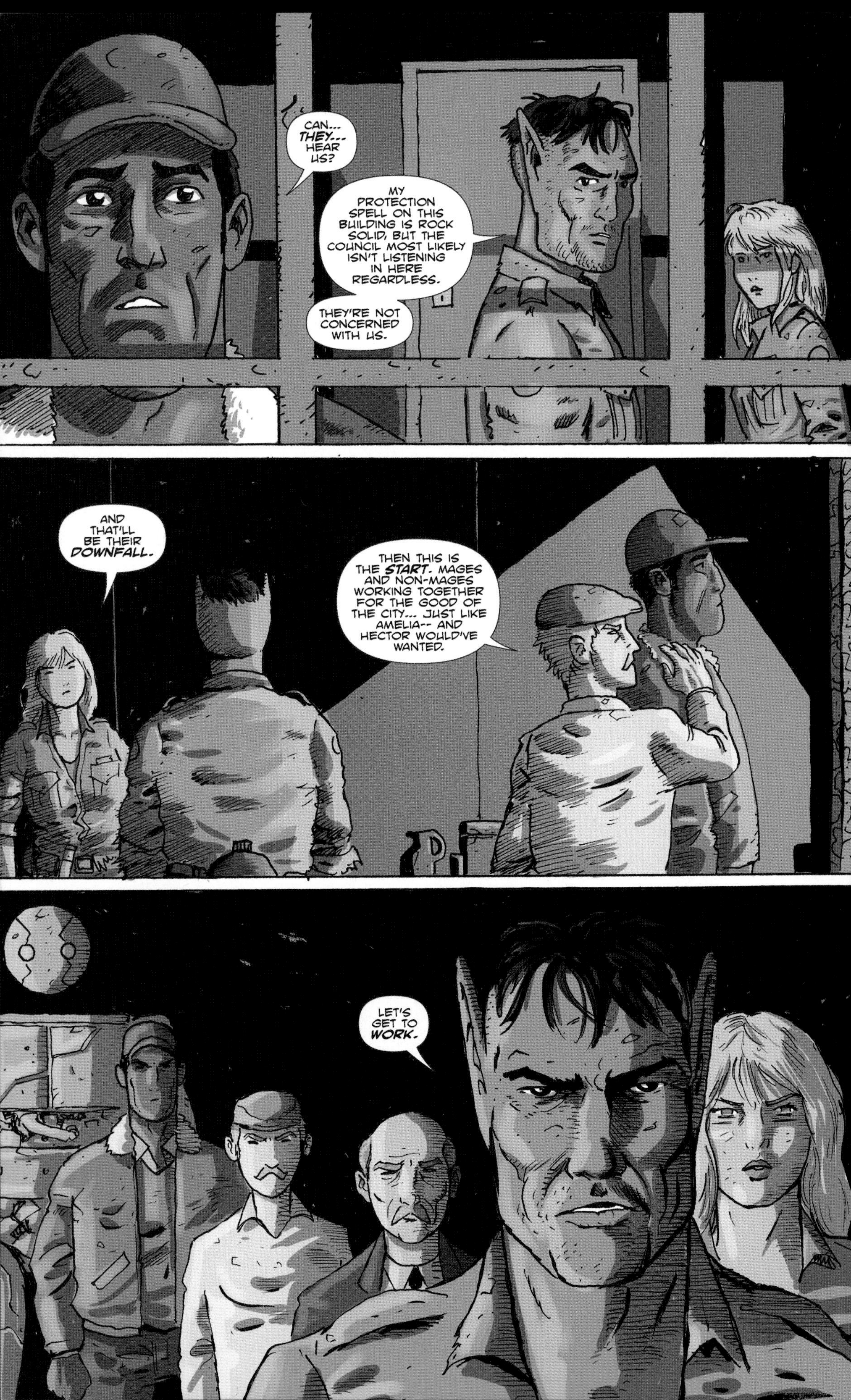
CAN... THEY... HEAR US?
MY PROTECTION SPELL ON THIS BUILDING IS ROCK SOLID, BUT THE COUNCIL MOST LIKELY ISN'T LISTENING IN HERE REGARDLESS.
THEY'RE NOT CONCERNED WITH US.
AND THAT'LL BE THEIR DOWNFALL.
THEN THIS IS THE START. MAGES AND NON-MAGES WORKING TOGETHER FOR THE GOOD OF THE CITY... JUST LIKE AMELIA-- AND HECTOR WOULD'VE WANTED.
LET'S GET TO WORK.

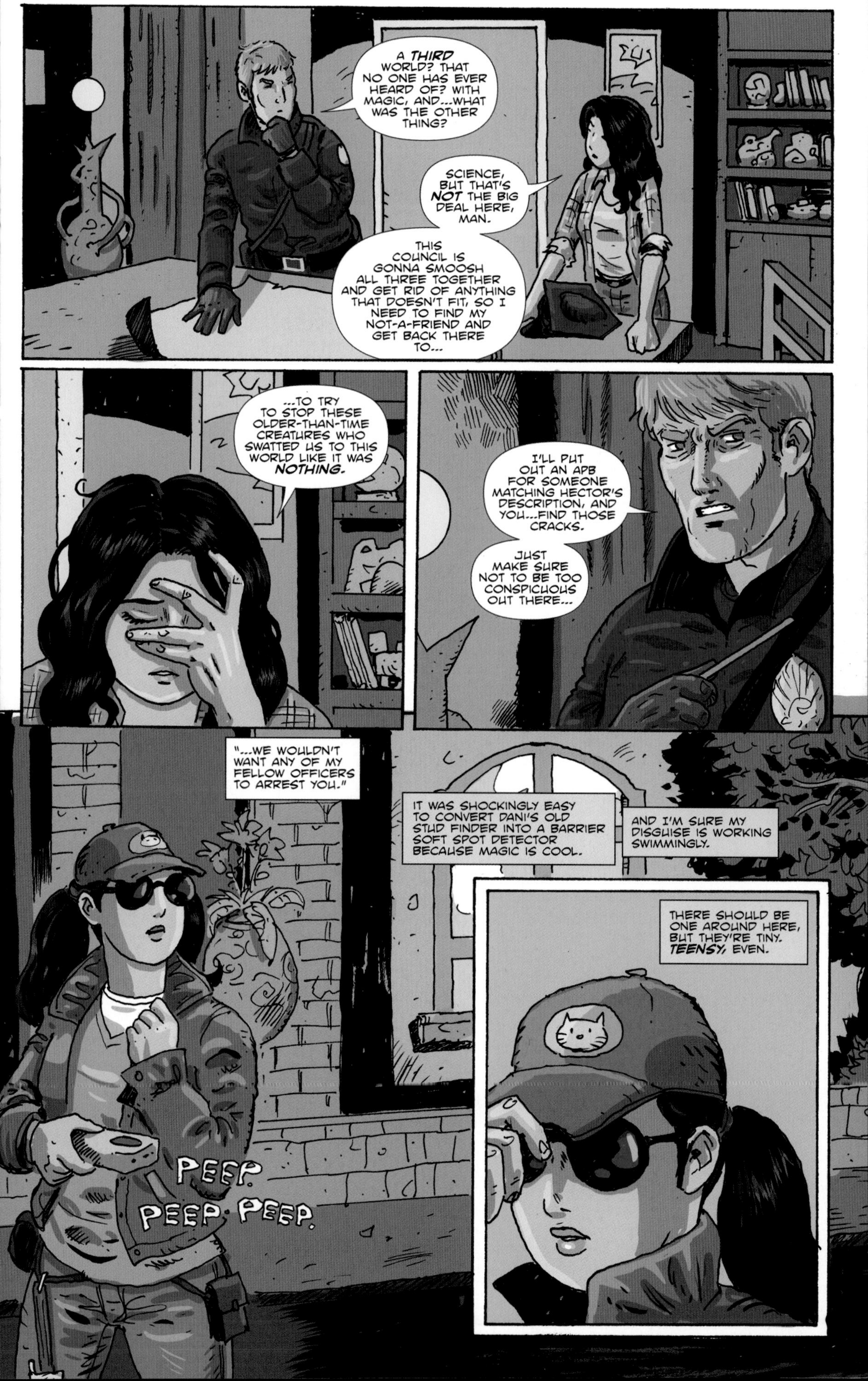
A THIRD WORLD? THAT NO ONE HAS EVER HEARD OF? WITH MAGIC, AND...WHAT WAS THE OTHER THING?
SCIENCE, BUT THAT'S NOT THE BIG DEAL HERE, MAN.
THIS COUNCIL IS GONNA SMOOSH ALL THREE TOGETHER AND GET RID OF ANYTHING THAT DOESN'T FIT, SO I NEED TO FIND MY NOT-A-FRIEND AND GET BACK THERE TO...
...TO TRY TO STOP THESE OLDER-THAN-TIME CREATURES WHO SWATTED US TO THIS WORLD LIKE IT WAS NOTHING.
I'LL PUT OUT AN APB FOR SOMEONE MATCHING HECTOR'S DESCRIPTION, AND YOU...FIND THOSE CRACKS.
JUST MAKE SURE NOT TO BE TOO CONSPICUOUS OUT THERE...
"...WE WOULDN'T WANT ANY OF MY FELLOW OFFICERS TO ARREST YOU."
IT WAS SHOCKINGLY EASY TO CONVERT DANI'S OLD STUD FINDER INTO A BARRIER SOFT SPOT DETECTOR BECAUSE MAGIC IS COOL.
AND I'M SURE MY DISGUISE IS WORKING SWIMMINGLY.
PEEP.
PEEP. PEEP.
THERE SHOULD BE ONE AROUND HERE, BUT THEY'RE TINY. TEENSY, EVEN.

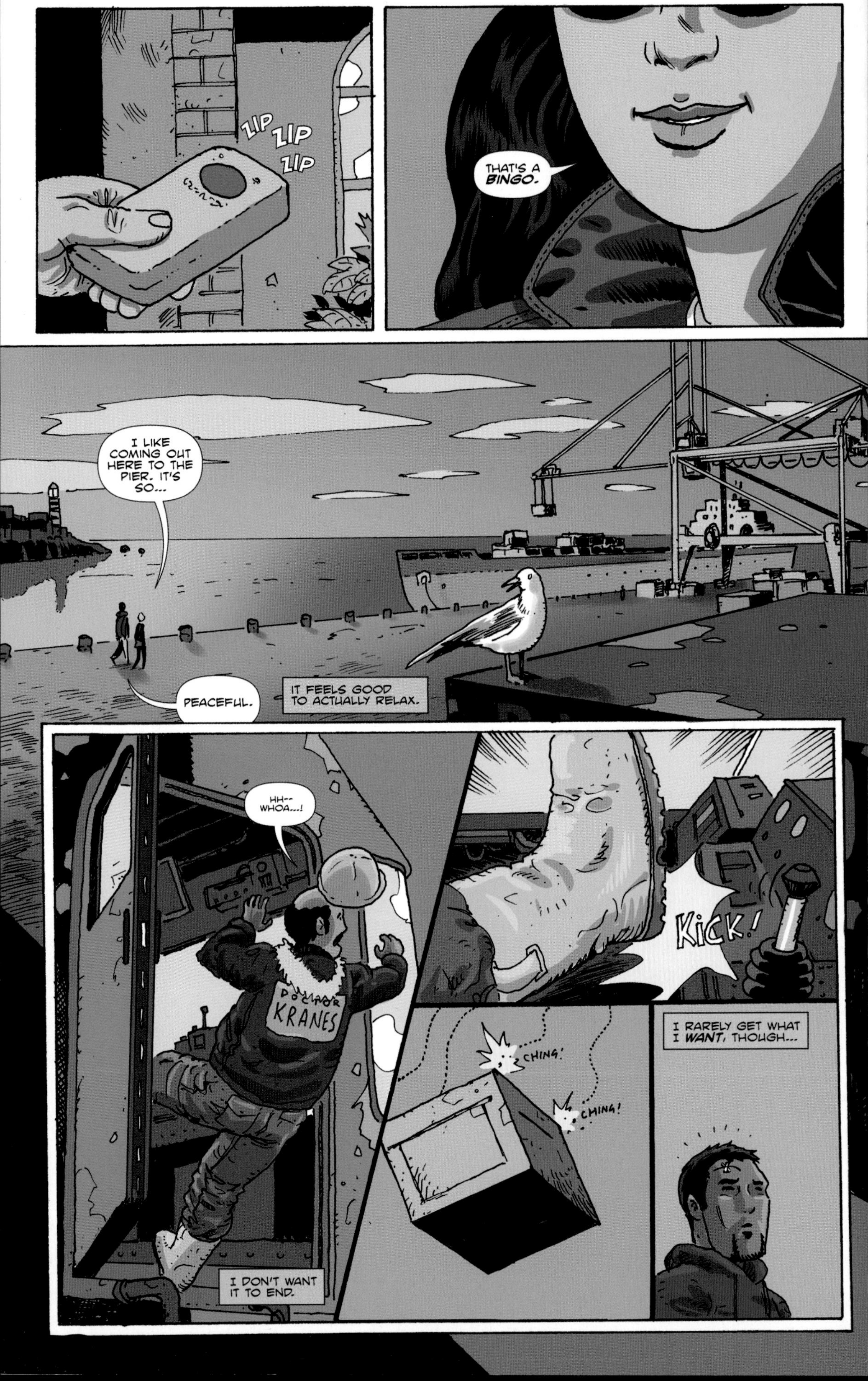
ZIP ZIP ZIP
THAT'S A *BINGO*.
I LIKE COMING OUT HERE TO THE PIER. IT'S SO...
PEACEFUL.
IT FEELS GOOD TO ACTUALLY RELAX.
HH-- WHOA...!
DOCTOR KRANES
I DON'T WANT IT TO END.
KICK!
CHING!
CHING!
I RARELY GET WHAT I *WANT*, THOUGH...

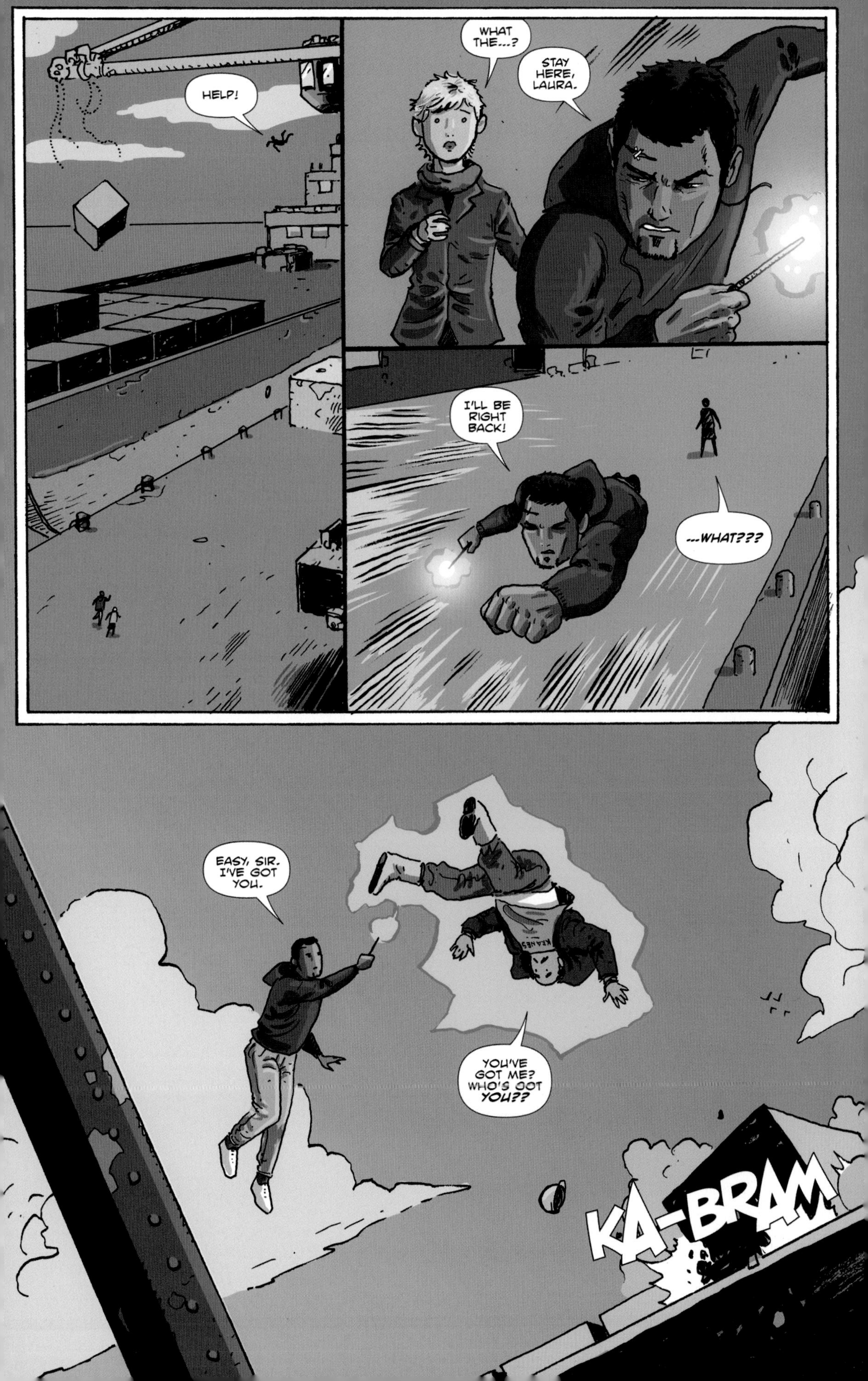
HELP!
WHAT THE...?
STAY HERE, LAURA.
I'LL BE RIGHT BACK!
...WHAT???
EASY, SIR. I'VE GOT YOU.
KRANES
YOU'VE GOT ME? WHO'S GOT YOU??
KA-BRAM

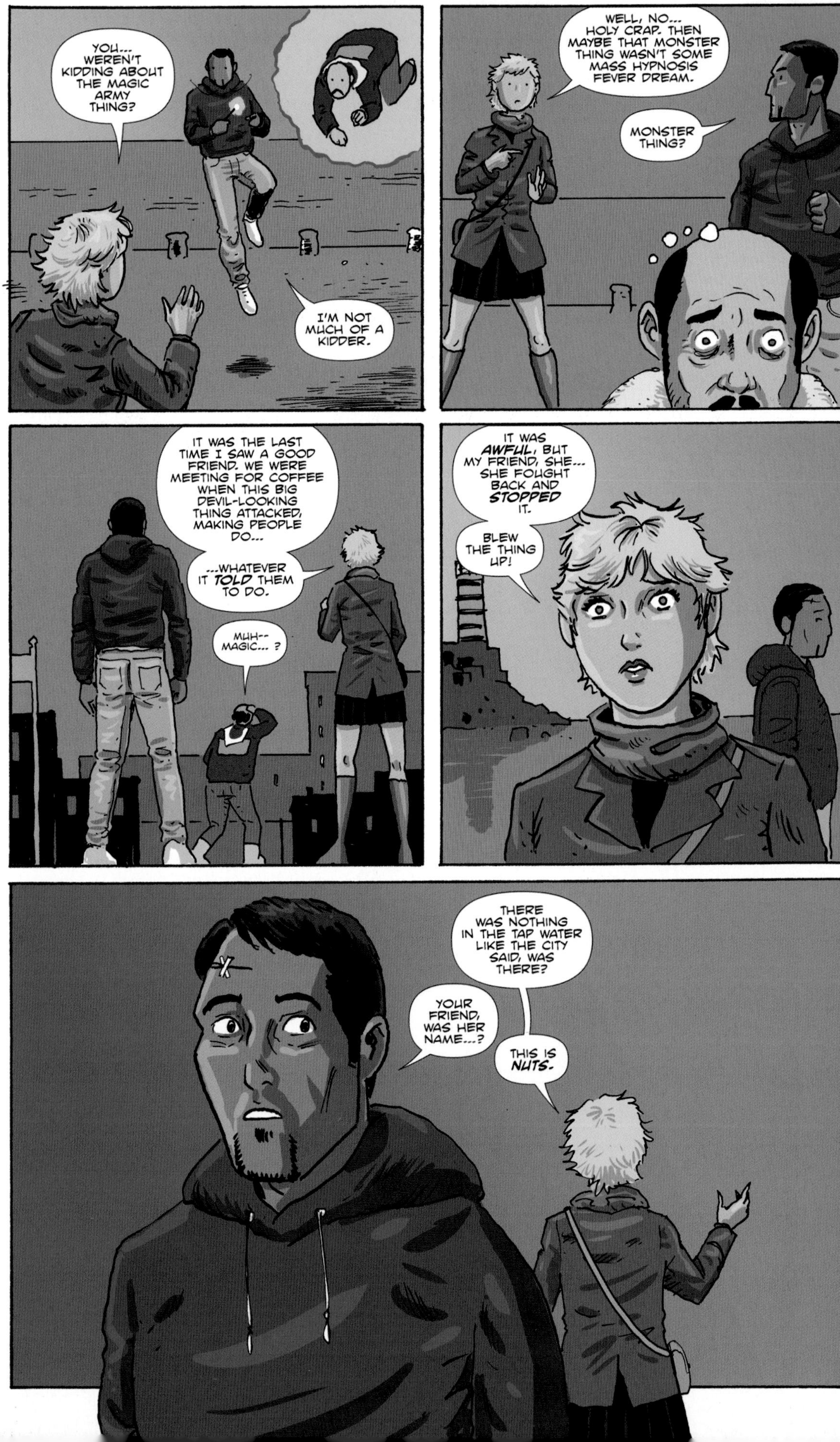
YOU... WEREN'T KIDDING ABOUT THE MAGIC ARMY THING?
I'M NOT MUCH OF A KIDDER.
WELL, NO... HOLY CRAP. THEN MAYBE THAT MONSTER THING WASN'T SOME MASS HYPNOSIS FEVER DREAM.
MONSTER THING?
IT WAS THE LAST TIME I SAW A GOOD FRIEND. WE WERE MEETING FOR COFFEE WHEN THIS BIG DEVIL-LOOKING THING ATTACKED, MAKING PEOPLE DO...
...WHATEVER IT TOLD THEM TO DO.
MUH-- MAGIC... ?
IT WAS AWFUL, BUT MY FRIEND, SHE... SHE FOUGHT BACK AND STOPPED IT.
BLEW THE THING UP!
THERE WAS NOTHING IN THE TAP WATER LIKE THE CITY SAID, WAS THERE?
YOUR FRIEND, WAS HER NAME...?
THIS IS NUTS.

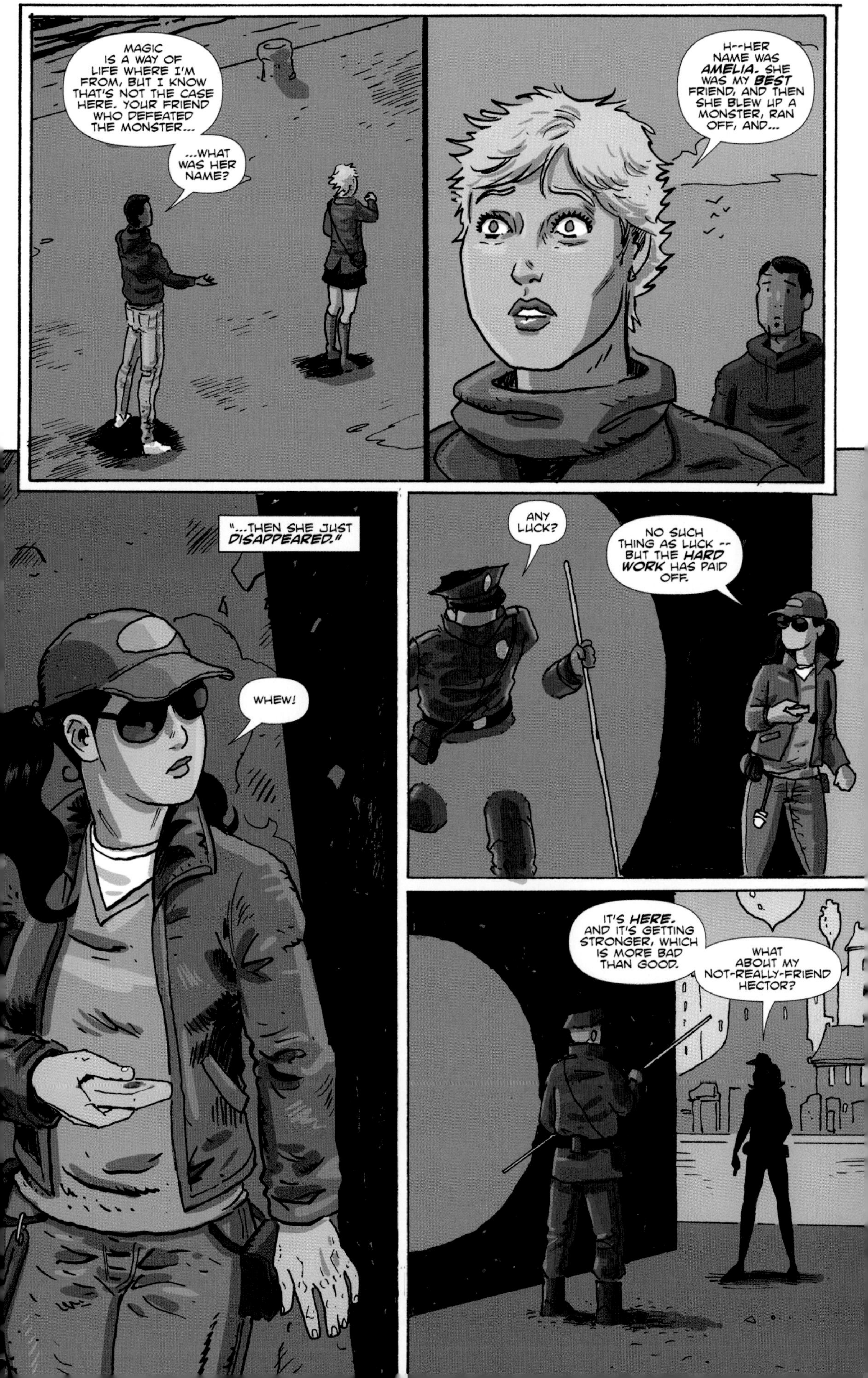
MAGIC IS A WAY OF LIFE WHERE I'M FROM, BUT I KNOW THAT'S NOT THE CASE HERE. YOUR FRIEND WHO DEFEATED THE MONSTER...
...WHAT WAS HER NAME?
H--HER NAME WAS AMELIA. SHE WAS MY BEST FRIEND, AND THEN SHE BLEW UP A MONSTER, RAN OFF, AND...
"...THEN SHE JUST DISAPPEARED."
WHEW!
ANY LUCK?
NO SUCH THING AS LUCK -- BUT THE HARD WORK HAS PAID OFF.
IT'S HERE. AND IT'S GETTING STRONGER, WHICH IS MORE BAD THAN GOOD.
WHAT ABOUT MY NOT-REALLY-FRIEND HECTOR?

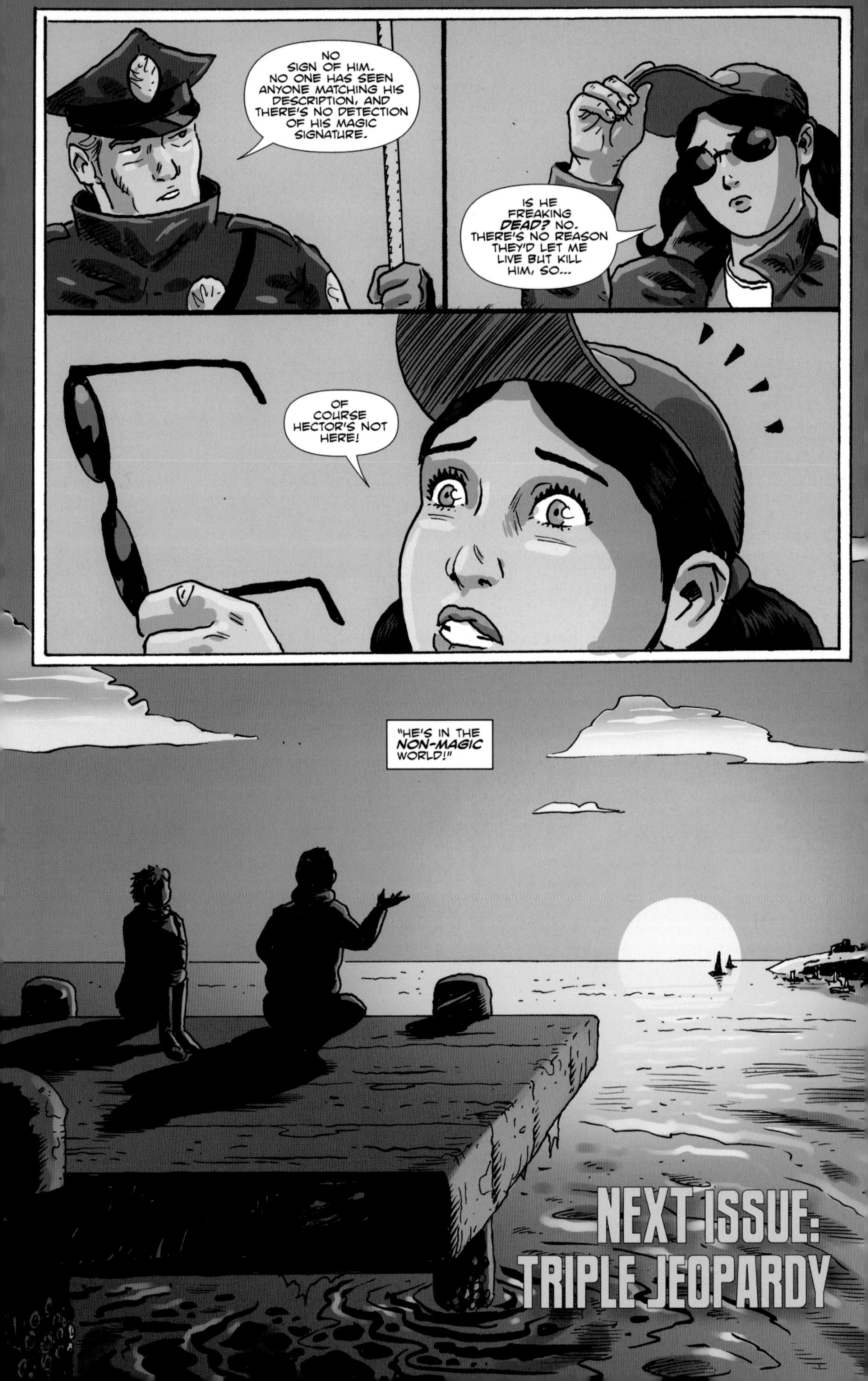
NO SIGN OF HIM. NO ONE HAS SEEN ANYONE MATCHING HIS DESCRIPTION, AND THERE'S NO DETECTION OF HIS MAGIC SIGNATURE.
IS HE FREAKING DEAD? NO. THERE'S NO REASON THEY'D LET ME LIVE BUT KILL HIM, SO...
OF COURSE HECTOR'S NOT HERE!
"HE'S IN THE NON-MAGIC WORLD!"
NEXT ISSUE: TRIPLE JEOPARDY

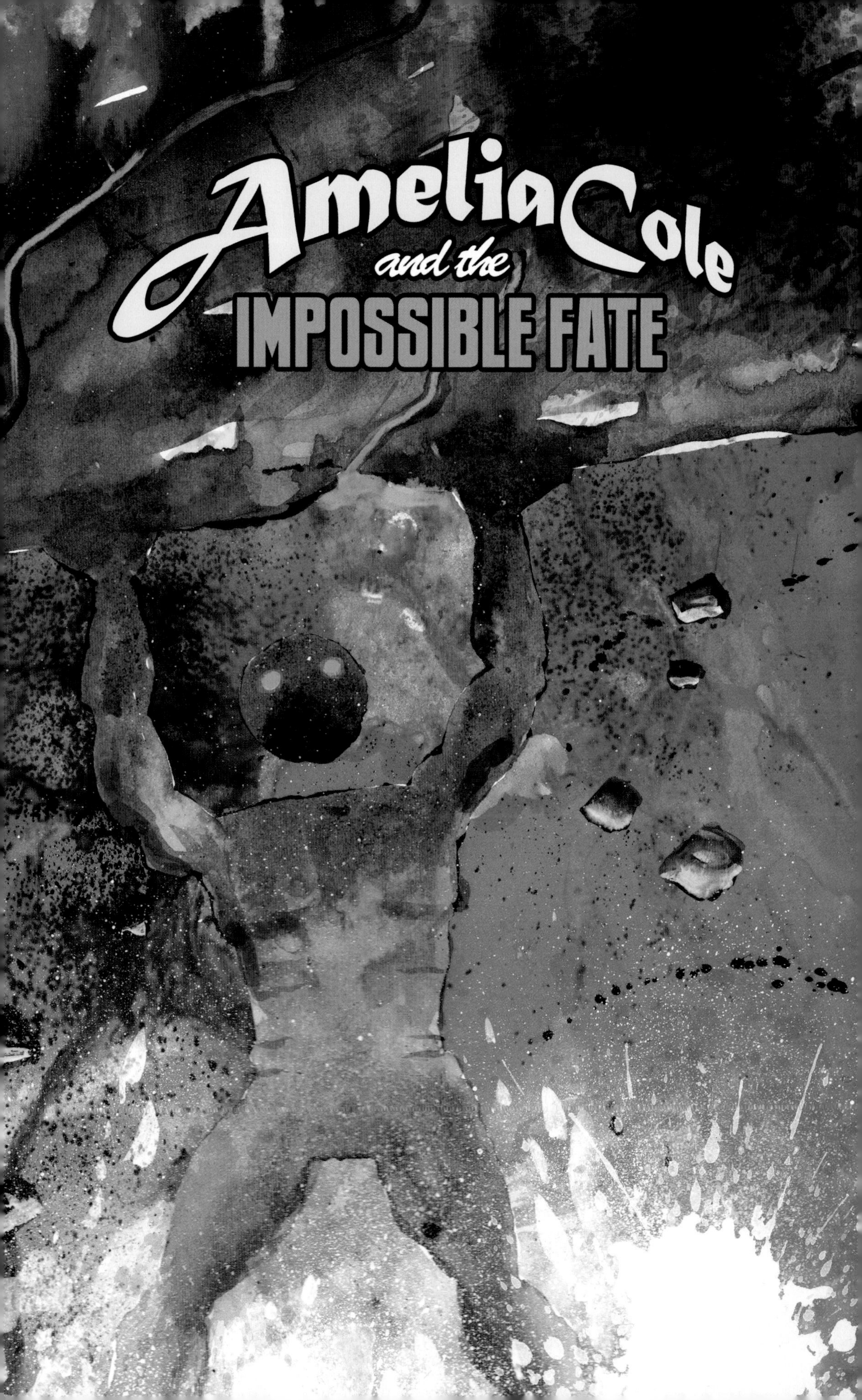
Amelia Cole
and the
IMPOSSIBLE FATE

CHAPTER 3

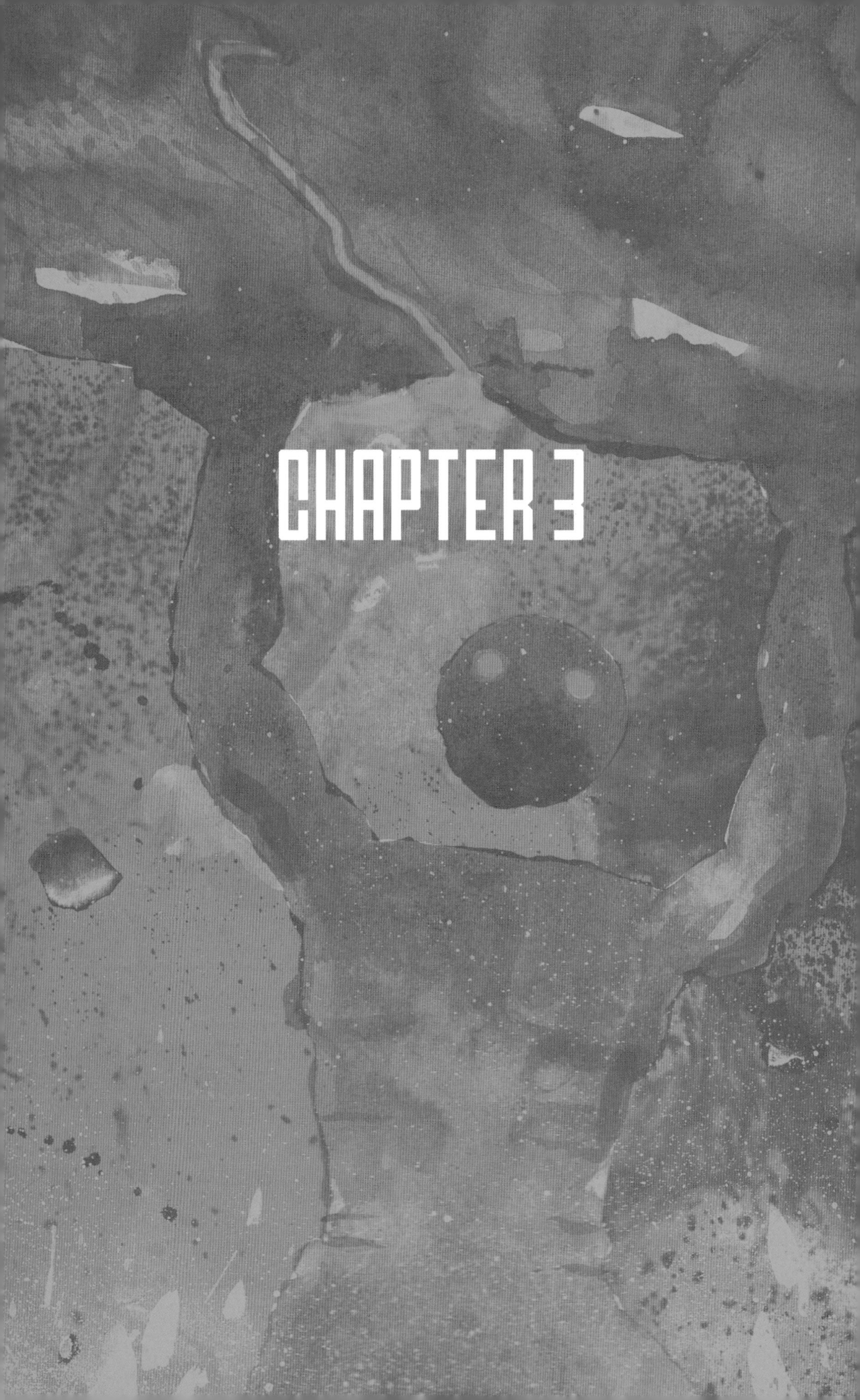

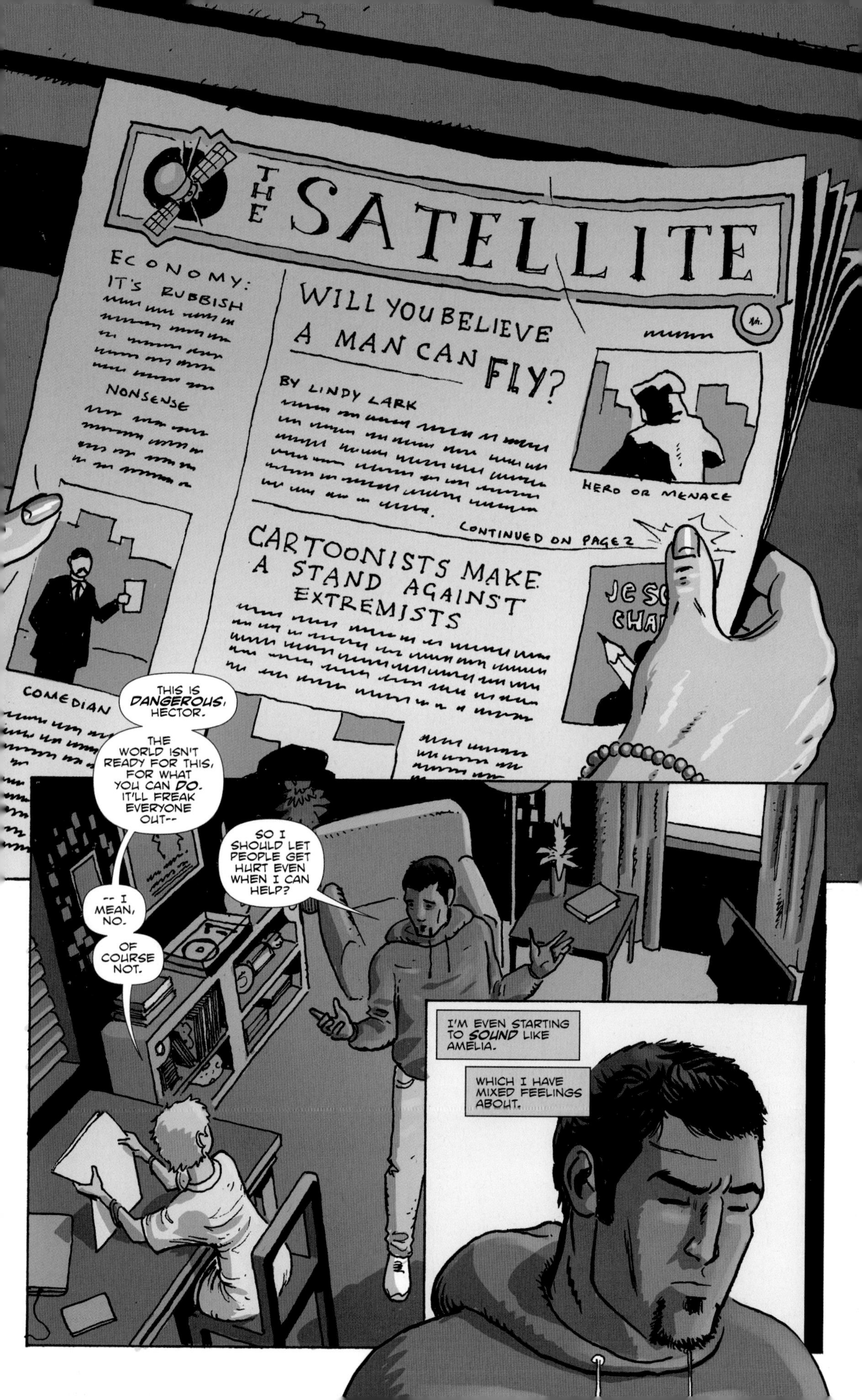
THE SATELLITE
ECONOMY: IT'S RUBBISH
NONSENSE
WILL YOU BELIEVE A MAN CAN FLY?
BY LINDY LARK
HERO OR MENACE
CONTINUED ON PAGE 2
CARTOONISTS MAKE A STAND AGAINST EXTREMISTS
COMEDIAN
THIS IS DANGEROUS, HECTOR.
THE WORLD ISN'T READY FOR THIS, FOR WHAT YOU CAN DO. IT'LL FREAK EVERYONE OUT--
SO I SHOULD LET PEOPLE GET HURT EVEN WHEN I CAN HELP?
-- I MEAN, NO.
OF COURSE NOT.
I'M EVEN STARTING TO SOUND LIKE AMELIA.
WHICH I HAVE MIXED FEELINGS ABOUT.

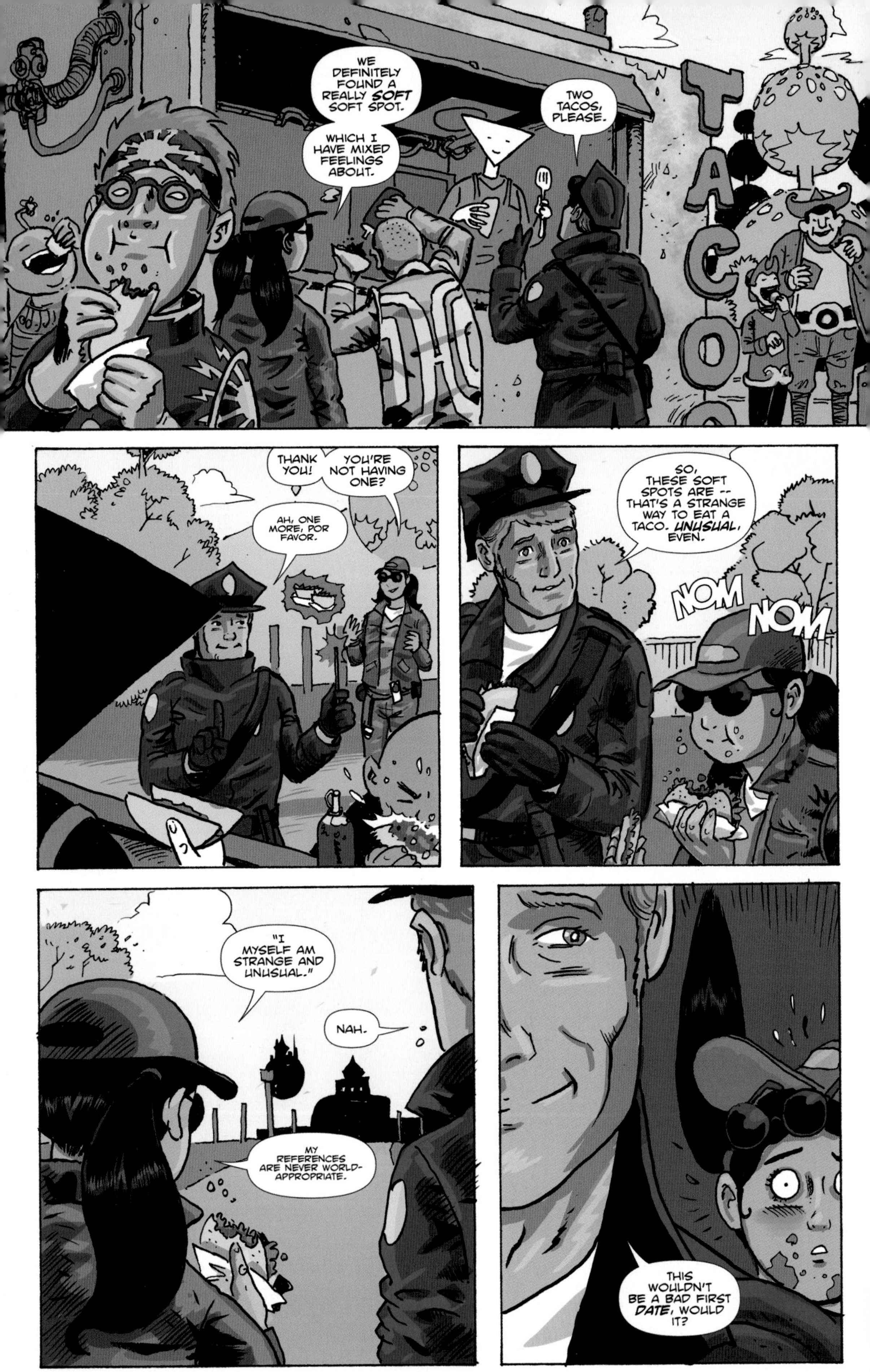
WE DEFINITELY FOUND A REALLY SOFT SOFT SPOT.
WHICH I HAVE MIXED FEELINGS ABOUT.
TWO TACOS, PLEASE.
TACO
THANK YOU!
YOU'RE NOT HAVING ONE?
AH, ONE MORE, POR FAVOR.
SO, THESE SOFT SPOTS ARE -- THAT'S A STRANGE WAY TO EAT A TACO. UNUSUAL, EVEN.
NOM
NOM
"I MYSELF AM STRANGE AND UNUSUAL."
NAH.
MY REFERENCES ARE NEVER WORLD-APPROPRIATE.
THIS WOULDN'T BE A BAD FIRST DATE, WOULD IT?

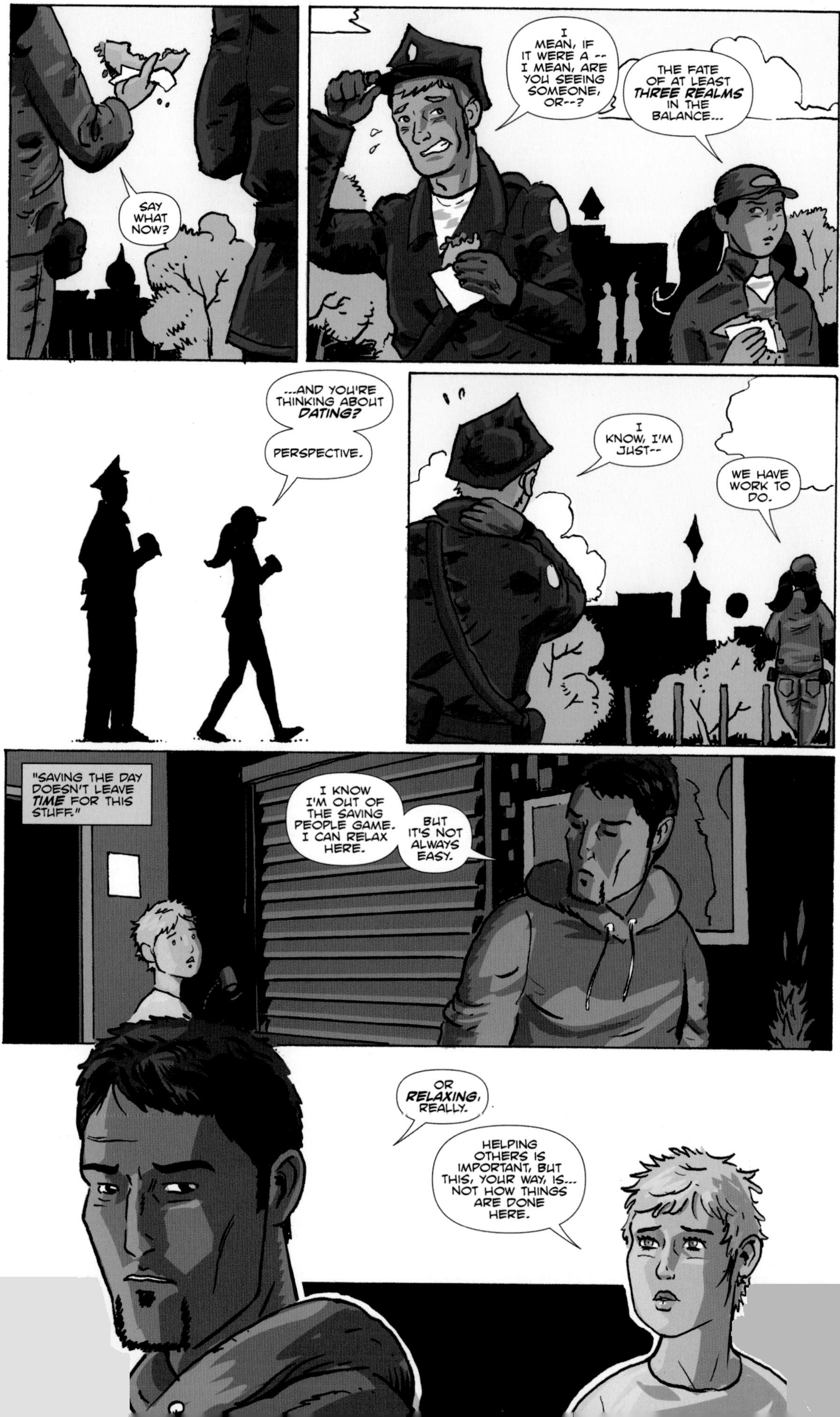
SAY WHAT NOW?
I MEAN, IF IT WERE A -- I MEAN, ARE YOU SEEING SOMEONE, OR--?
THE FATE OF AT LEAST THREE REALMS IN THE BALANCE...
...AND YOU'RE THINKING ABOUT DATING?
PERSPECTIVE.
I KNOW, I'M JUST--
WE HAVE WORK TO DO.
"SAVING THE DAY DOESN'T LEAVE TIME FOR THIS STUFF."
I KNOW I'M OUT OF THE SAVING PEOPLE GAME. I CAN RELAX HERE.
BUT IT'S NOT ALWAYS EASY.
OR RELAXING, REALLY.
HELPING OTHERS IS IMPORTANT, BUT THIS, YOUR WAY, IS... NOT HOW THINGS ARE DONE HERE.

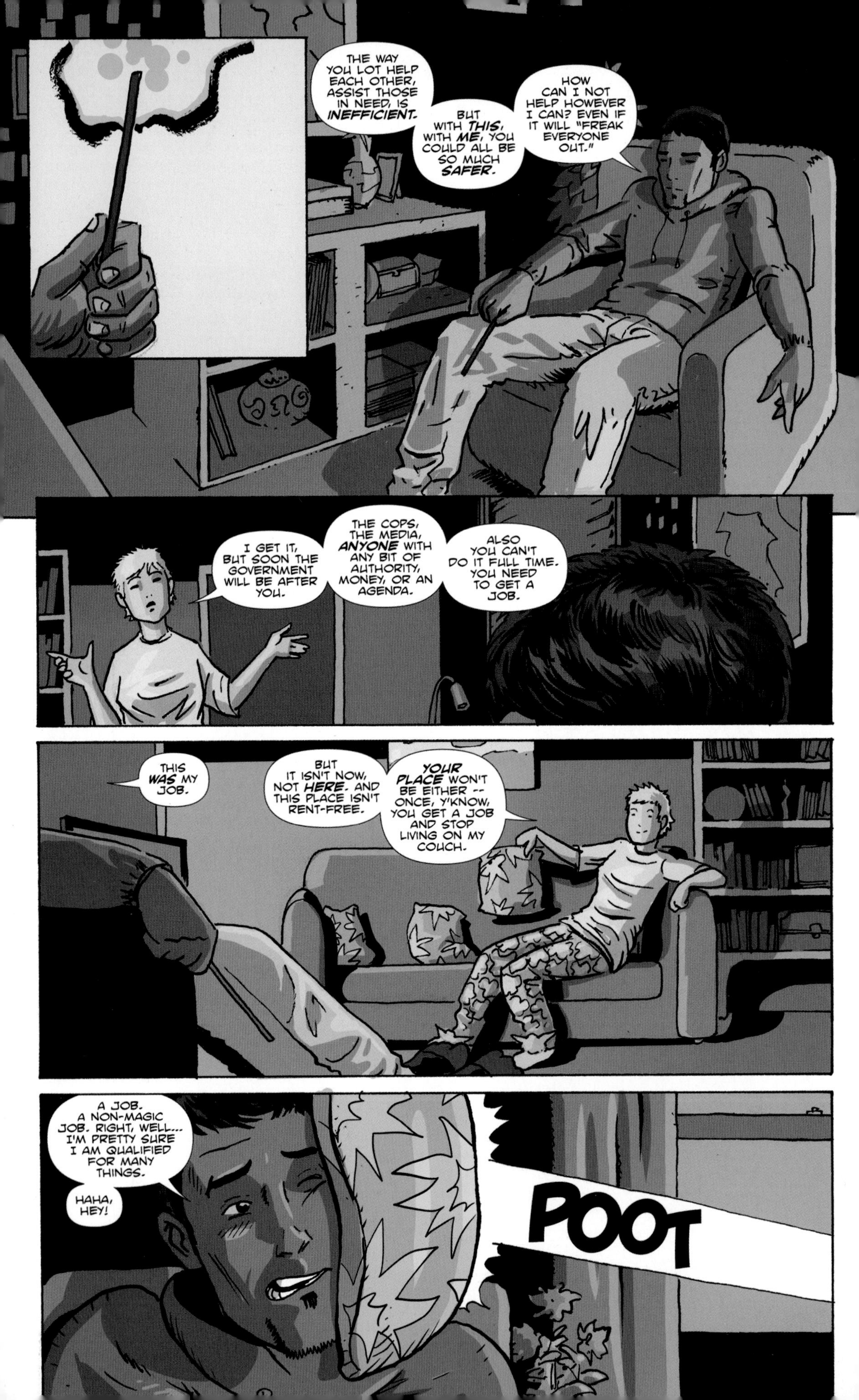
THE WAY YOU LOT HELP EACH OTHER, ASSIST THOSE IN NEED, IS INEFFICIENT.
BUT WITH THIS, WITH ME, YOU COULD ALL BE SO MUCH SAFER.
HOW CAN I NOT HELP HOWEVER I CAN? EVEN IF IT WILL "FREAK EVERYONE OUT."
I GET IT, BUT SOON THE GOVERNMENT WILL BE AFTER YOU.
THE COPS, THE MEDIA, ANYONE WITH ANY BIT OF AUTHORITY, MONEY, OR AN AGENDA.
ALSO YOU CAN'T DO IT FULL TIME. YOU NEED TO GET A JOB.
THIS WAS MY JOB.
BUT IT ISN'T NOW, NOT HERE. AND THIS PLACE ISN'T RENT-FREE.
YOUR PLACE WON'T BE EITHER -- ONCE, Y'KNOW, YOU GET A JOB AND STOP LIVING ON MY COUCH.
A JOB. A NON-MAGIC JOB. RIGHT, WELL... I'M PRETTY SURE I AM QUALIFIED FOR MANY THINGS.
HAHA, HEY!
POOT

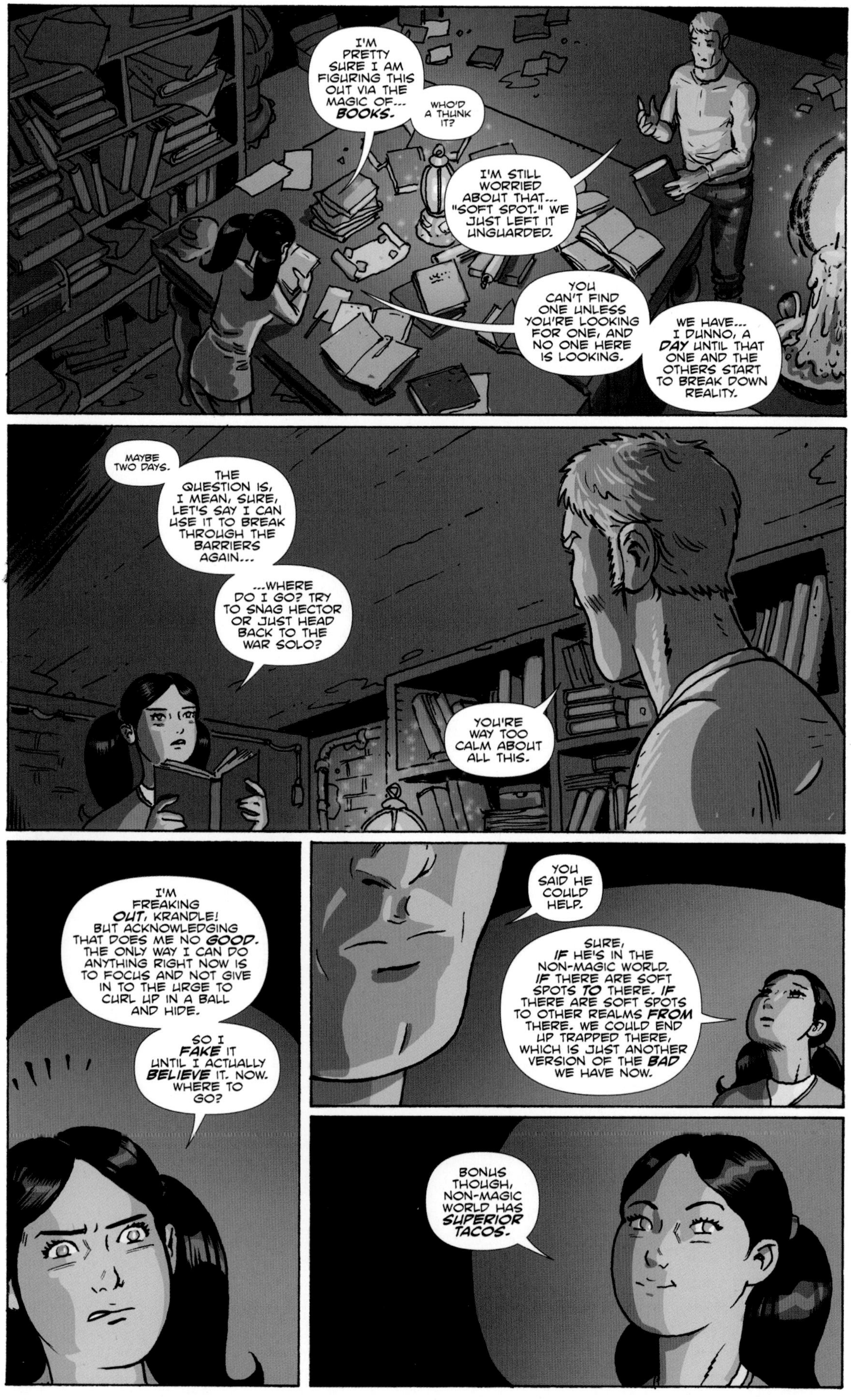
I'M PRETTY SURE I AM FIGURING THIS OUT VIA THE MAGIC OF--- BOOKS.
WHO'D A THUNK IT?
I'M STILL WORRIED ABOUT THAT--- "SOFT SPOT." WE JUST LEFT IT UNGUARDED.
YOU CAN'T FIND ONE UNLESS YOU'RE LOOKING FOR ONE, AND NO ONE HERE IS LOOKING.
WE HAVE--- I DUNNO, A DAY UNTIL THAT ONE AND THE OTHERS START TO BREAK DOWN REALITY.
MAYBE TWO DAYS.
THE QUESTION IS, I MEAN, SURE, LET'S SAY I CAN USE IT TO BREAK THROUGH THE BARRIERS AGAIN---
---WHERE DO I GO? TRY TO SNAG HECTOR OR JUST HEAD BACK TO THE WAR SOLO?
YOU'RE WAY TOO CALM ABOUT ALL THIS.
I'M FREAKING OUT, KRANDLE! BUT ACKNOWLEDGING THAT DOES ME NO GOOD. THE ONLY WAY I CAN DO ANYTHING RIGHT NOW IS TO FOCUS AND NOT GIVE IN TO THE URGE TO CURL UP IN A BALL AND HIDE.
SO I FAKE IT UNTIL I ACTUALLY BELIEVE IT. NOW. WHERE TO GO?
YOU SAID HE COULD HELP.
SURE, IF HE'S IN THE NON-MAGIC WORLD. IF THERE ARE SOFT SPOTS TO THERE. IF THERE ARE SOFT SPOTS TO OTHER REALMS FROM THERE. WE COULD END UP TRAPPED THERE, WHICH IS JUST ANOTHER VERSION OF THE BAD WE HAVE NOW.
BONUS THOUGH, NON-MAGIC WORLD HAS SUPERIOR TACOS.

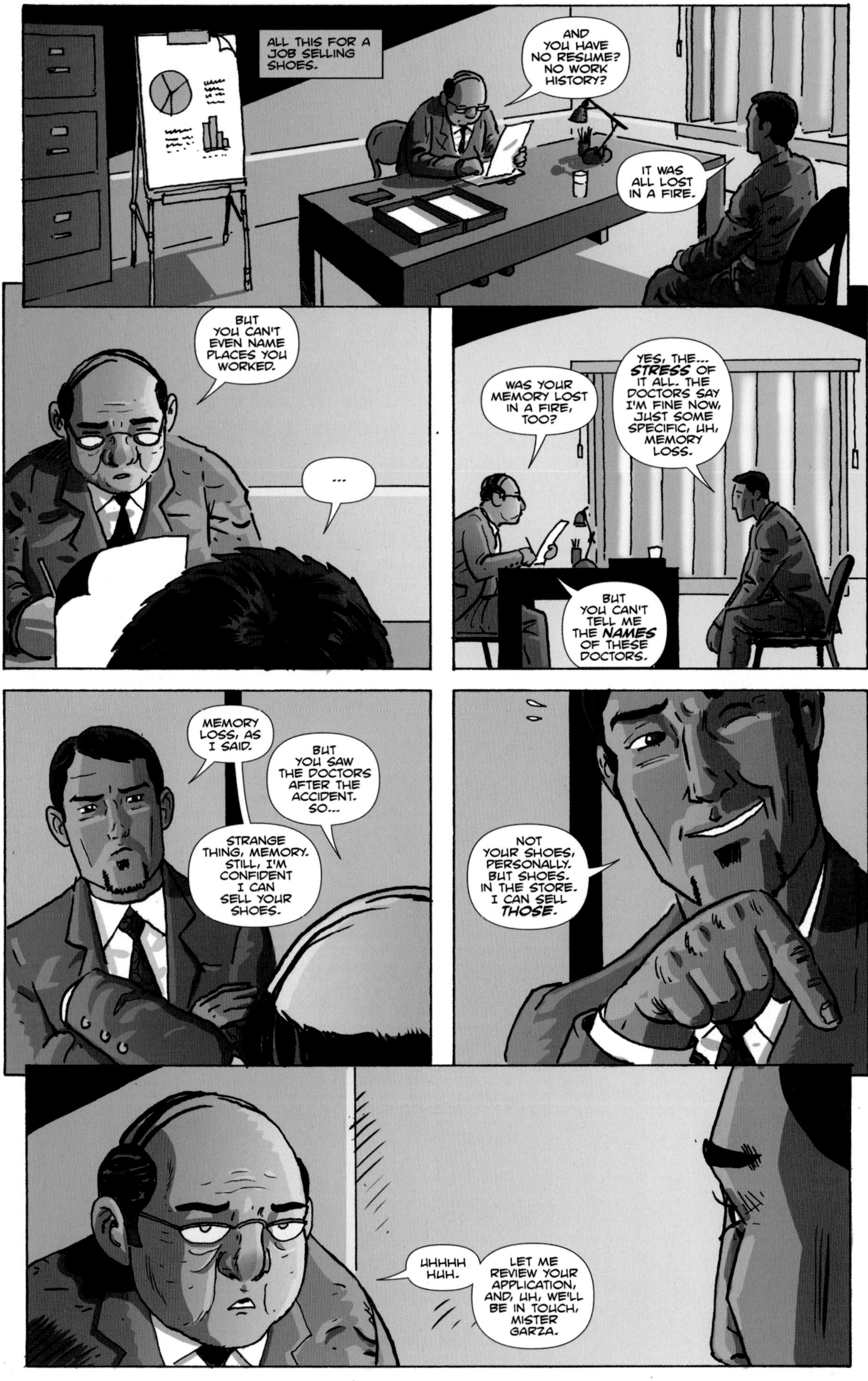
ALL THIS FOR A JOB SELLING SHOES.
AND YOU HAVE NO RESUME? NO WORK HISTORY?
IT WAS ALL LOST IN A FIRE.
BUT YOU CAN'T EVEN NAME PLACES YOU WORKED.
...
WAS YOUR MEMORY LOST IN A FIRE, TOO?
YES, THE... STRESS OF IT ALL. THE DOCTORS SAY I'M FINE NOW, JUST SOME SPECIFIC, UH, MEMORY LOSS.
BUT YOU CAN'T TELL ME THE NAMES OF THESE DOCTORS.
MEMORY LOSS, AS I SAID.
BUT YOU SAW THE DOCTORS AFTER THE ACCIDENT. SO...
STRANGE THING, MEMORY. STILL, I'M CONFIDENT I CAN SELL YOUR SHOES.
NOT YOUR SHOES, PERSONALLY. BUT SHOES. IN THE STORE. I CAN SELL THOSE.
UHHHH HUH.
LET ME REVIEW YOUR APPLICATION, AND, UH, WE'LL BE IN TOUCH, MISTER GARZA.

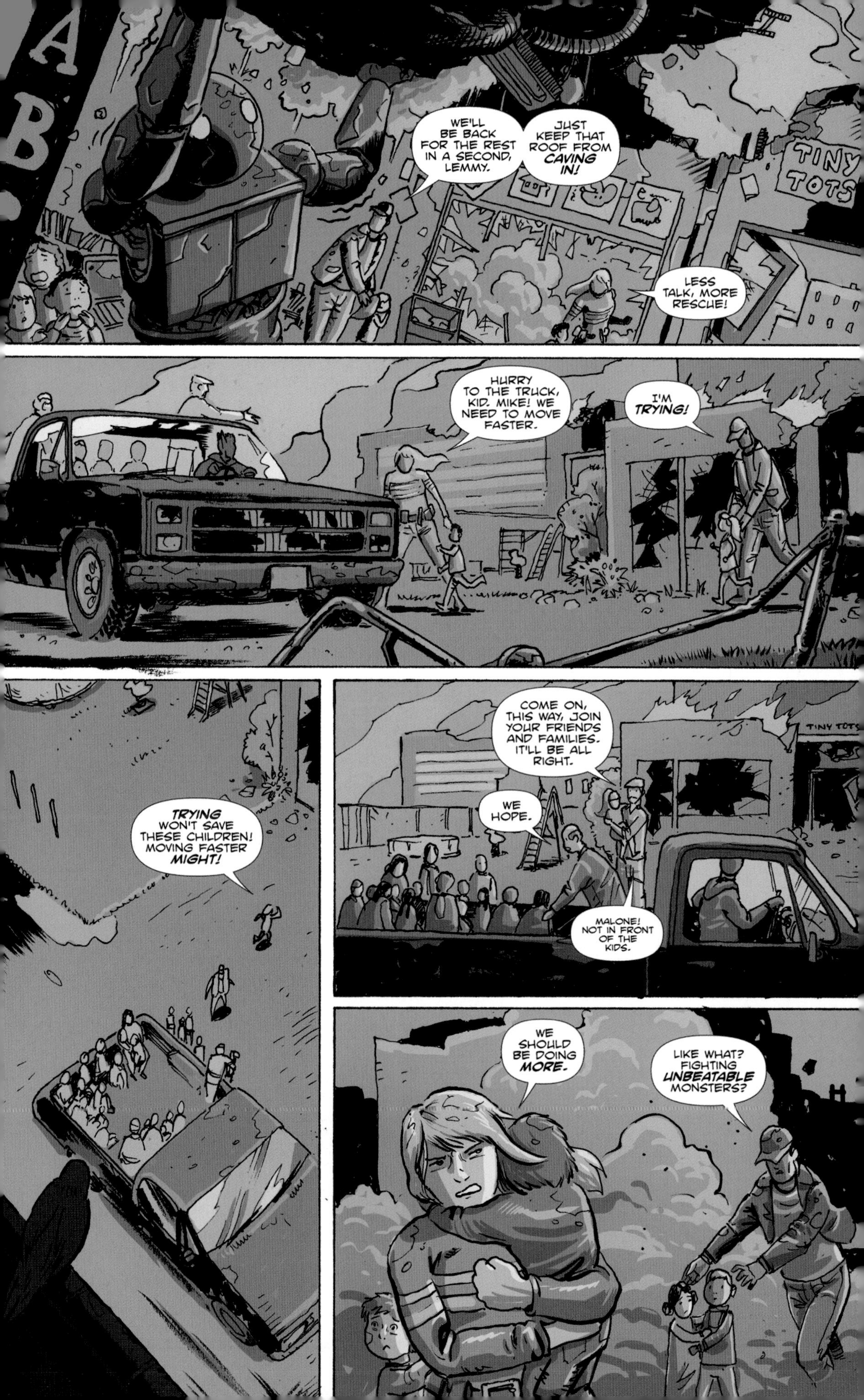
A
B
WE'LL BE BACK FOR THE REST IN A SECOND, LEMMY.
JUST KEEP THAT ROOF FROM CAVING IN!
TINY TOTS
LESS TALK, MORE RESCUE!
HURRY TO THE TRUCK, KID. MIKE! WE NEED TO MOVE FASTER.
I'M TRYING!
TRYING WON'T SAVE THESE CHILDREN! MOVING FASTER MIGHT!
COME ON, THIS WAY, JOIN YOUR FRIENDS AND FAMILIES. IT'LL BE ALL RIGHT.
TINY TOTS
WE HOPE.
MALONE! NOT IN FRONT OF THE KIDS.
WE SHOULD BE DOING MORE.
LIKE WHAT? FIGHTING UNBEATABLE MONSTERS?

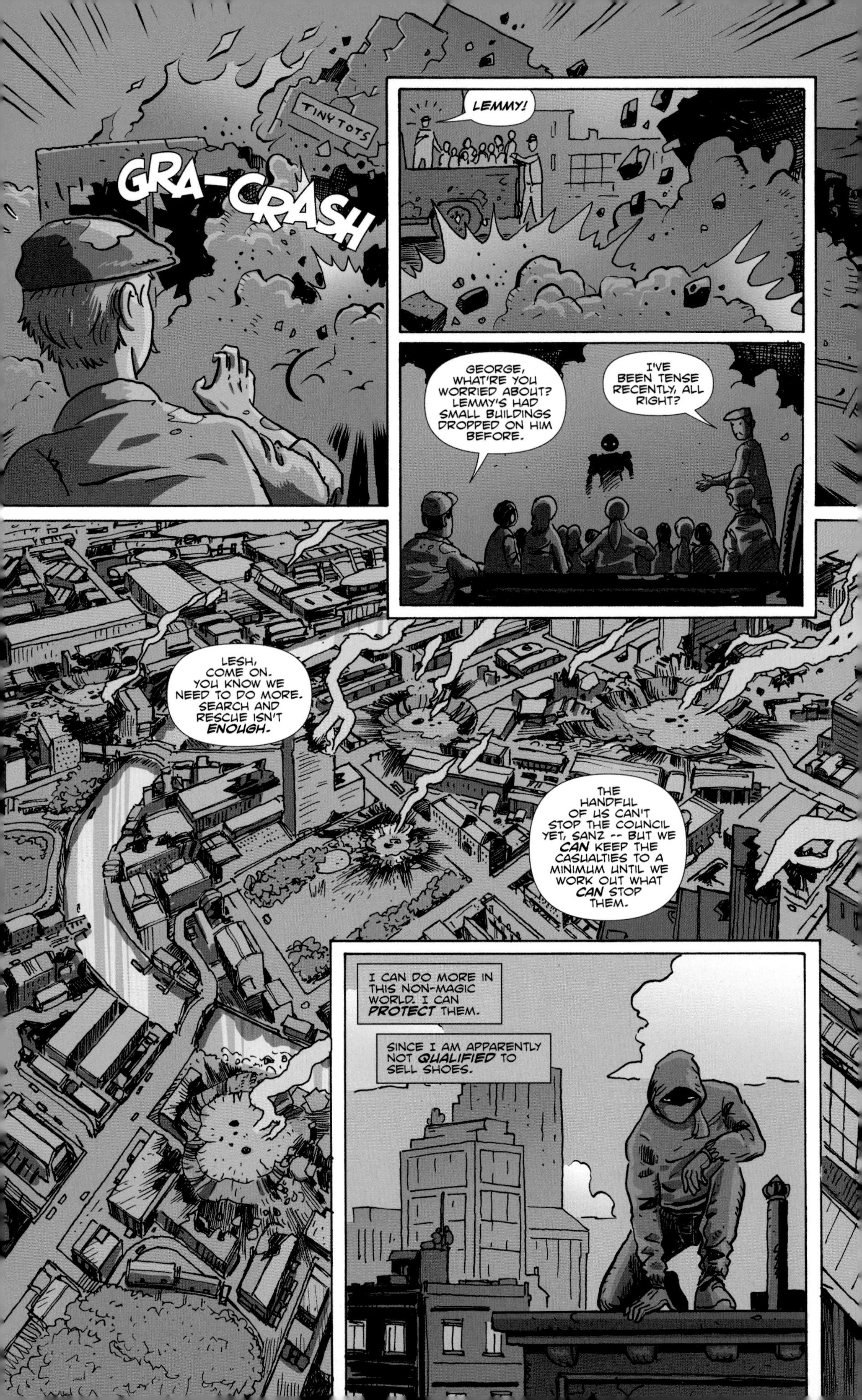
TINY TOTS
GRA-CRASH
LEMMY!
GEORGE, WHAT'RE YOU WORRIED ABOUT? LEMMY'S HAD SMALL BUILDINGS DROPPED ON HIM BEFORE.
I'VE BEEN TENSE RECENTLY, ALL RIGHT?
LESH, COME ON. YOU KNOW WE NEED TO DO MORE. SEARCH AND RESCUE ISN'T ENOUGH.
THE HANDFUL OF US CAN'T STOP THE COUNCIL YET, SANZ -- BUT WE CAN KEEP THE CASUALTIES TO A MINIMUM UNTIL WE WORK OUT WHAT CAN STOP THEM.
I CAN DO MORE IN THIS NON-MAGIC WORLD. I CAN PROTECT THEM.
SINCE I AM APPARENTLY NOT QUALIFIED TO SELL SHOES.

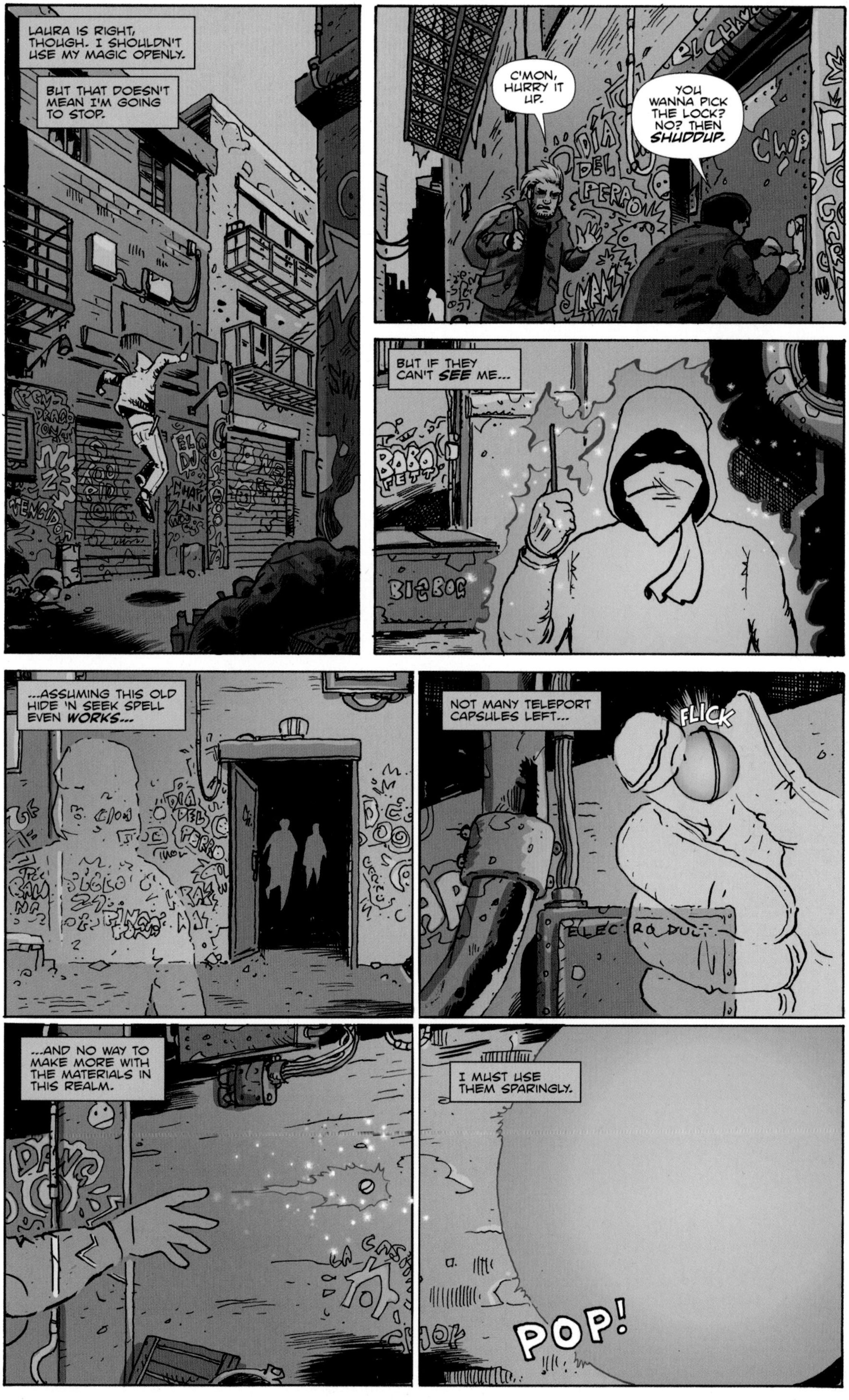
LAURA IS RIGHT, THOUGH. I SHOULDN'T USE MY MAGIC OPENLY.
BUT THAT DOESN'T MEAN I'M GOING TO STOP.
C'MON, HURRY IT UP.
YOU WANNA PICK THE LOCK? NO? THEN **SHUDDUP.**
BUT IF THEY CAN'T ***SEE*** ME...
...ASSUMING THIS OLD HIDE 'N SEEK SPELL EVEN ***WORKS...***
NOT MANY TELEPORT CAPSULES LEFT...
FLICK
...AND NO WAY TO MAKE MORE WITH THE MATERIALS IN THIS REALM.
I MUST USE THEM SPARINGLY.
POP!

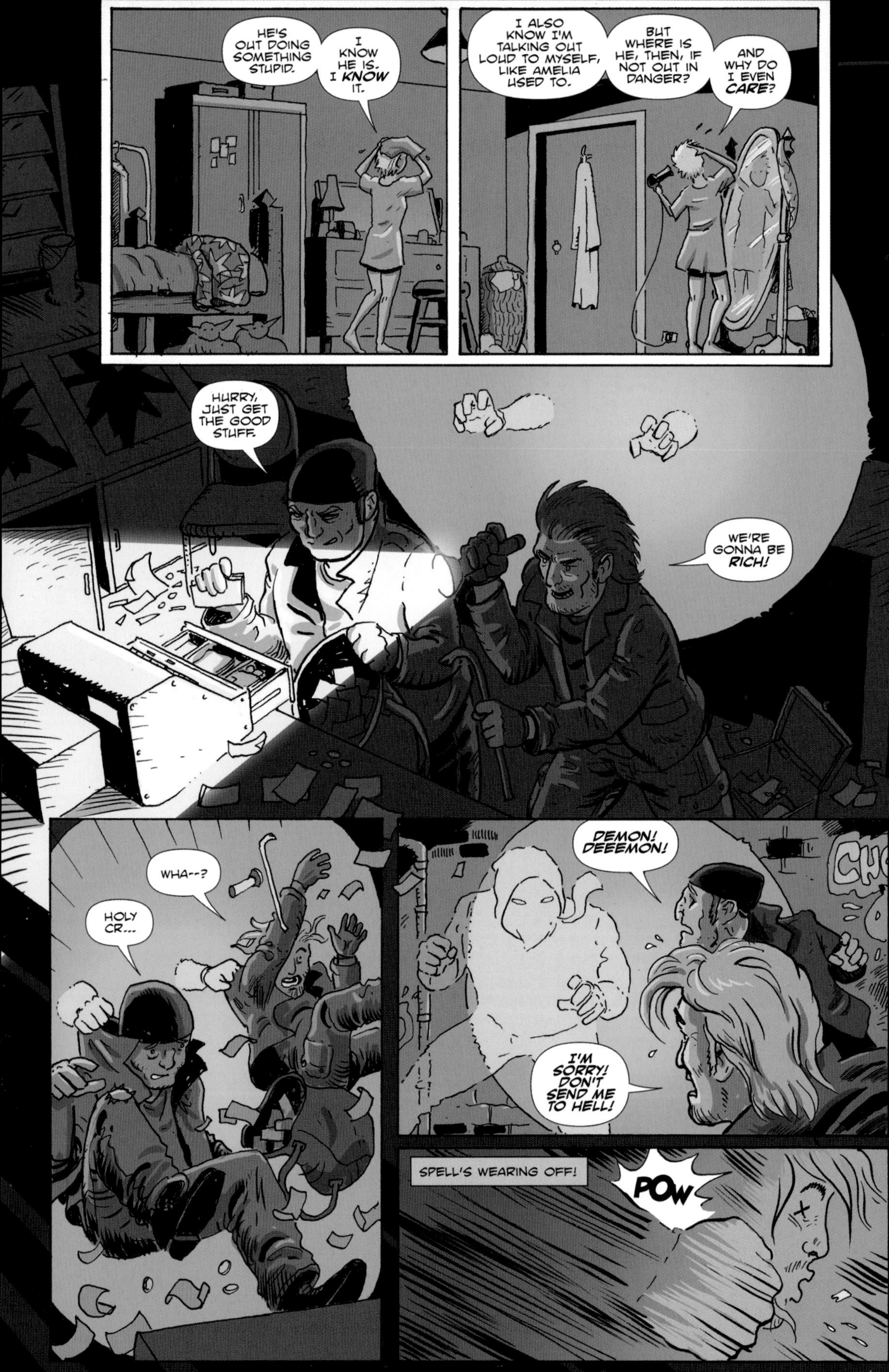
HE'S OUT DOING SOMETHING STUPID.
I KNOW HE IS. I KNOW IT.
I ALSO KNOW I'M TALKING OUT LOUD TO MYSELF, LIKE AMELIA USED TO.
BUT WHERE IS HE, THEN, IF NOT OUT IN DANGER?
AND WHY DO I EVEN CARE?
HURRY, JUST GET THE GOOD STUFF.
WE'RE GONNA BE RICH!
WHA--?
HOLY CR...
DEMON! DEEEMON!
I'M SORRY! DON'T SEND ME TO HELL!
SPELL'S WEARING OFF!
POW

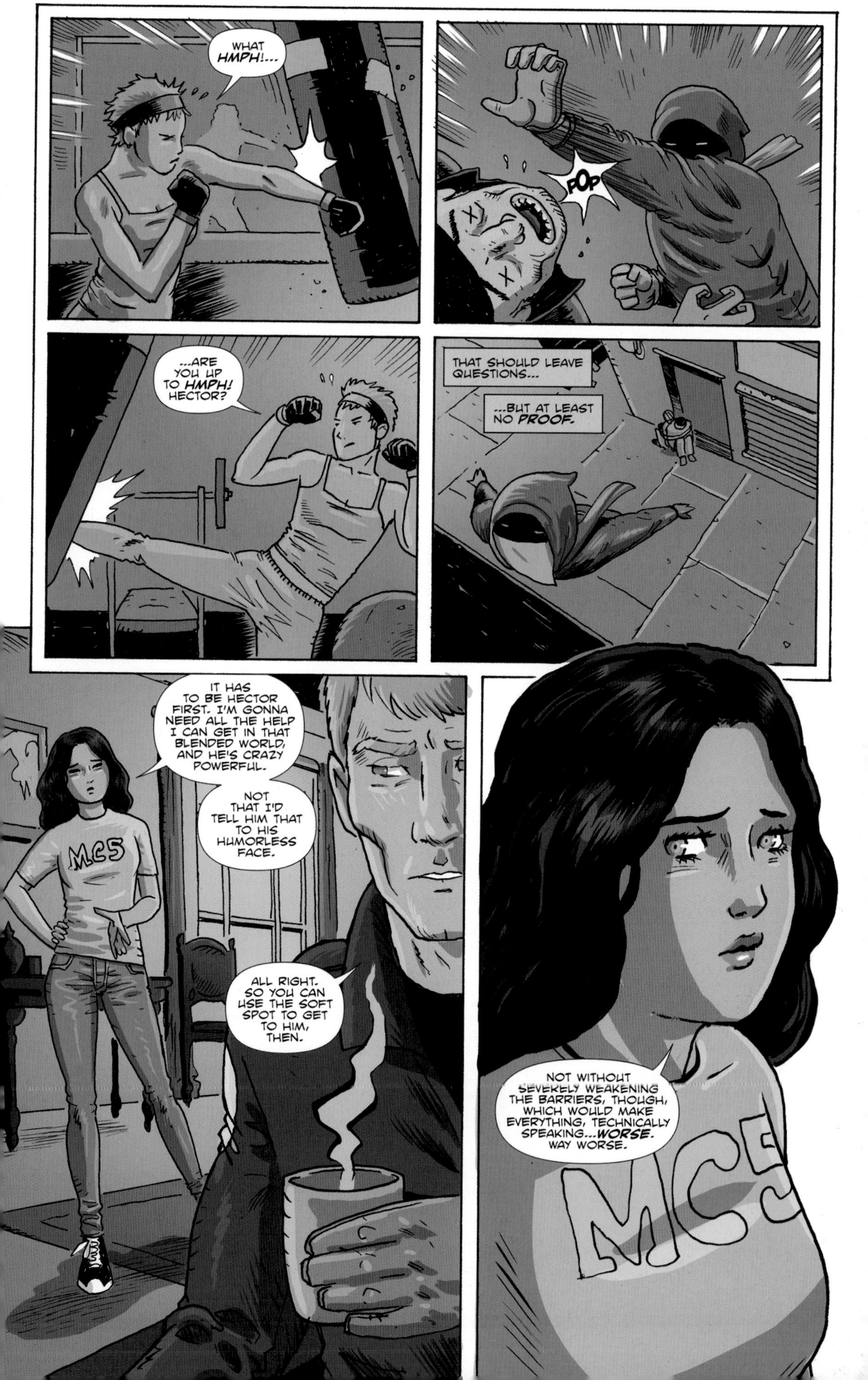
WHAT HMPH!...
POP
...ARE YOU UP TO HMPH! HECTOR?
THAT SHOULD LEAVE QUESTIONS...
...BUT AT LEAST NO PROOF.
IT HAS TO BE HECTOR FIRST. I'M GONNA NEED ALL THE HELP I CAN GET IN THAT BLENDED WORLD, AND HE'S CRAZY POWERFUL.
NOT THAT I'D TELL HIM THAT TO HIS HUMORLESS FACE.
ALL RIGHT. SO YOU CAN USE THE SOFT SPOT TO GET TO HIM, THEN.
NOT WITHOUT SEVERELY WEAKENING THE BARRIERS, THOUGH, WHICH WOULD MAKE EVERYTHING, TECHNICALLY SPEAKING...WORSE. WAY WORSE.
MC5
MC5

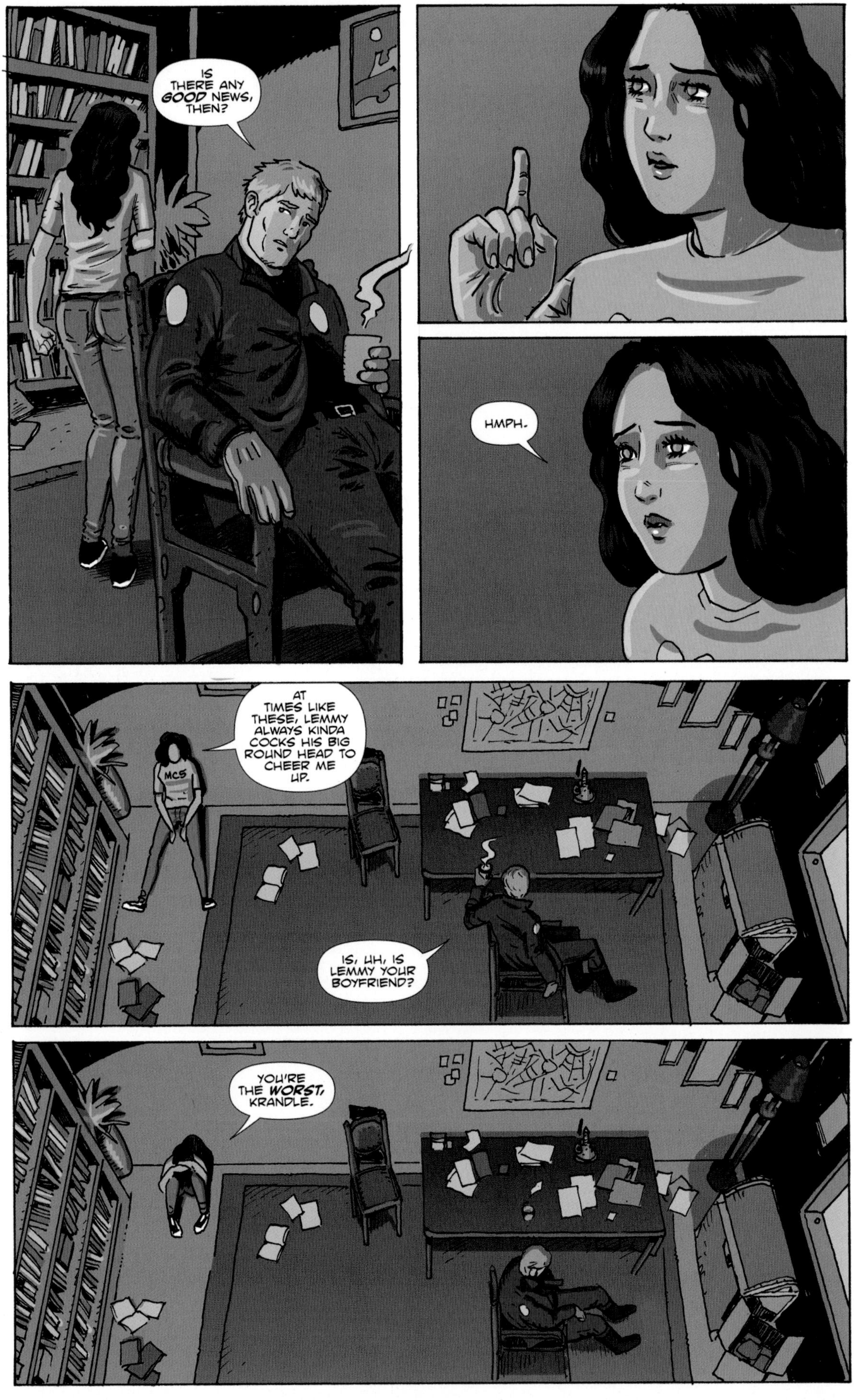
IS THERE ANY GOOD NEWS, THEN?
HMPH.
AT TIMES LIKE THESE, LEMMY ALWAYS KINDA COCKS HIS BIG ROUND HEAD TO CHEER ME UP.
MCS
IS, UH, IS LEMMY YOUR BOYFRIEND?
YOU'RE THE WORST, KRANDLE.

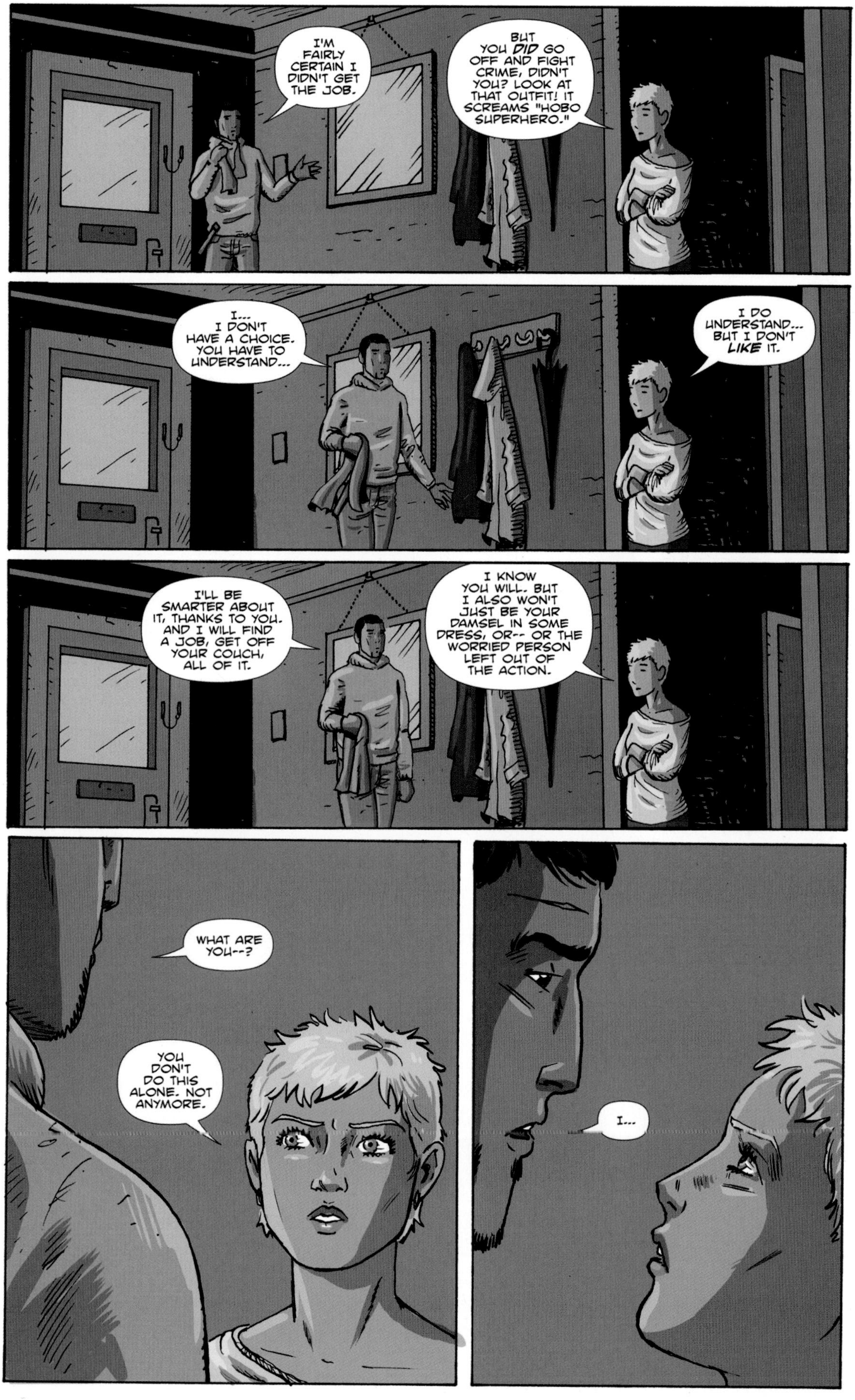
I'M FAIRLY CERTAIN I DIDN'T GET THE JOB.
BUT YOU DID GO OFF AND FIGHT CRIME, DIDN'T YOU? LOOK AT THAT OUTFIT! IT SCREAMS "HOBO SUPERHERO."
I... I DON'T HAVE A CHOICE. YOU HAVE TO UNDERSTAND...
I DO UNDERSTAND... BUT I DON'T LIKE IT.
I'LL BE SMARTER ABOUT IT, THANKS TO YOU. AND I WILL FIND A JOB, GET OFF YOUR COUCH, ALL OF IT.
I KNOW YOU WILL. BUT I ALSO WON'T JUST BE YOUR DAMSEL IN SOME DRESS, OR-- OR THE WORRIED PERSON LEFT OUT OF THE ACTION.
WHAT ARE YOU--?
YOU DON'T DO THIS ALONE. NOT ANYMORE.
I...

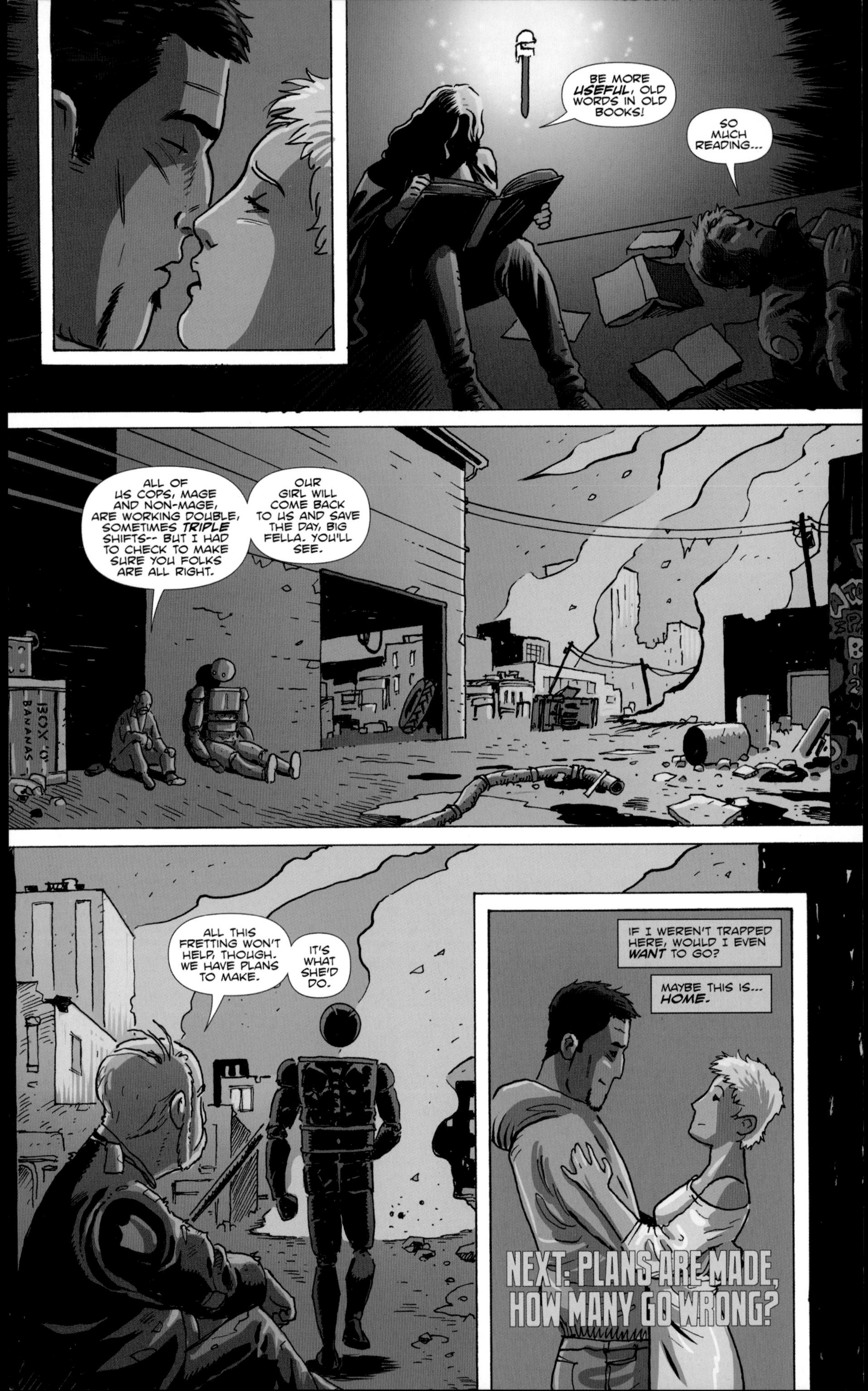
BE MORE USEFUL, OLD WORDS IN OLD BOOKS!
SO MUCH READING...
ALL OF US COPS, MAGE AND NON-MAGE, ARE WORKING DOUBLE, SOMETIMES TRIPLE SHIFTS-- BUT I HAD TO CHECK TO MAKE SURE YOU FOLKS ARE ALL RIGHT.
OUR GIRL WILL COME BACK TO US AND SAVE THE DAY, BIG FELLA. YOU'LL SEE.
BOX 'O' BANANAS
ALL THIS FRETTING WON'T HELP, THOUGH. WE HAVE PLANS TO MAKE.
IT'S WHAT SHE'D DO.
IF I WEREN'T TRAPPED HERE, WOULD I EVEN WANT TO GO?
MAYBE THIS IS... HOME.
NEXT: PLANS ARE MADE, HOW MANY GO WRONG?

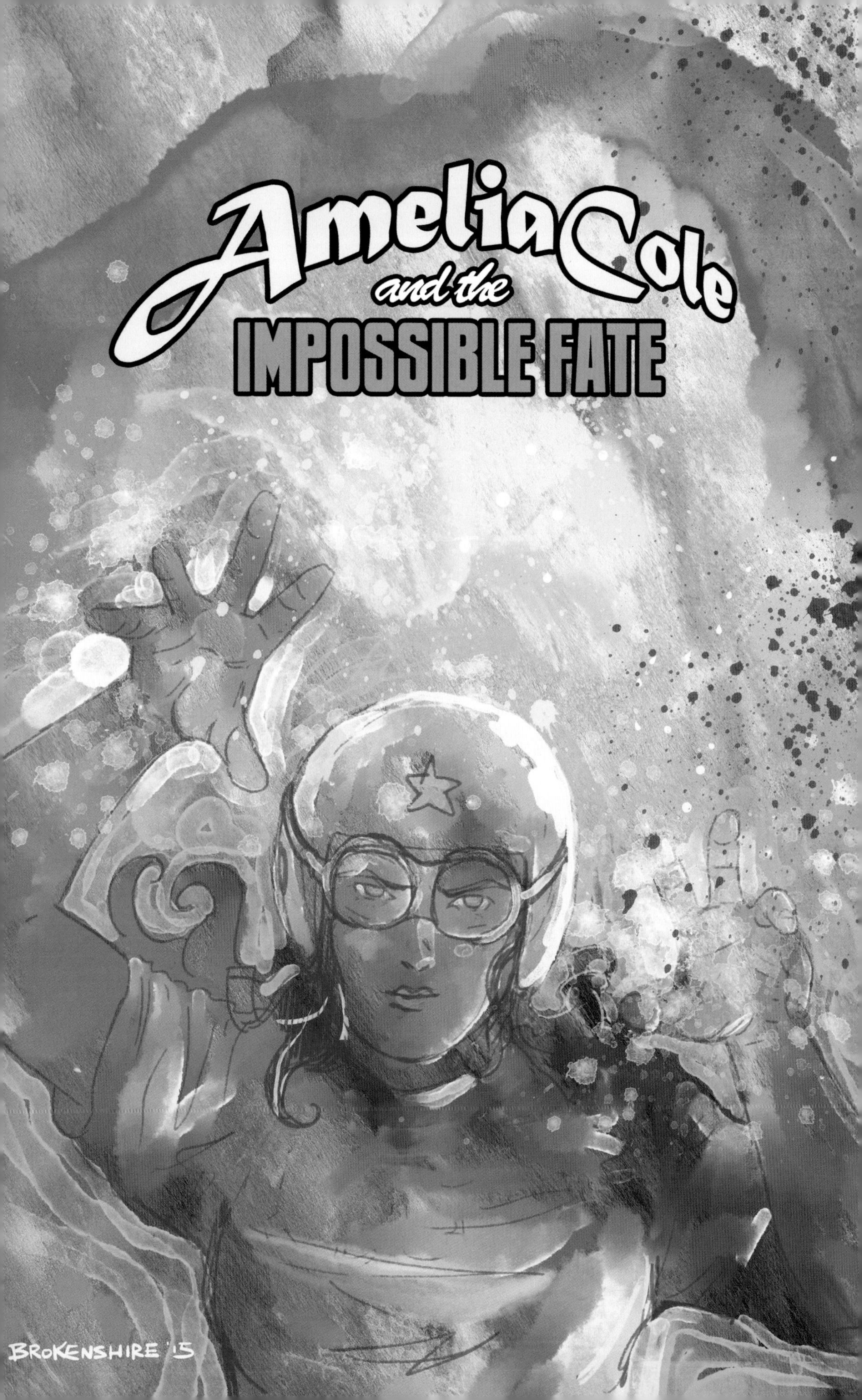

Amelia Cole
and the
IMPOSSIBLE FATE
BROKENSHIRE '15

CHAPTER 4

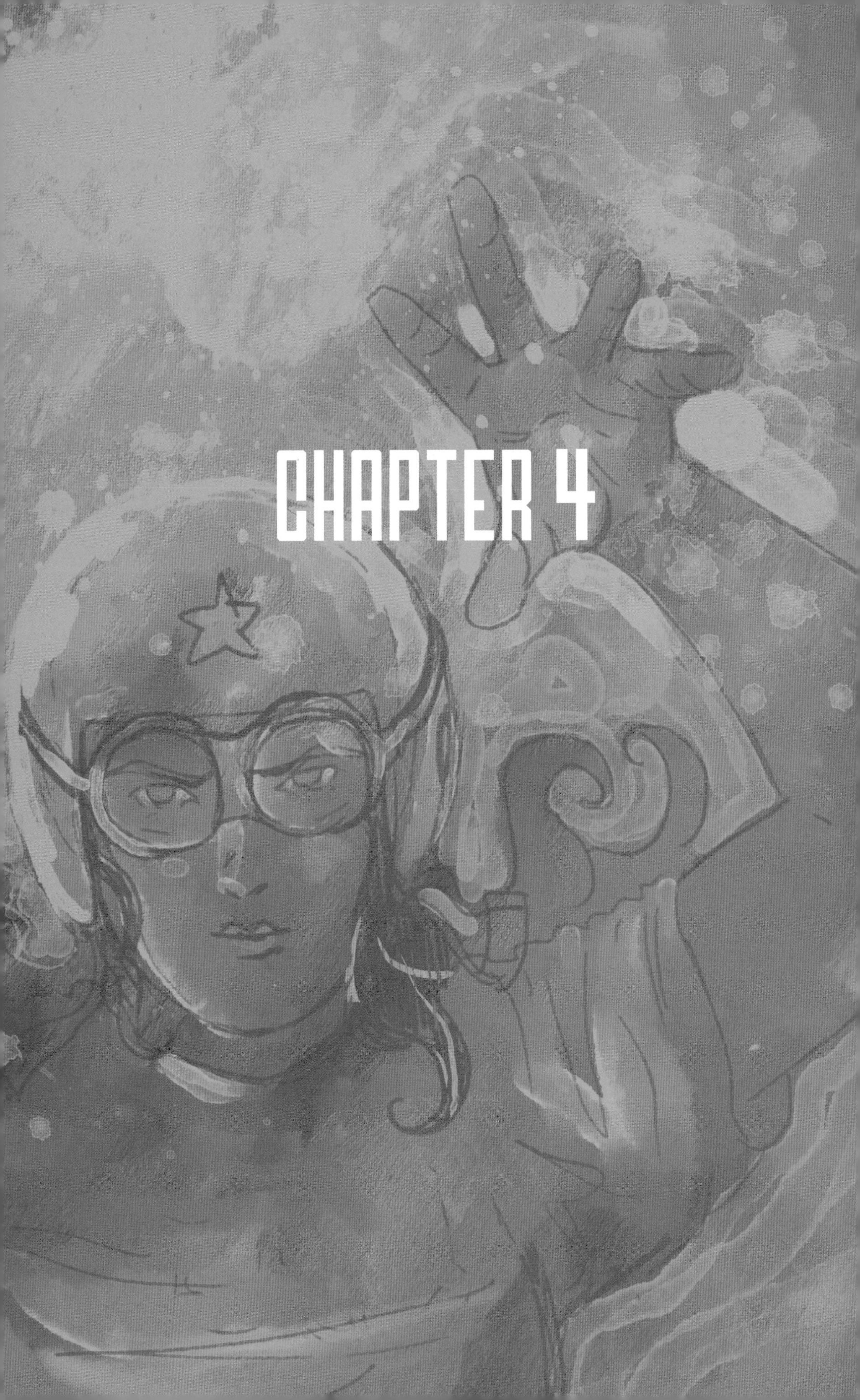

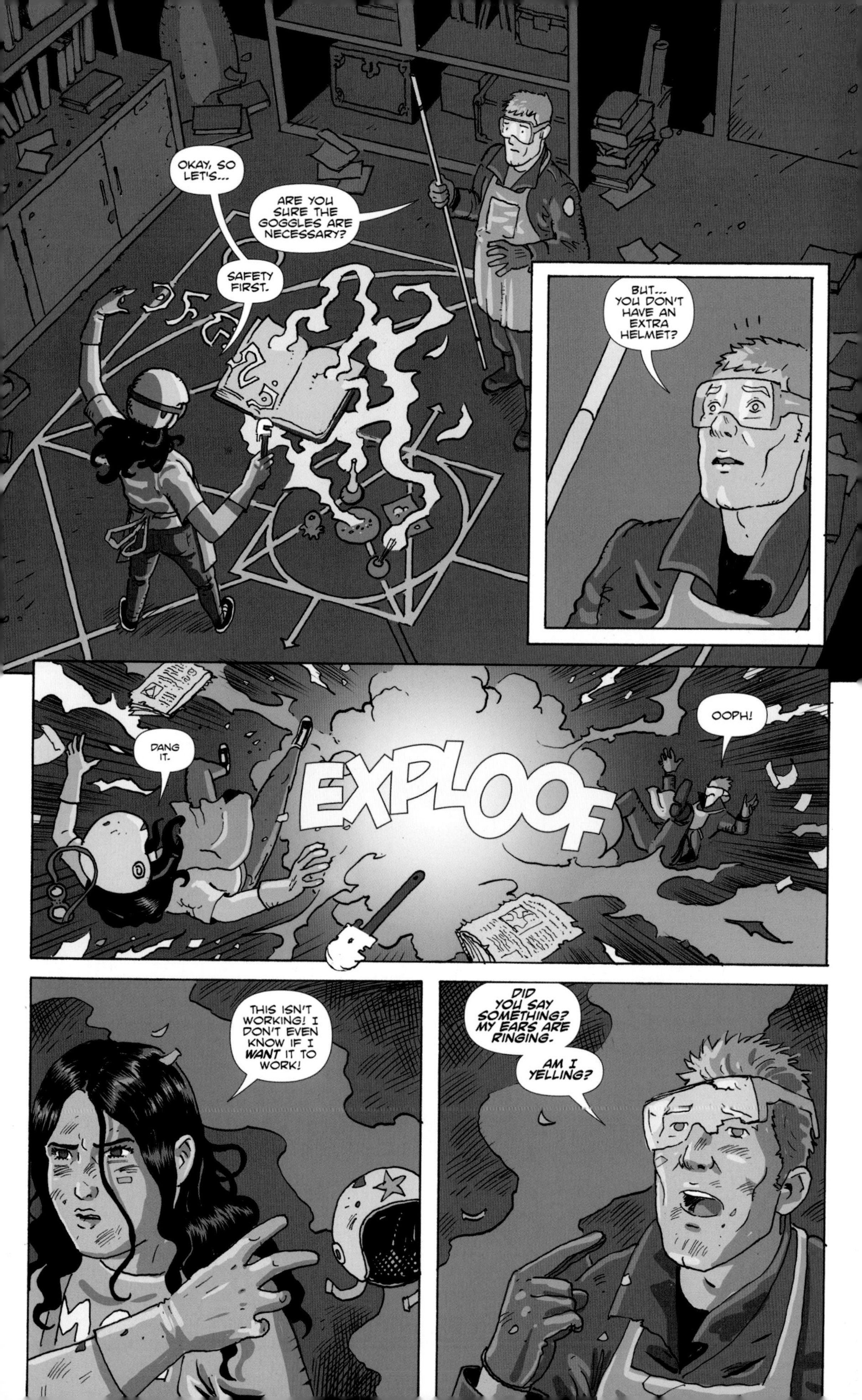

OKAY, SO LET'S...
ARE YOU SURE THE GOGGLES ARE NECESSARY?
SAFETY FIRST.
BUT... YOU DON'T HAVE AN EXTRA HELMET?
DANG IT.
EXPLOOF
OOPH!
THIS ISN'T WORKING! I DON'T EVEN KNOW IF I WANT IT TO WORK!
DID YOU SAY SOMETHING? MY EARS ARE RINGING.
AM I YELLING?

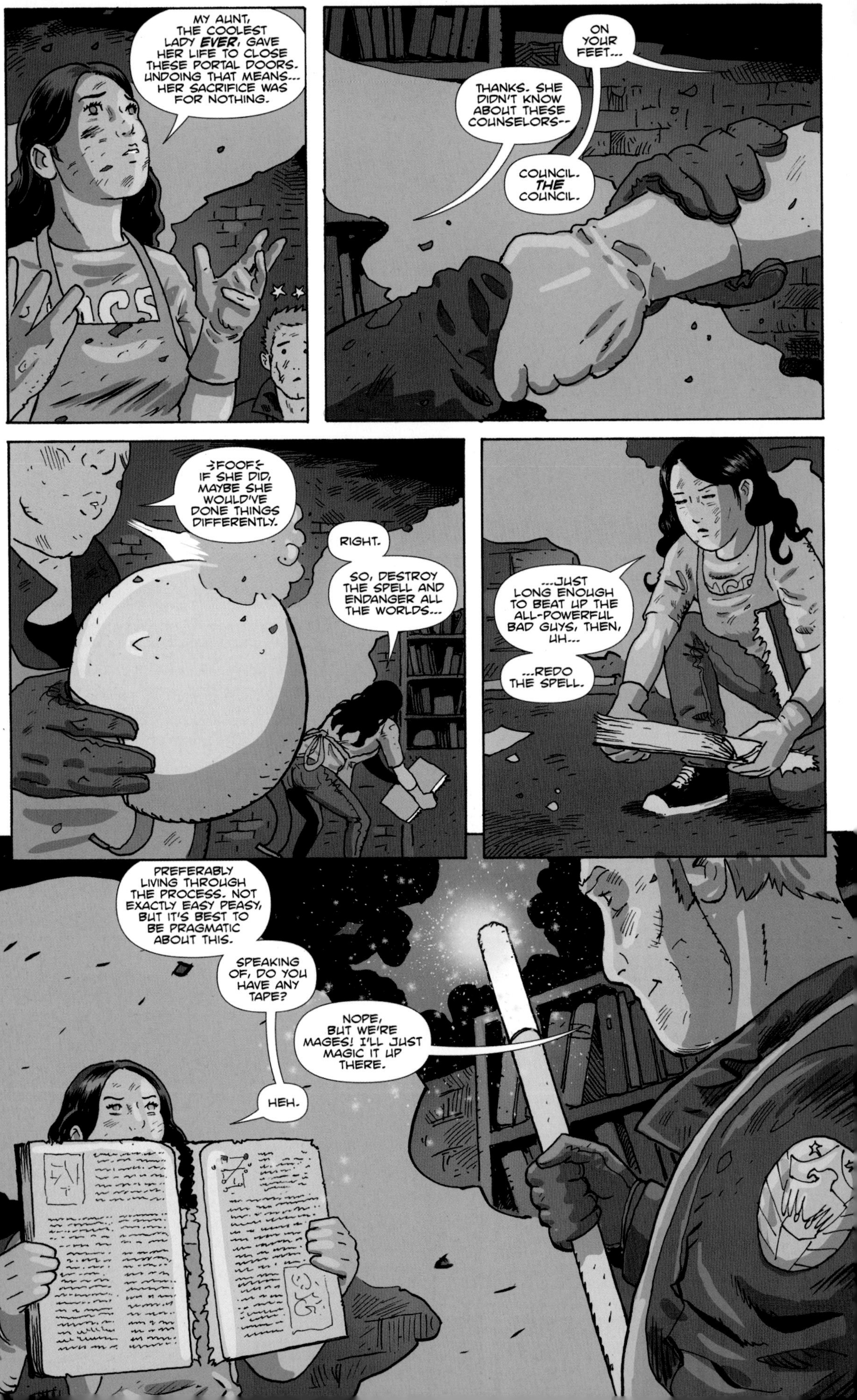
MY AUNT, THE COOLEST LADY EVER, GAVE HER LIFE TO CLOSE THESE PORTAL DOORS. UNDOING THAT MEANS... HER SACRIFICE WAS FOR NOTHING.
ON YOUR FEET...
THANKS. SHE DIDN'T KNOW ABOUT THESE COUNSELORS--
COUNCIL. THE COUNCIL.
FOOF
IF SHE DID, MAYBE SHE WOULD'VE DONE THINGS DIFFERENTLY.
RIGHT.
SO, DESTROY THE SPELL AND ENDANGER ALL THE WORLDS...
...JUST LONG ENOUGH TO BEAT UP THE ALL-POWERFUL BAD GUYS, THEN, UH...
...REDO THE SPELL.
PREFERABLY LIVING THROUGH THE PROCESS. NOT EXACTLY EASY PEASY, BUT IT'S BEST TO BE PRAGMATIC ABOUT THIS.
SPEAKING OF, DO YOU HAVE ANY TAPE?
NOPE, BUT WE'RE MAGES! I'LL JUST MAGIC IT UP THERE.
HEH.

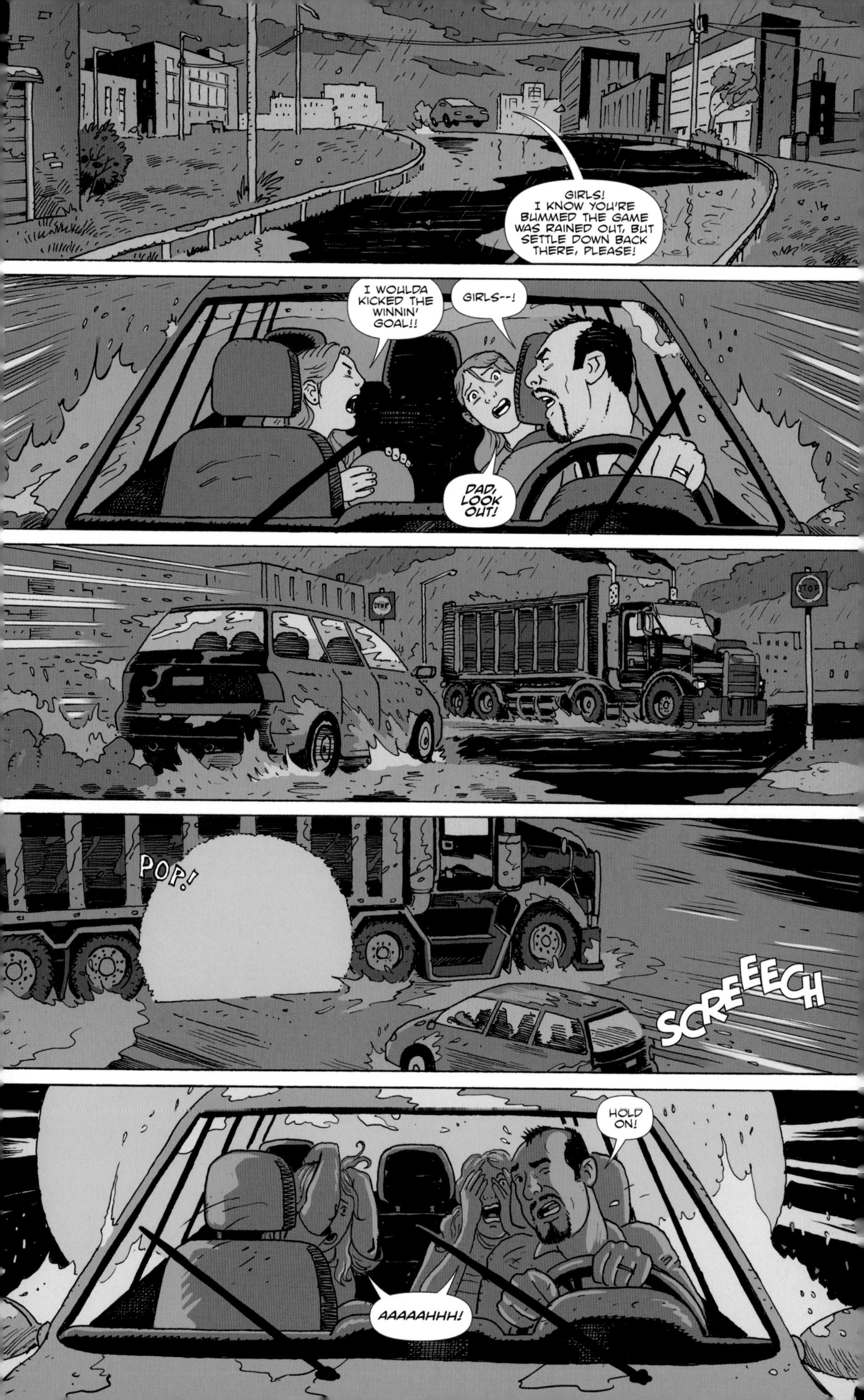
GIRLS! I KNOW YOU'RE BUMMED THE GAME WAS RAINED OUT, BUT SETTLE DOWN BACK THERE, PLEASE!
I WOULDA KICKED THE WINNIN' GOAL!!
GIRLS--!
DAD, LOOK OUT!
STOP
STOP
POP!
SCREEEECH
HOLD ON!
AAAAAHHH!

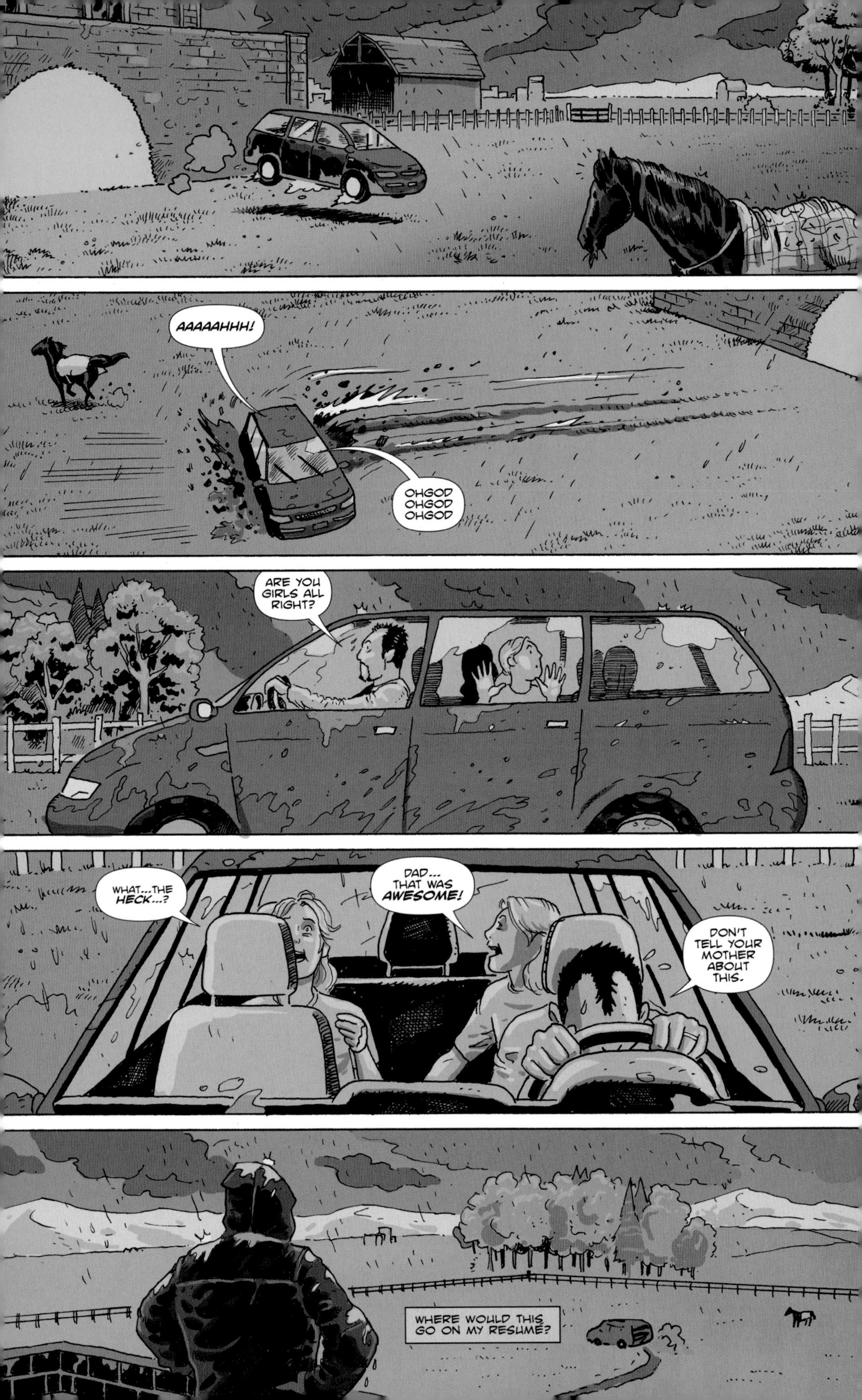
AAAAAHHH!
OHGOD OHGOD OHGOD
ARE YOU GIRLS ALL RIGHT?
WHAT...THE HECK...?
DAD... THAT WAS AWESOME!
DON'T TELL YOUR MOTHER ABOUT THIS.
WHERE WOULD THIS GO ON MY RESUME?

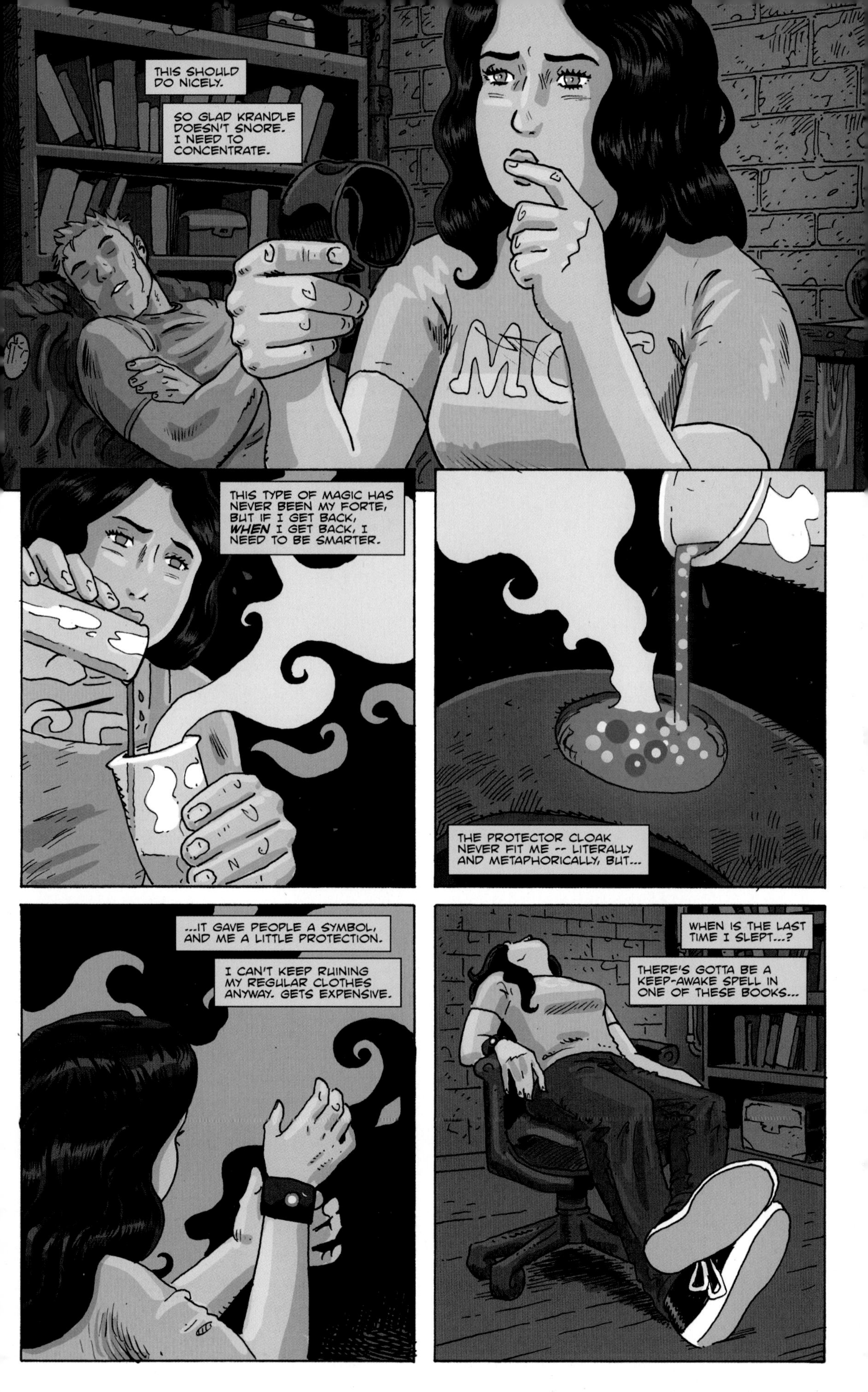
THIS SHOULD DO NICELY.
SO GLAD KRANDLE DOESN'T SNORE. I NEED TO CONCENTRATE.
THIS TYPE OF MAGIC HAS NEVER BEEN MY FORTE, BUT IF I GET BACK, ***WHEN*** I GET BACK, I NEED TO BE SMARTER.
THE PROTECTOR CLOAK NEVER FIT ME -- LITERALLY AND METAPHORICALLY, BUT...
...IT GAVE PEOPLE A SYMBOL, AND ME A LITTLE PROTECTION.
I CAN'T KEEP RUINING MY REGULAR CLOTHES ANYWAY. GETS EXPENSIVE.
WHEN IS THE LAST TIME I SLEPT...?
THERE'S GOTTA BE A KEEP-AWAKE SPELL IN ONE OF THESE BOOKS...

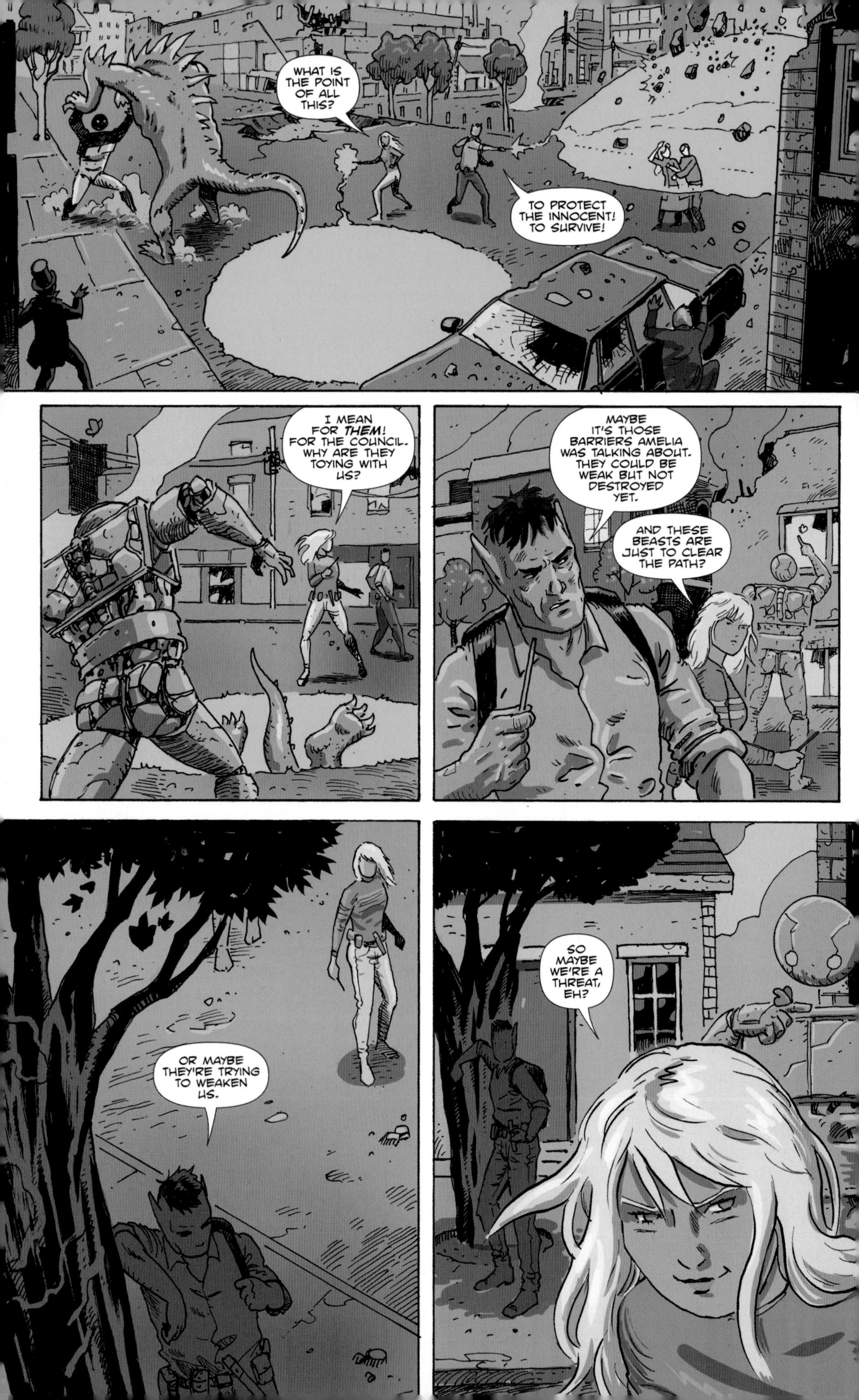
WHAT IS THE POINT OF ALL THIS?
TO PROTECT THE INNOCENT! TO SURVIVE!
I MEAN FOR *THEM*! FOR THE COUNCIL. WHY ARE THEY TOYING WITH US?
MAYBE IT'S THOSE BARRIERS AMELIA WAS TALKING ABOUT. THEY COULD BE WEAK BUT NOT DESTROYED YET.
AND THESE BEASTS ARE JUST TO CLEAR THE PATH?
OR MAYBE THEY'RE TRYING TO WEAKEN US.
SO MAYBE WE'RE A THREAT, EH?

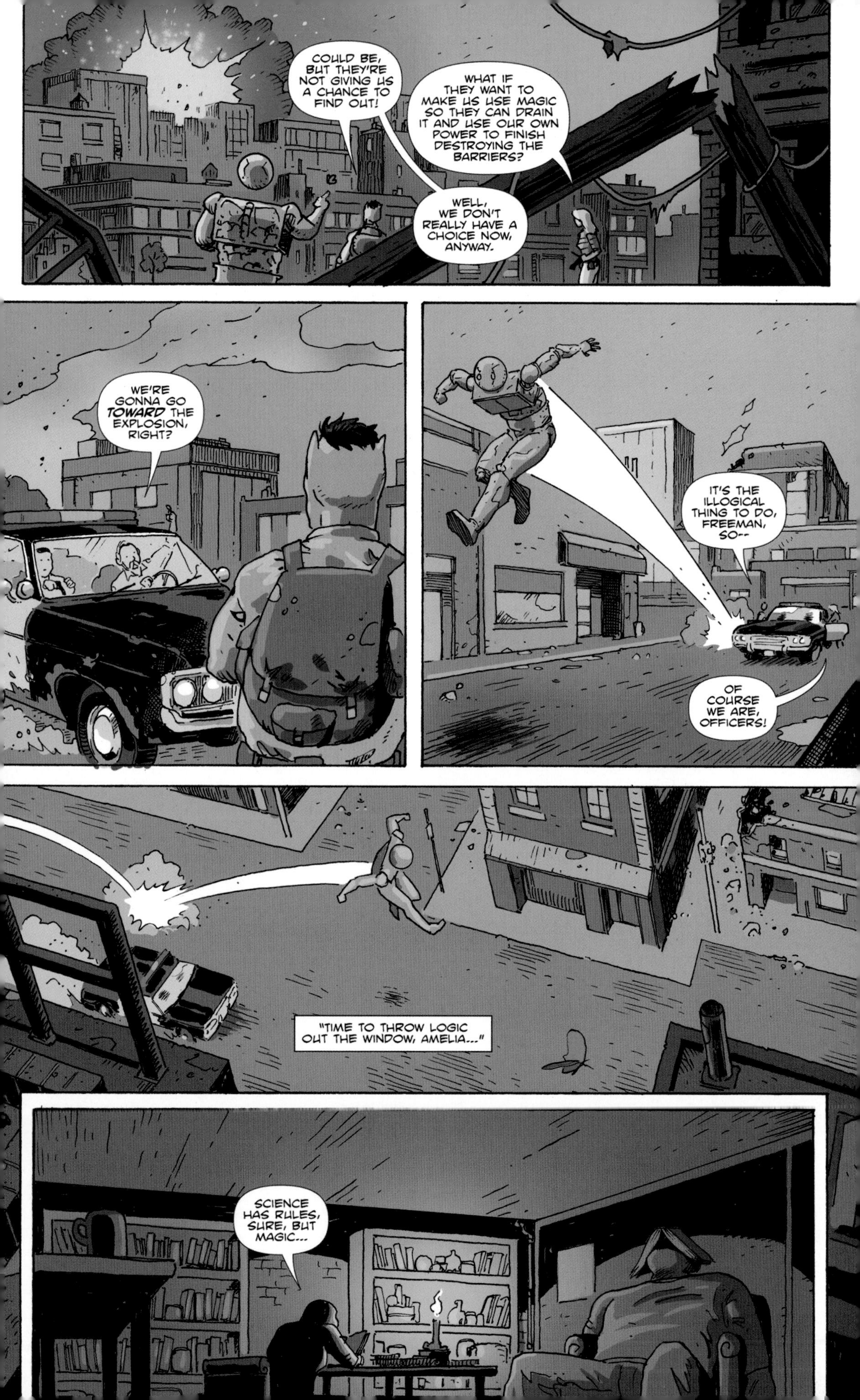
COULD BE, BUT THEY'RE NOT GIVING US A CHANCE TO FIND OUT!
WHAT IF THEY WANT TO MAKE US USE MAGIC SO THEY CAN DRAIN IT AND USE OUR OWN POWER TO FINISH DESTROYING THE BARRIERS?
WELL, WE DON'T REALLY HAVE A CHOICE NOW, ANYWAY.
WE'RE GONNA GO TOWARD THE EXPLOSION, RIGHT?
IT'S THE ILLOGICAL THING TO DO, FREEMAN, SO--
OF COURSE WE ARE, OFFICERS!
"TIME TO THROW LOGIC OUT THE WINDOW, AMELIA..."
SCIENCE HAS RULES, SURE, BUT MAGIC...

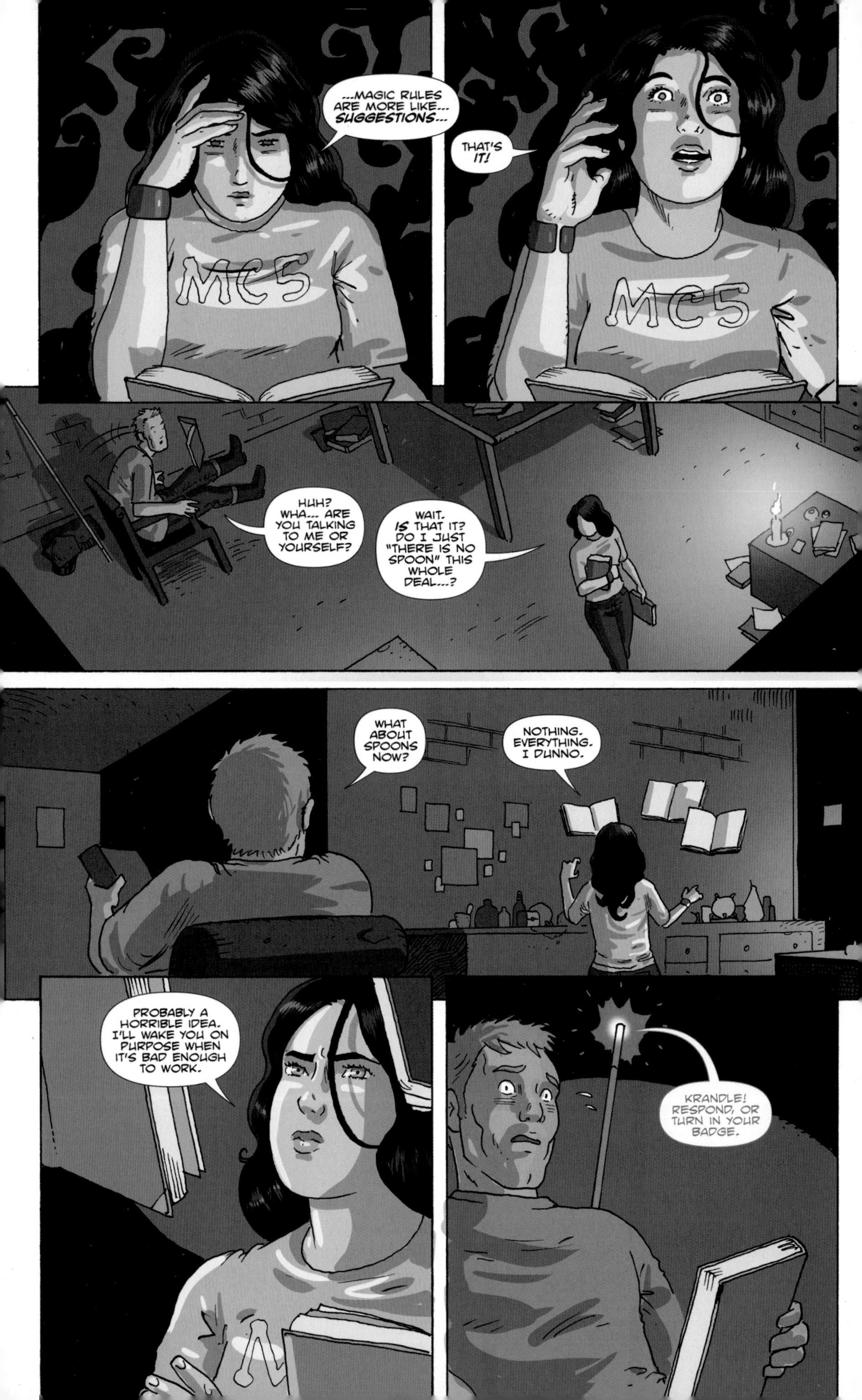
...MAGIC RULES ARE MORE LIKE... SUGGESTIONS...
THAT'S IT!
HUH? WHA... ARE YOU TALKING TO ME OR YOURSELF?
WAIT. IS THAT IT? DO I JUST "THERE IS NO SPOON" THIS WHOLE DEAL...?
WHAT ABOUT SPOONS NOW?
NOTHING. EVERYTHING. I DUNNO.
PROBABLY A HORRIBLE IDEA. I'LL WAKE YOU ON PURPOSE WHEN IT'S BAD ENOUGH TO WORK.
KRANDLE! RESPOND, OR TURN IN YOUR BADGE.
MC5

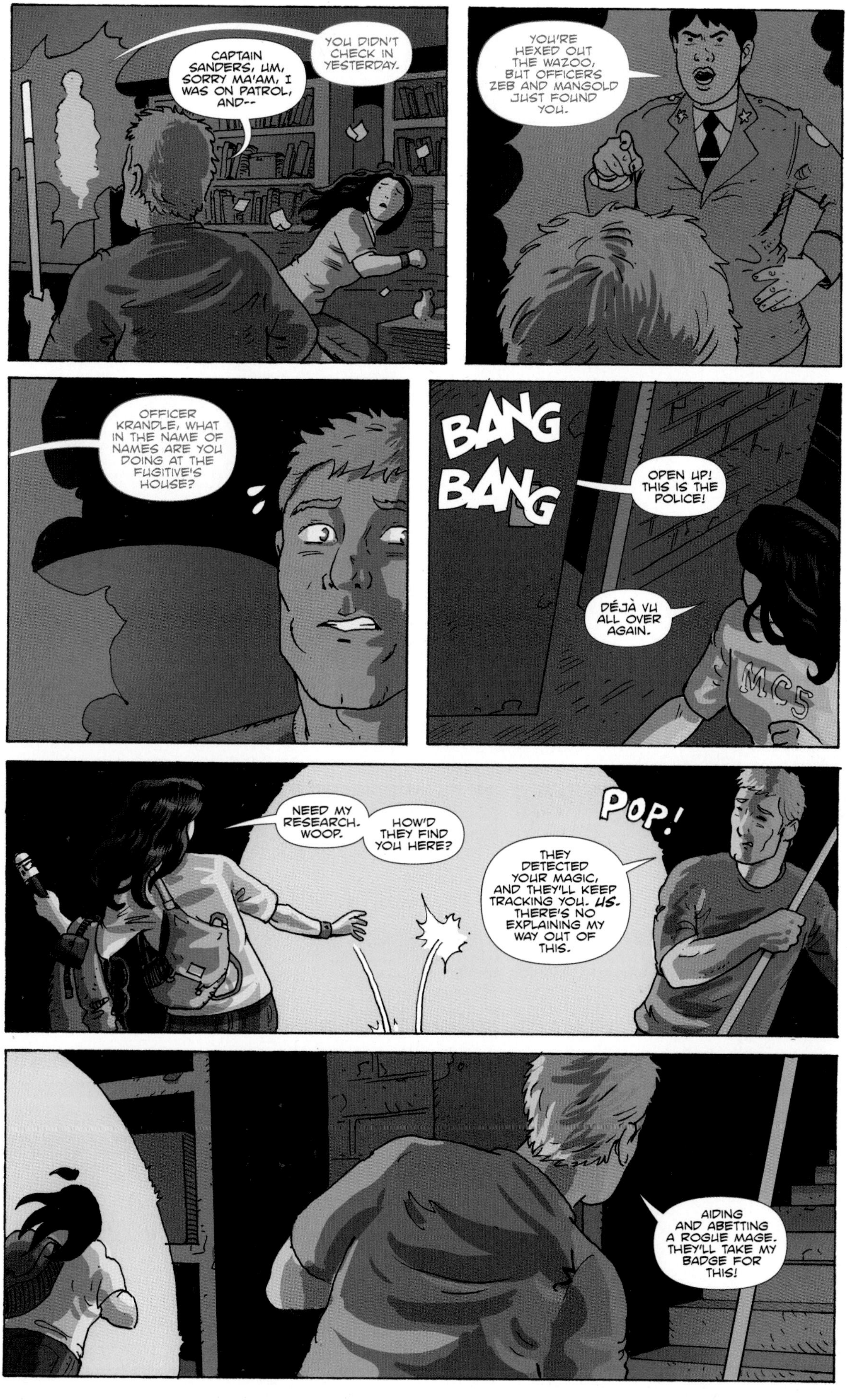
CAPTAIN SANDERS, UM, SORRY MA'AM, I WAS ON PATROL, AND--
YOU DIDN'T CHECK IN YESTERDAY.
YOU'RE HEXED OUT THE WAZOO, BUT OFFICERS ZEB AND MANGOLD JUST FOUND YOU.
OFFICER KRANDLE, WHAT IN THE NAME OF NAMES ARE YOU DOING AT THE FUGITIVE'S HOUSE?
BANG BANG
OPEN UP! THIS IS THE POLICE!
DÉJÀ VU ALL OVER AGAIN.
MC5
NEED MY RESEARCH. WOOP.
HOW'D THEY FIND YOU HERE?
POP!
THEY DETECTED YOUR MAGIC, AND THEY'LL KEEP TRACKING YOU. US. THERE'S NO EXPLAINING MY WAY OUT OF THIS.
AIDING AND ABETTING A ROGUE MAGE. THEY'LL TAKE MY BADGE FOR THIS!

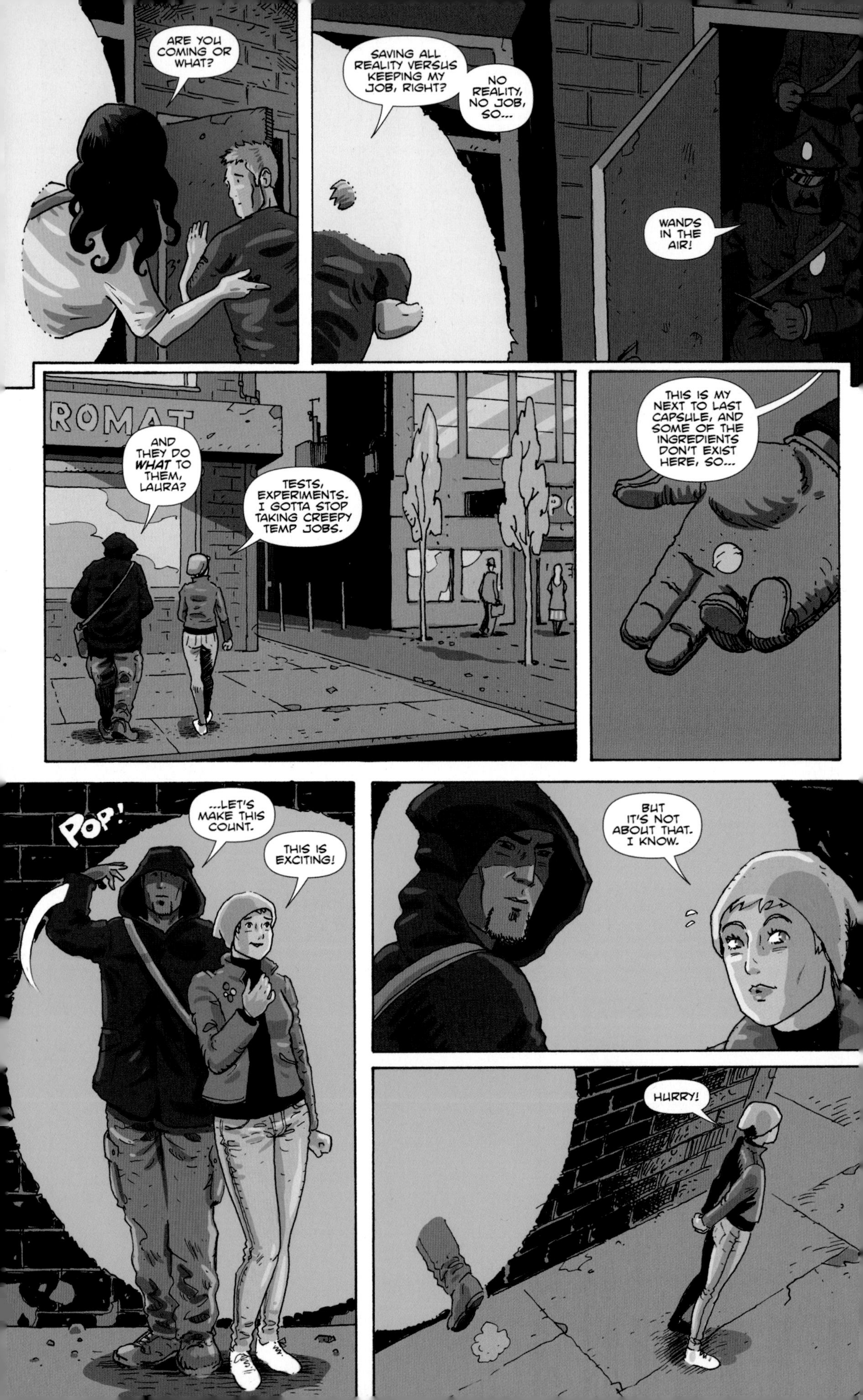
ARE YOU COMING OR WHAT?
SAVING ALL REALITY VERSUS KEEPING MY JOB, RIGHT?
NO REALITY, NO JOB, SO...
WANDS IN THE AIR!
ROMAT
AND THEY DO *WHAT* TO THEM, LAURA?
TESTS, EXPERIMENTS. I GOTTA STOP TAKING CREEPY TEMP JOBS.
THIS IS MY NEXT TO LAST CAPSULE, AND SOME OF THE INGREDIENTS DON'T EXIST HERE, SO...
POP!
...LET'S MAKE THIS COUNT.
THIS IS EXCITING!
BUT IT'S NOT ABOUT THAT. I KNOW.
HURRY!

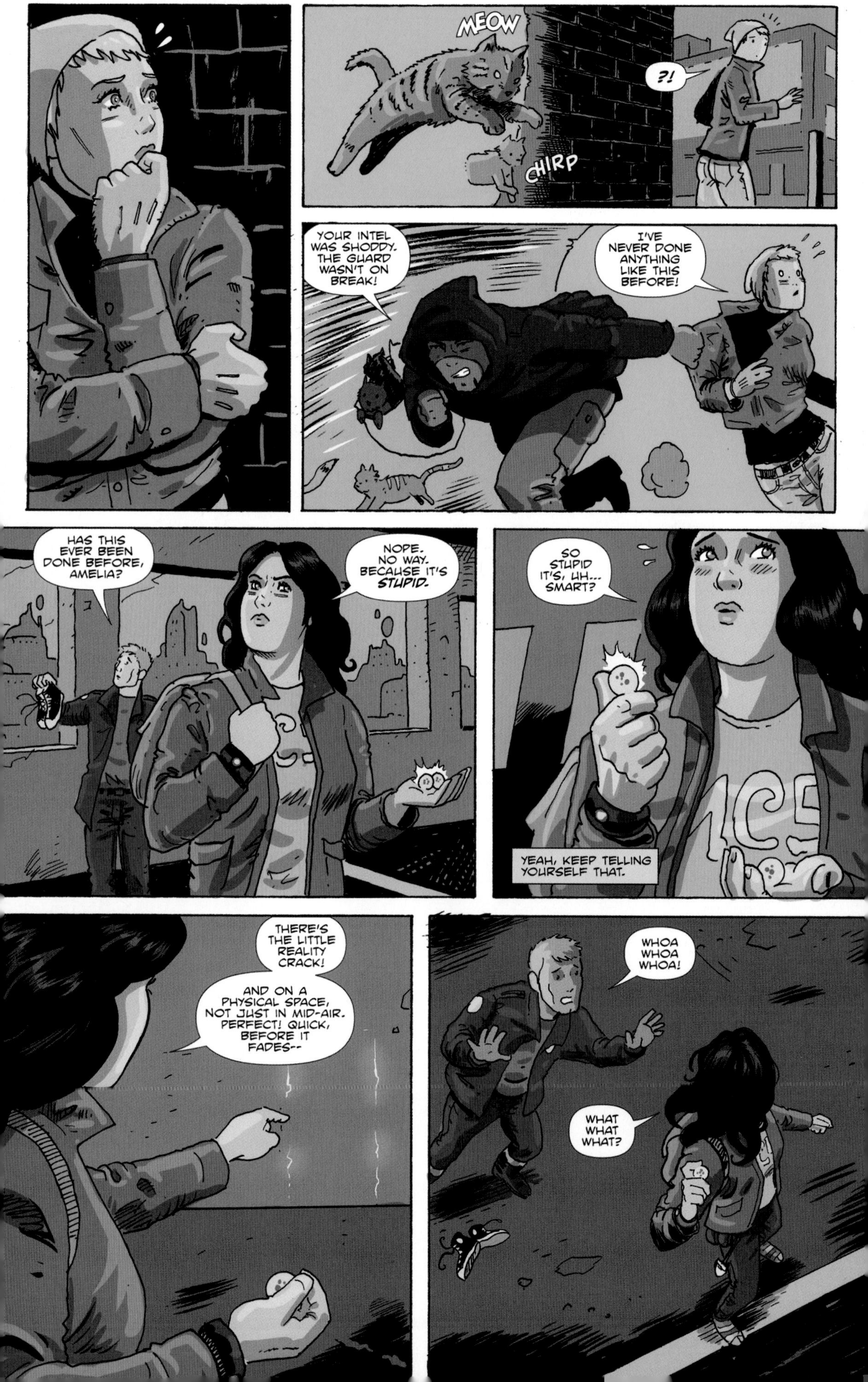

MEOW
CHIRP
?!
YOUR INTEL WAS SHODDY. THE GUARD WASN'T ON BREAK!
I'VE NEVER DONE ANYTHING LIKE THIS BEFORE!
HAS THIS EVER BEEN DONE BEFORE, AMELIA?
NOPE. NO WAY. BECAUSE IT'S STUPID.
SO STUPID IT'S, UH... SMART?
YEAH, KEEP TELLING YOURSELF THAT.
THERE'S THE LITTLE REALITY CRACK!
AND ON A PHYSICAL SPACE, NOT JUST IN MID-AIR. PERFECT! QUICK, BEFORE IT FADES--
WHOA WHOA WHOA!
WHAT WHAT WHAT?

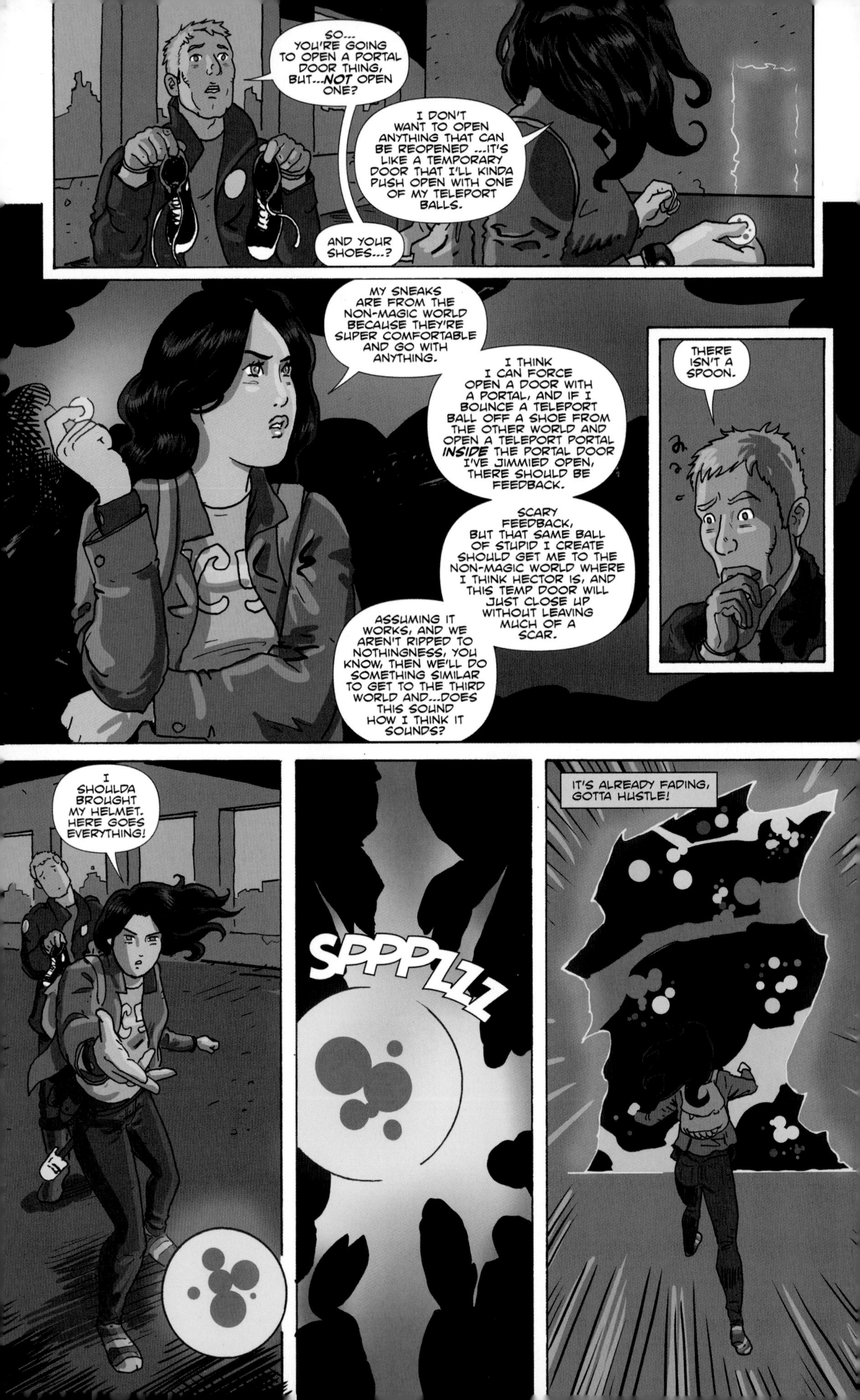
SO... YOU'RE GOING TO OPEN A PORTAL DOOR THING, BUT...NOT OPEN ONE?
I DON'T WANT TO OPEN ANYTHING THAT CAN BE REOPENED ...IT'S LIKE A TEMPORARY DOOR THAT I'LL KINDA PUSH OPEN WITH ONE OF MY TELEPORT BALLS.
AND YOUR SHOES...?
MY SNEAKS ARE FROM THE NON-MAGIC WORLD BECAUSE THEY'RE SUPER COMFORTABLE AND GO WITH ANYTHING.
I THINK I CAN FORCE OPEN A DOOR WITH A PORTAL, AND IF I BOUNCE A TELEPORT BALL OFF A SHOE FROM THE OTHER WORLD AND OPEN A TELEPORT PORTAL INSIDE THE PORTAL DOOR I'VE JIMMIED OPEN, THERE SHOULD BE FEEDBACK.
SCARY FEEDBACK, BUT THAT SAME BALL OF STUPID I CREATE SHOULD GET ME TO THE NON-MAGIC WORLD WHERE I THINK HECTOR IS, AND THIS TEMP DOOR WILL JUST CLOSE UP WITHOUT LEAVING MUCH OF A SCAR.
ASSUMING IT WORKS, AND WE AREN'T RIPPED TO NOTHINGNESS, YOU KNOW, THEN WE'LL DO SOMETHING SIMILAR TO GET TO THE THIRD WORLD AND...DOES THIS SOUND HOW I THINK IT SOUNDS?
THERE ISN'T A SPOON.
I SHOULDA BROUGHT MY HELMET. HERE GOES EVERYTHING!
SPPPZZZ
IT'S ALREADY FADING, GOTTA HUSTLE!

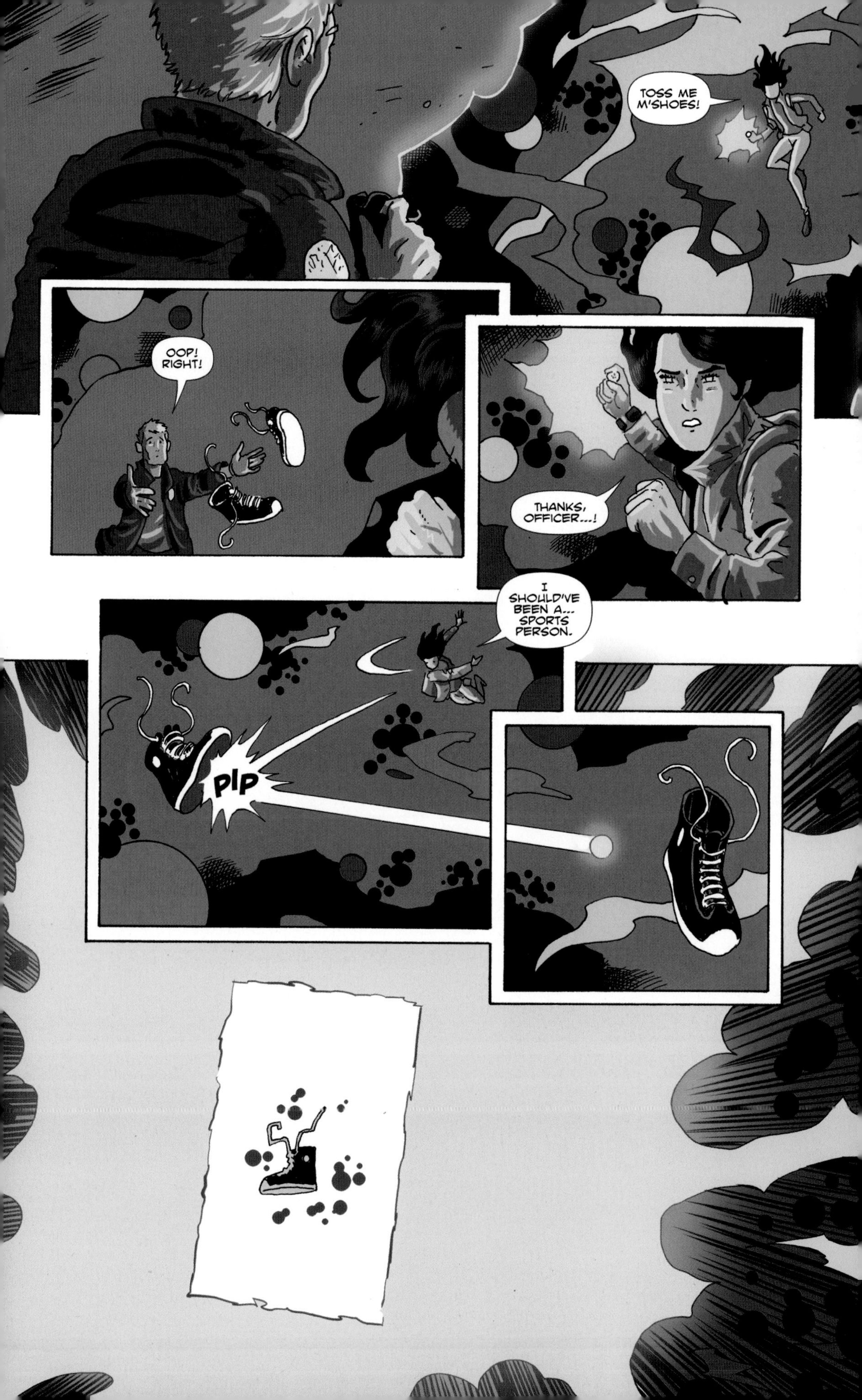
TOSS ME M'SHOES!
OOP! RIGHT!
THANKS, OFFICER...!
I SHOULD'VE BEEN A... SPORTS PERSON.
PIP

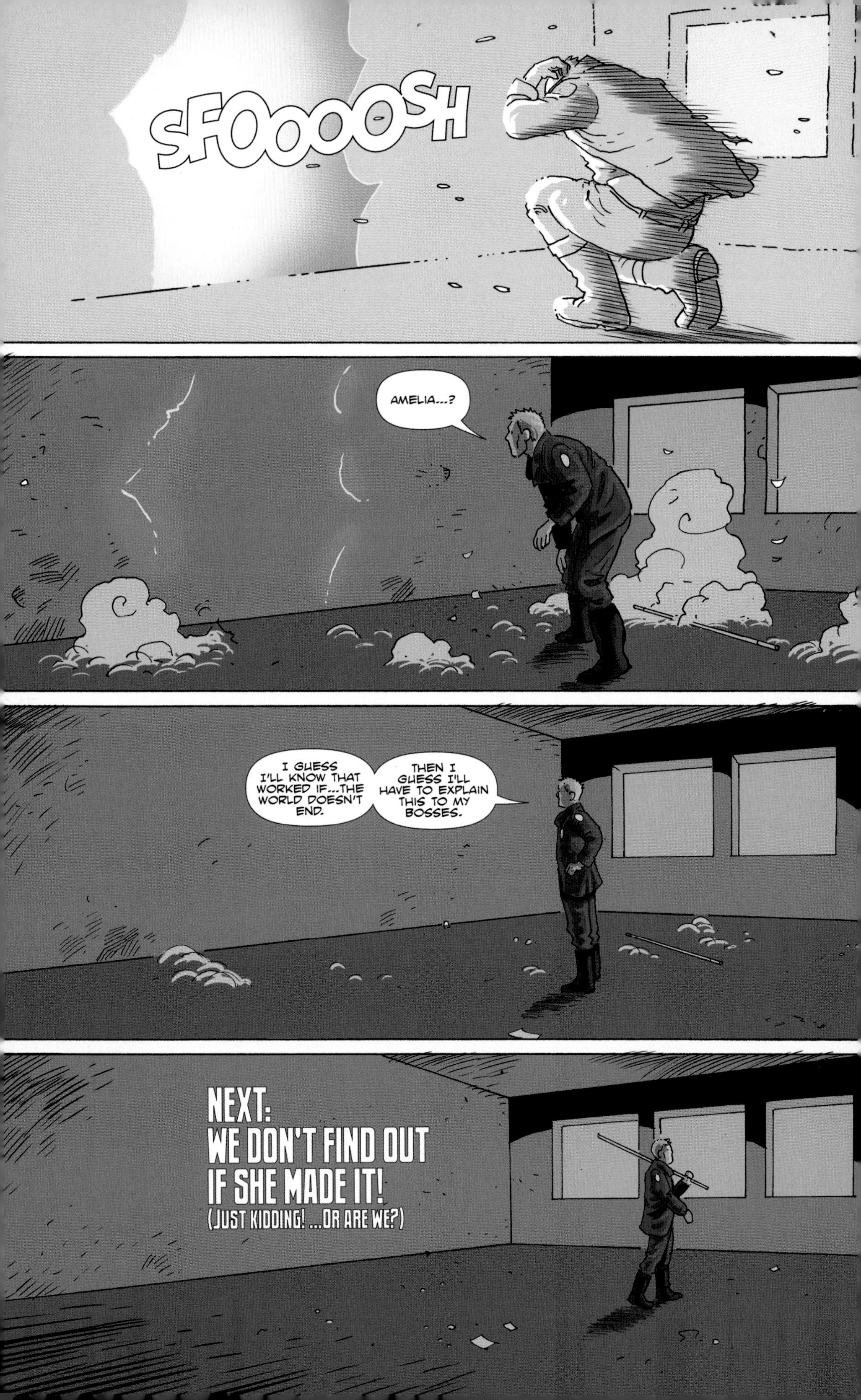
SFOOOOOSH
AMELIA...?
I GUESS I'LL KNOW THAT WORKED IF...THE WORLD DOESN'T END.
THEN I GUESS I'LL HAVE TO EXPLAIN THIS TO MY BOSSES.
NEXT: WE DON'T FIND OUT IF SHE MADE IT!
(JUST KIDDING! ...OR ARE WE?)

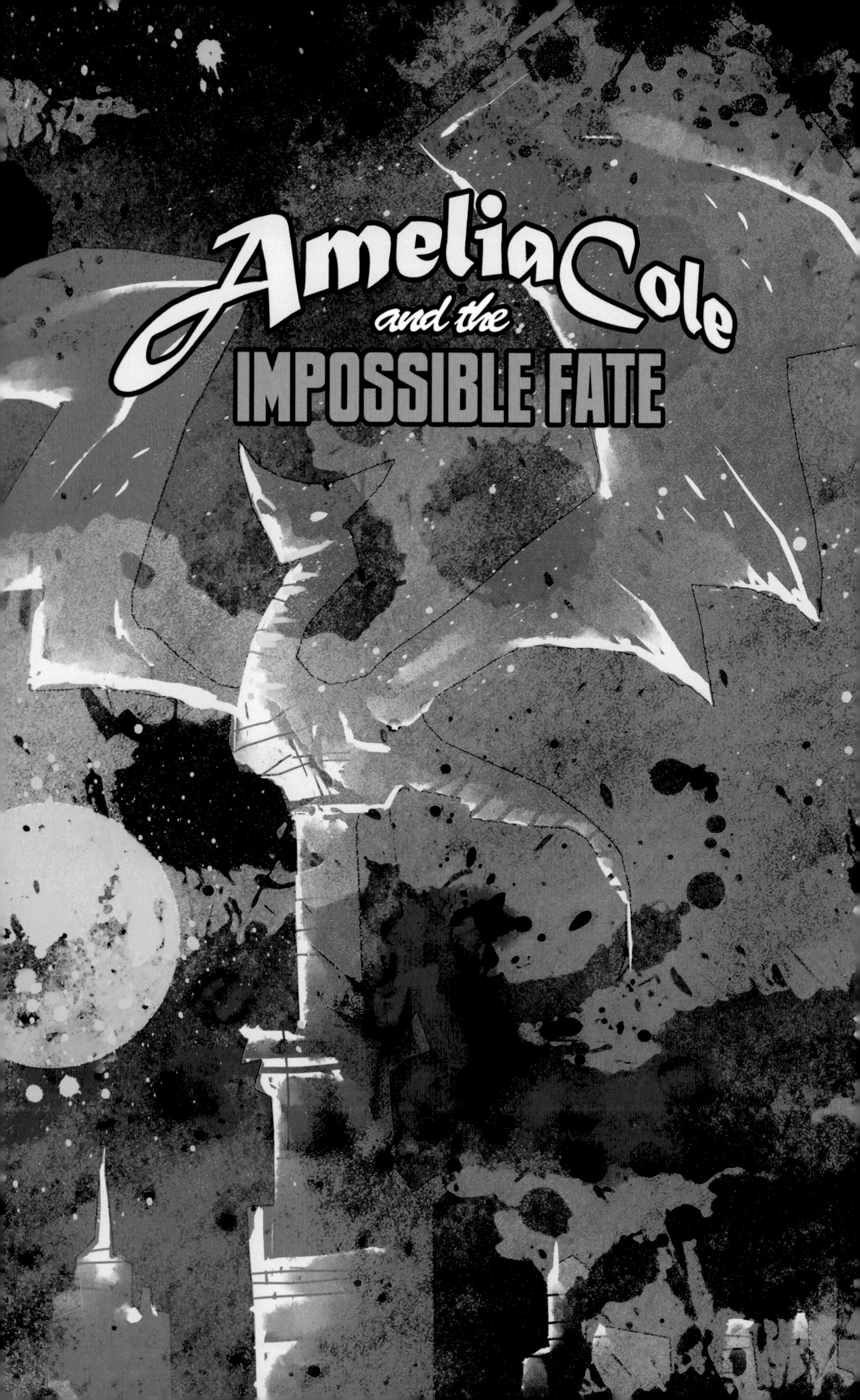
Amelia Cole
and the
IMPOSSIBLE FATE

CHAPTER 5

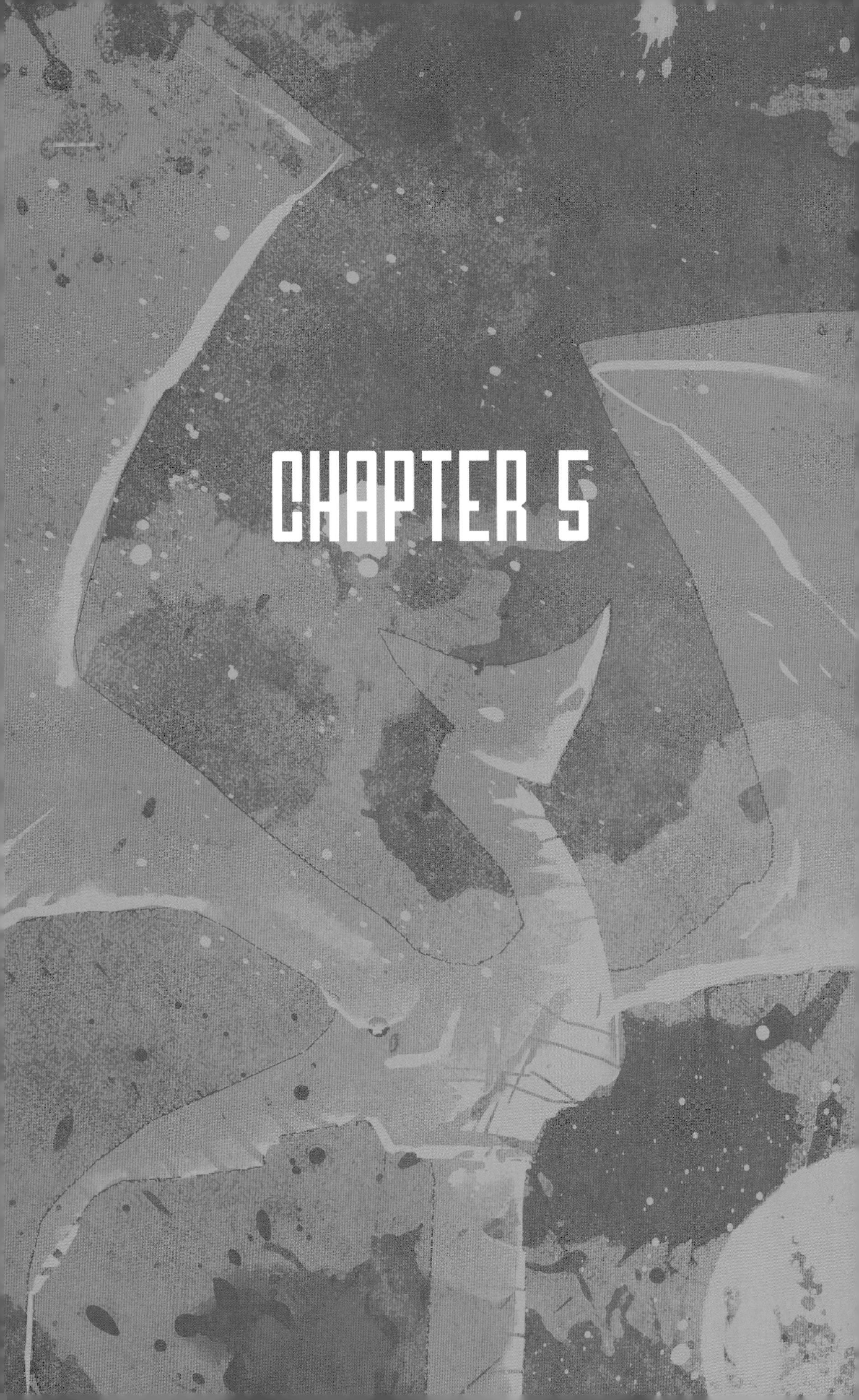

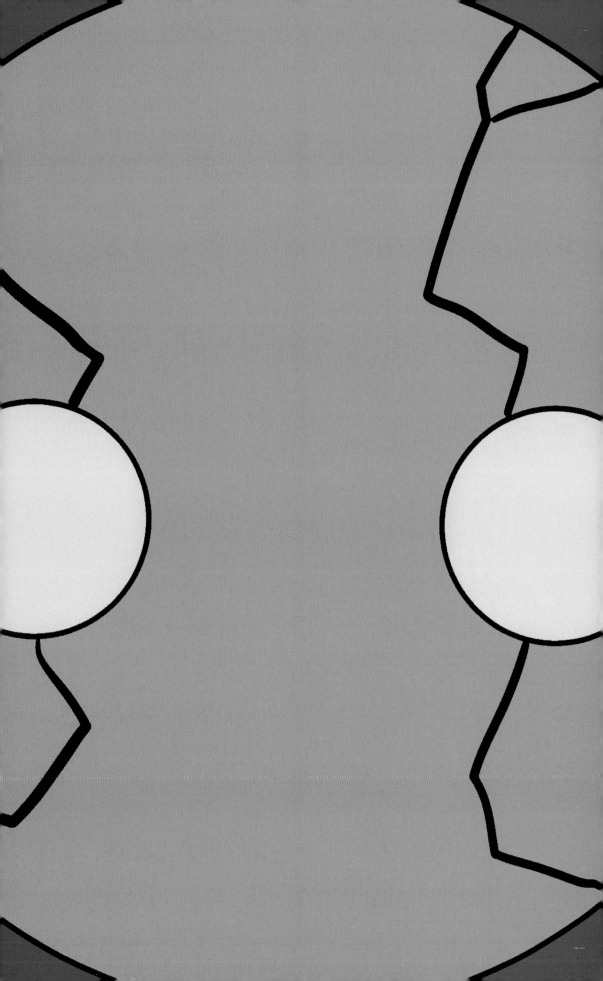

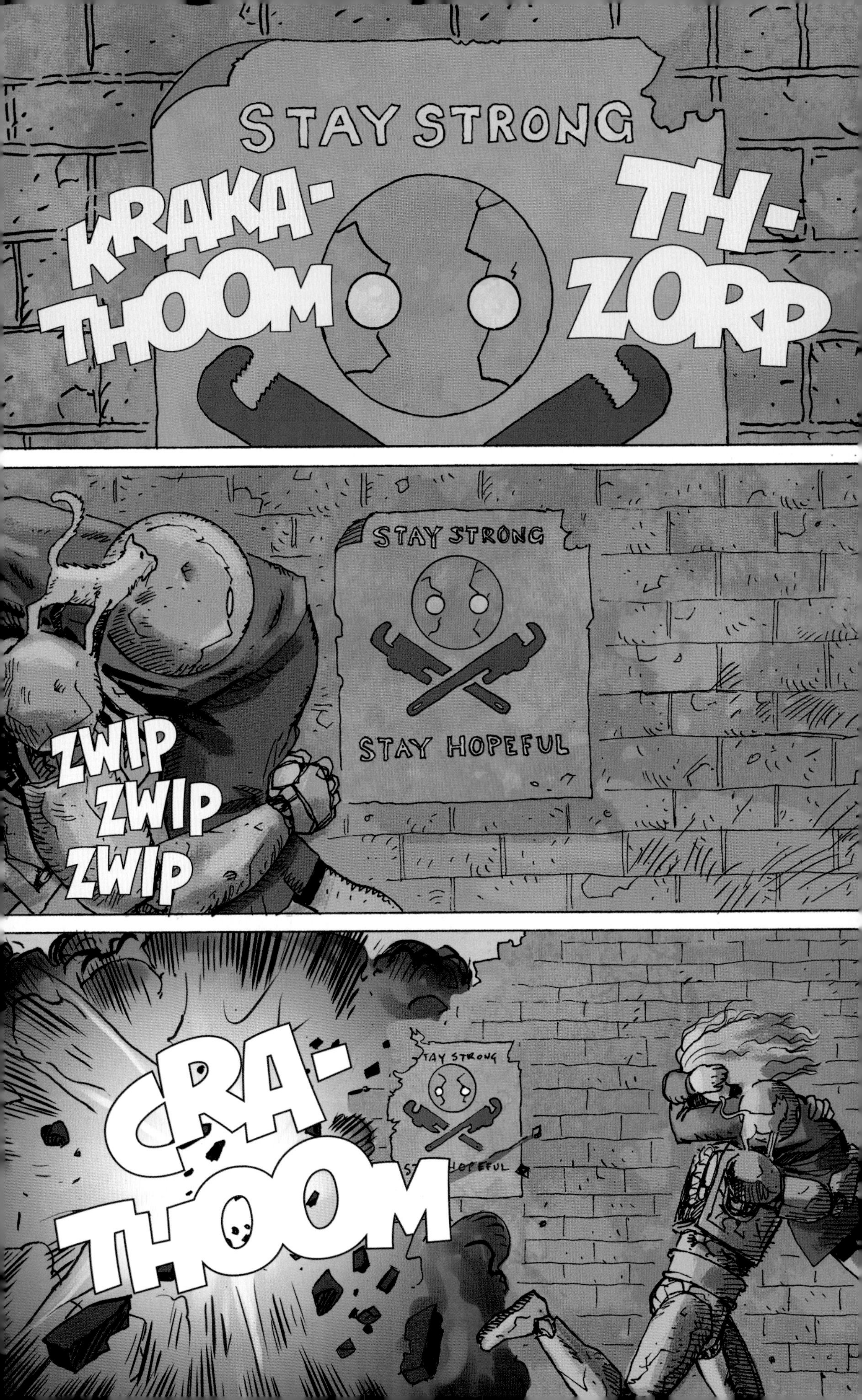
STAY STRONG
KRAKA-THOOM
TH-ZORP
STAY STRONG
STAY HOPEFUL
ZWIP
ZWIP
ZWIP
TAY STRONG
CRA-THOOM
S HOPEFUL

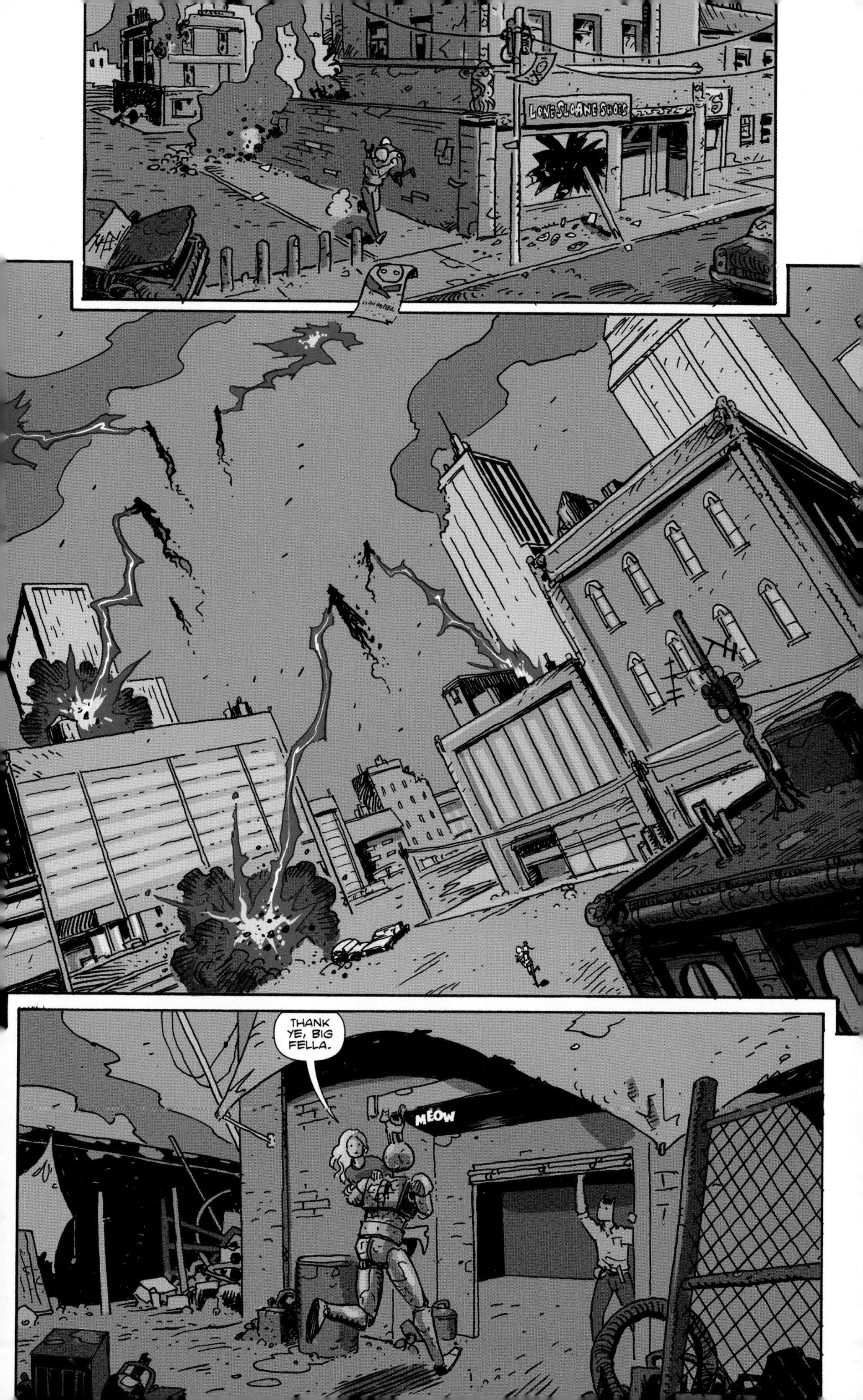
LONE SLOANE SHOES
THANK YE, BIG FELLA.
MEOW

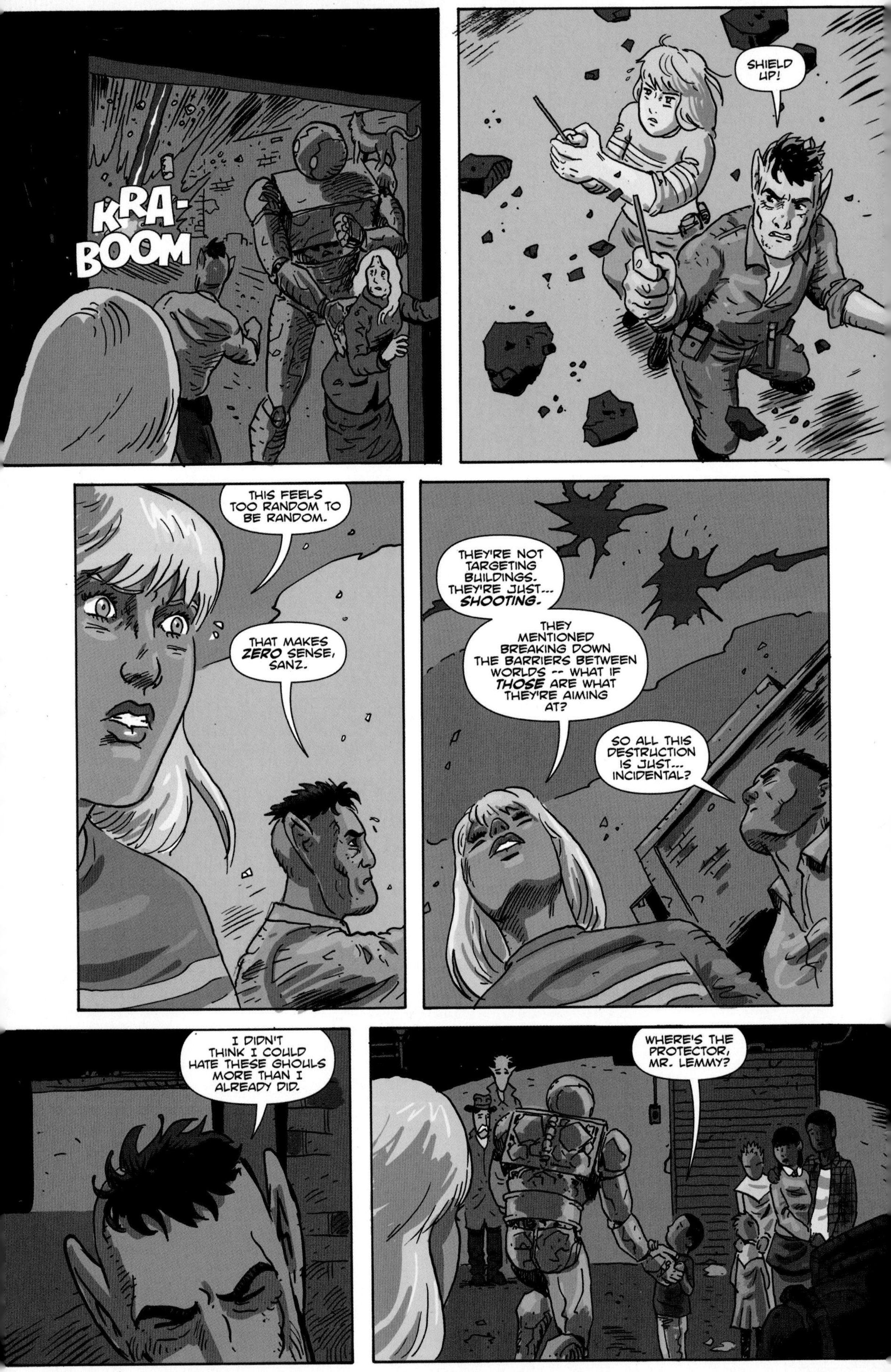
KRA-
BOOM
SHIELD UP!
THIS FEELS TOO RANDOM TO BE RANDOM.
THAT MAKES *ZERO* SENSE, SANZ.
THEY'RE NOT TARGETING BUILDINGS. THEY'RE JUST... *SHOOTING.*
THEY MENTIONED BREAKING DOWN THE BARRIERS BETWEEN WORLDS -- WHAT IF *THOSE* ARE WHAT THEY'RE AIMING AT?
SO ALL THIS DESTRUCTION IS JUST... INCIDENTAL?
I DIDN'T THINK I COULD HATE THESE GHOULS MORE THAN I ALREADY DID.
WHERE'S THE PROTECTOR, MR. LEMMY?

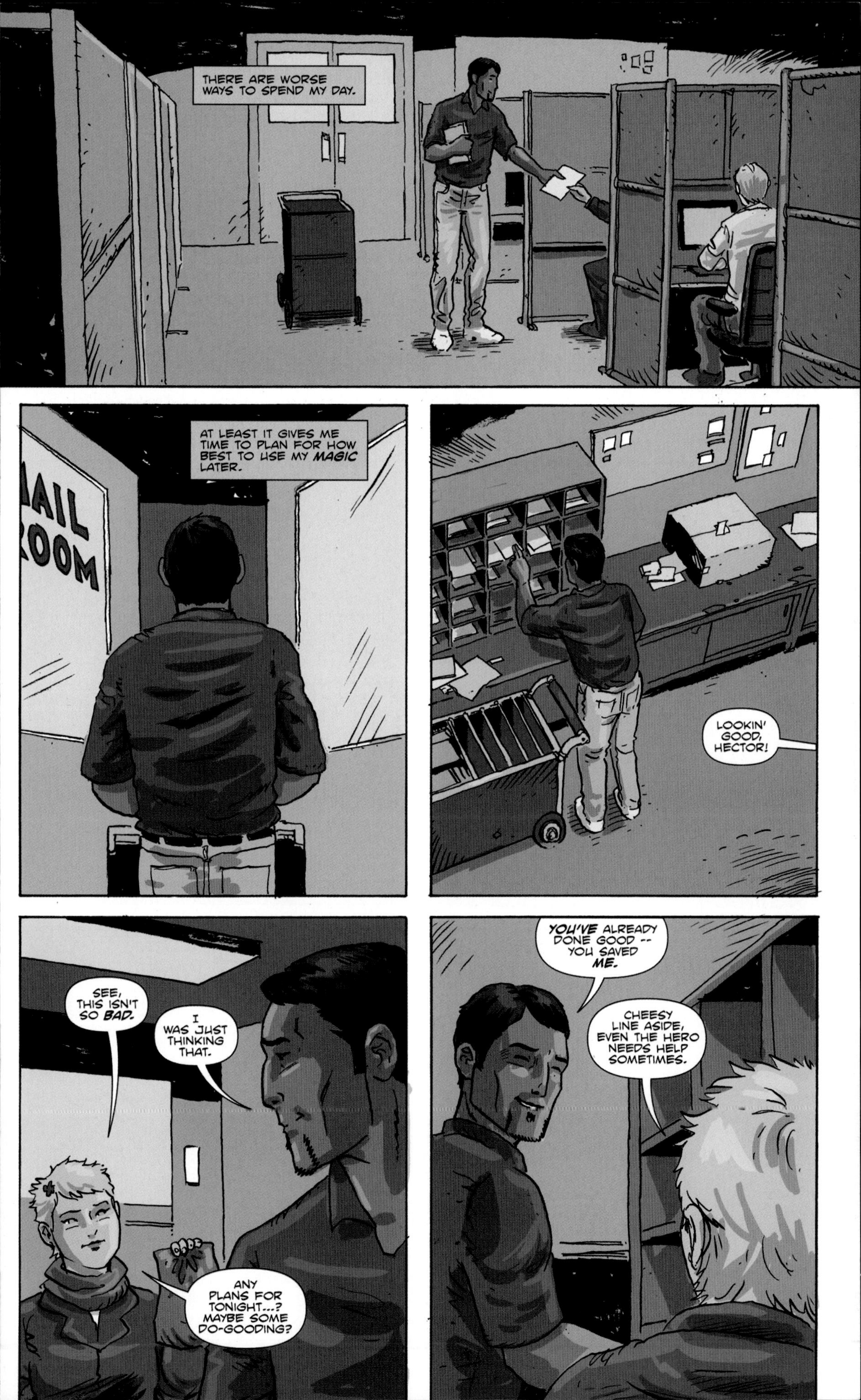
THERE ARE WORSE WAYS TO SPEND MY DAY.
AT LEAST IT GIVES ME TIME TO PLAN FOR HOW BEST TO USE MY MAGIC LATER.
MAIL ROOM
LOOKIN' GOOD, HECTOR!
SEE, THIS ISN'T SO BAD.
I WAS JUST THINKING THAT.
ANY PLANS FOR TONIGHT...? MAYBE SOME DO-GOODING?
YOU'VE ALREADY DONE GOOD -- YOU SAVED ME.
CHEESY LINE ASIDE, EVEN THE HERO NEEDS HELP SOMETIMES.

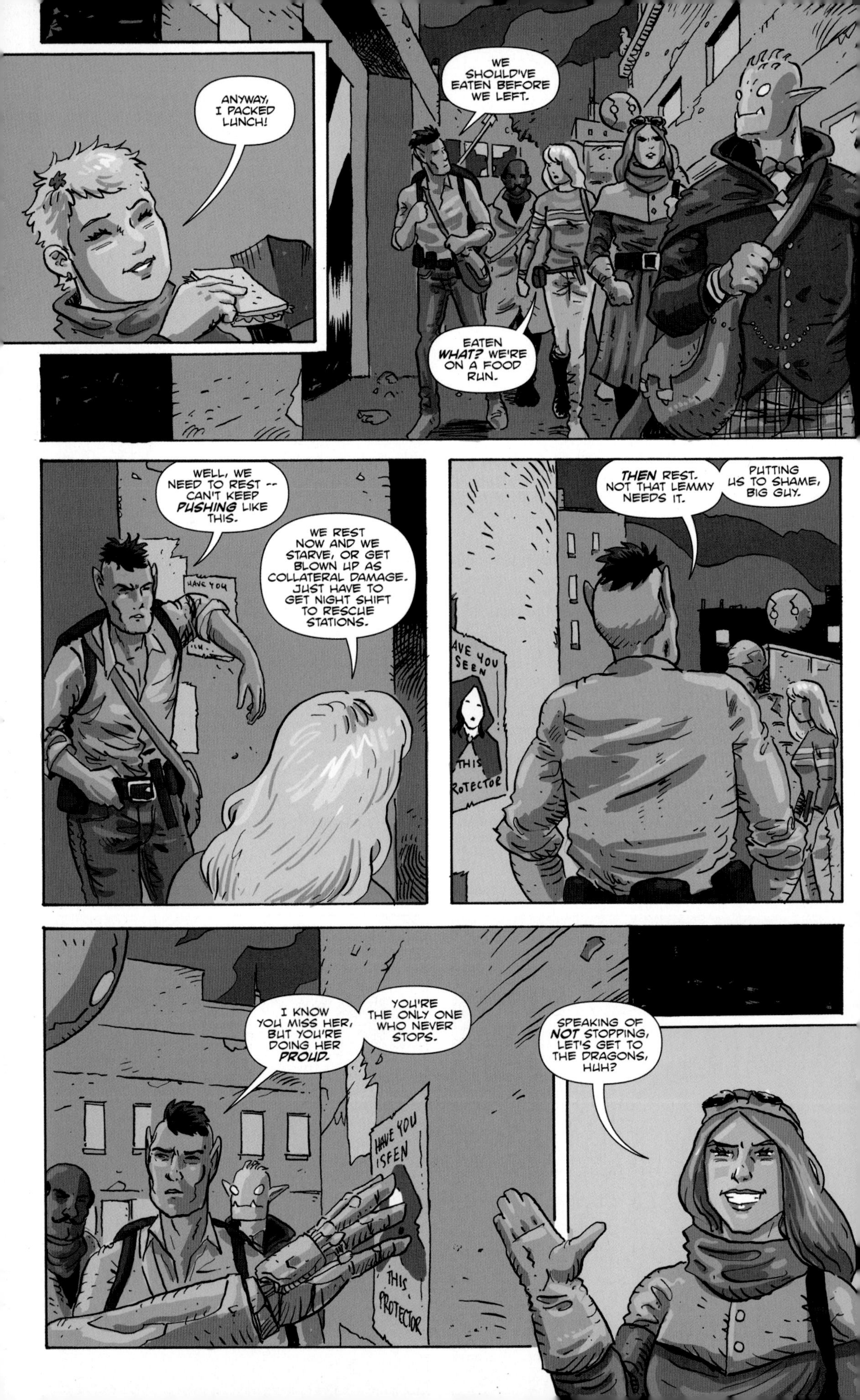
ANYWAY, I PACKED LUNCH!
WE SHOULD'VE EATEN BEFORE WE LEFT.
EATEN *WHAT?* WE'RE ON A FOOD RUN.
WELL, WE NEED TO REST -- CAN'T KEEP *PUSHING* LIKE THIS.
HAVE YOU
WE REST NOW AND WE STARVE, OR GET BLOWN UP AS COLLATERAL DAMAGE. JUST HAVE TO GET NIGHT SHIFT TO RESCUE STATIONS.
THEN REST. NOT THAT LEMMY NEEDS IT.
PUTTING US TO SHAME, BIG GUY.
AVE YOU SEEN
THIS
ROTECTOR
I KNOW YOU MISS HER, BUT YOU'RE DOING HER *PROUD.*
YOU'RE THE ONLY ONE WHO NEVER STOPS.
SPEAKING OF *NOT* STOPPING, LET'S GET TO THE DRAGONS, HUH?
HAVE YOU SEEN
THIS
PROTECTOR

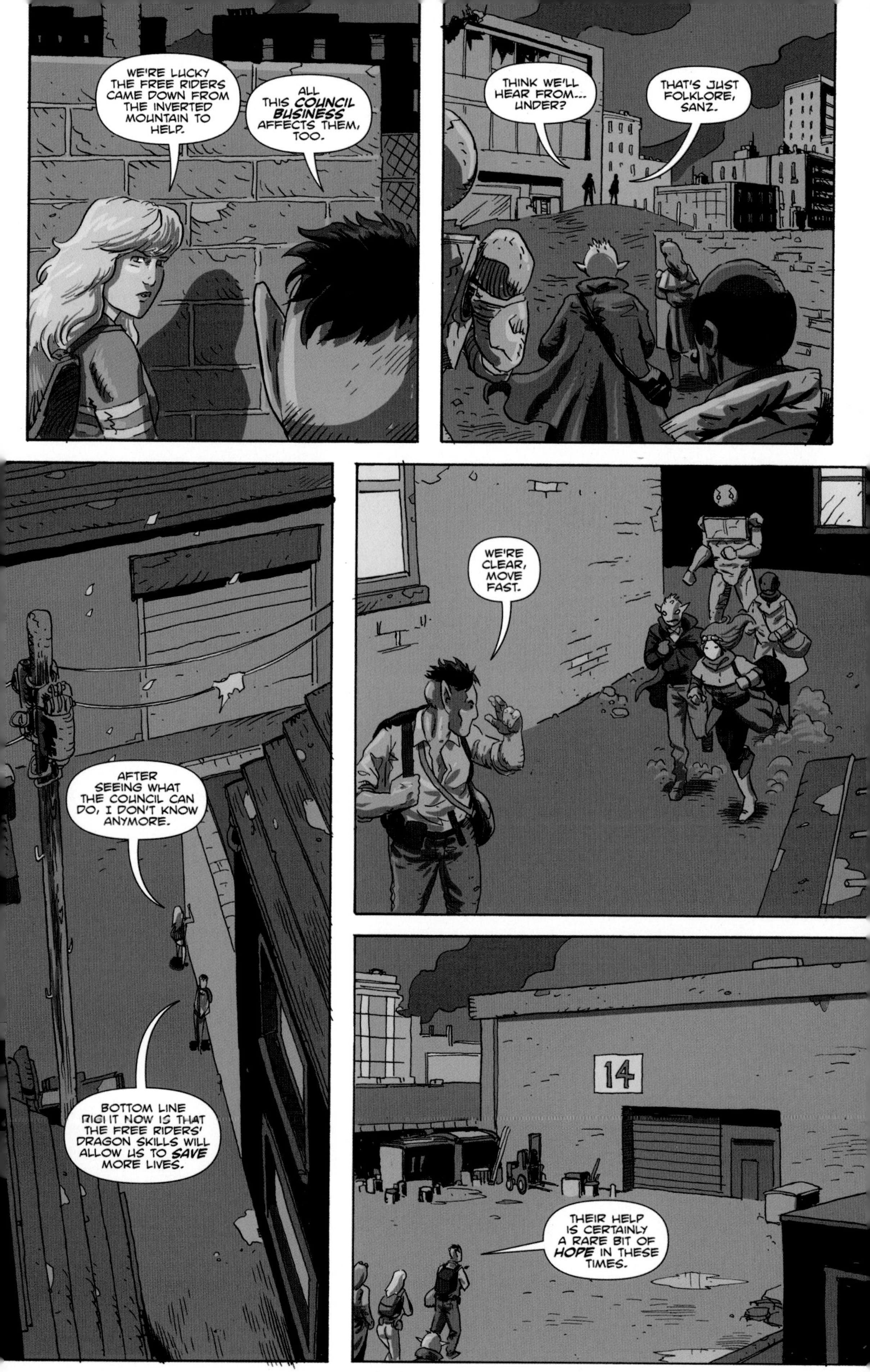
WE'RE LUCKY THE FREE RIDERS CAME DOWN FROM THE INVERTED MOUNTAIN TO HELP.
ALL THIS COUNCIL BUSINESS AFFECTS THEM, TOO.
THINK WE'LL HEAR FROM... UNDER?
THAT'S JUST FOLKLORE, SANZ.
AFTER SEEING WHAT THE COUNCIL CAN DO, I DON'T KNOW ANYMORE.
BOTTOM LINE RIGHT NOW IS THAT THE FREE RIDERS' DRAGON SKILLS WILL ALLOW US TO SAVE MORE LIVES.
WE'RE CLEAR, MOVE FAST.
14
THEIR HELP IS CERTAINLY A RARE BIT OF HOPE IN THESE TIMES.

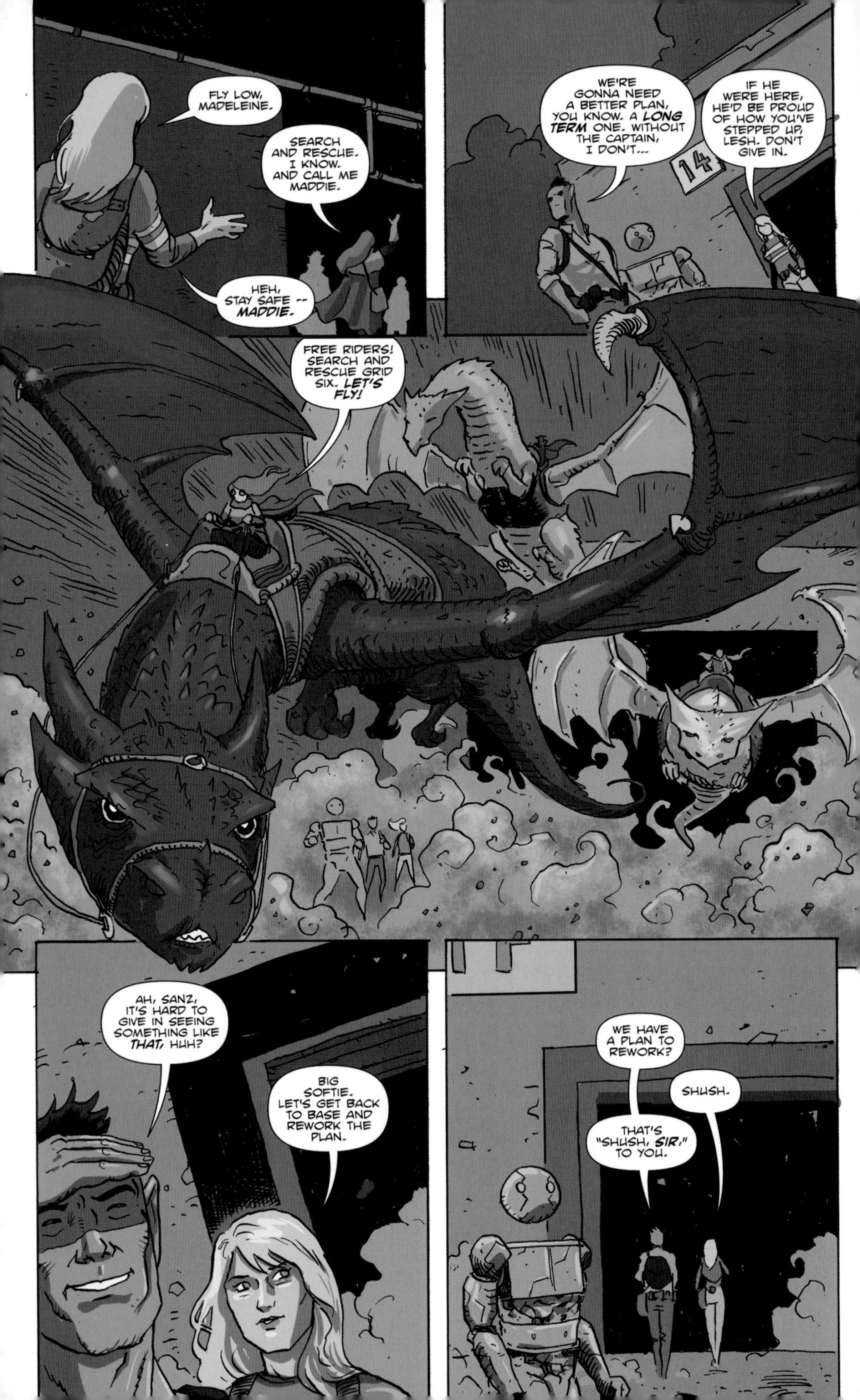

FLY LOW, MADELEINE.
SEARCH AND RESCUE. I KNOW. AND CALL ME MADDIE.
HEH, STAY SAFE -- MADDIE.
WE'RE GONNA NEED A BETTER PLAN, YOU KNOW. A LONG TERM ONE. WITHOUT THE CAPTAIN, I DON'T...
IF HE WERE HERE, HE'D BE PROUD OF HOW YOU'VE STEPPED UP, LESH. DON'T GIVE IN.
14
FREE RIDERS! SEARCH AND RESCUE GRID SIX. LET'S FLY!
AH, SANZ, IT'S HARD TO GIVE IN SEEING SOMETHING LIKE THAT, HUH?
BIG SOFTIE. LET'S GET BACK TO BASE AND REWORK THE PLAN.
WE HAVE A PLAN TO REWORK?
SHUSH.
THAT'S "SHUSH, SIR," TO YOU.

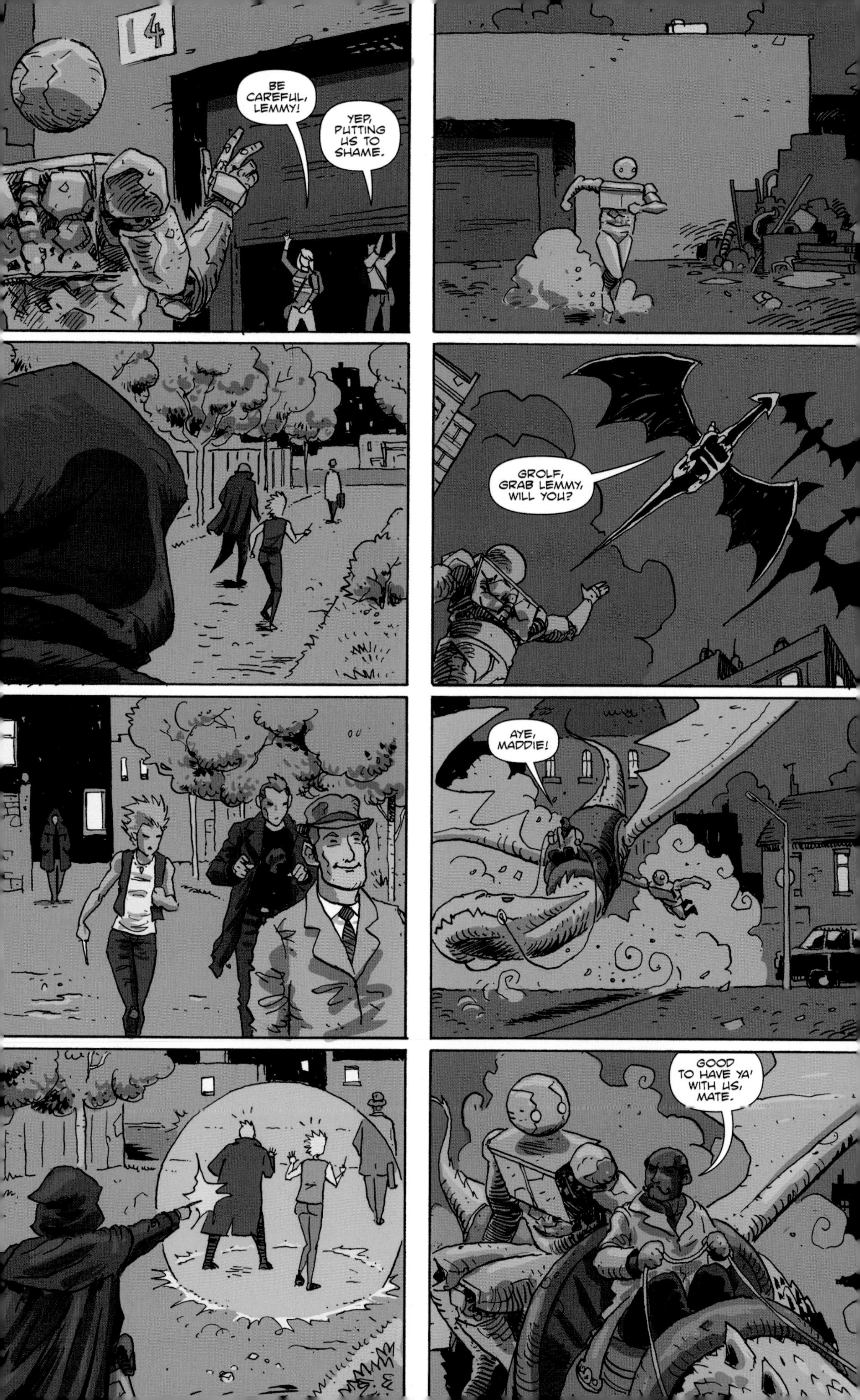
BE CAREFUL, LEMMY!
YEP, PUTTING US TO SHAME.
GROLF, GRAB LEMMY, WILL YOU?
AYE, MADDIE!
GOOD TO HAVE YA' WITH US, MATE.

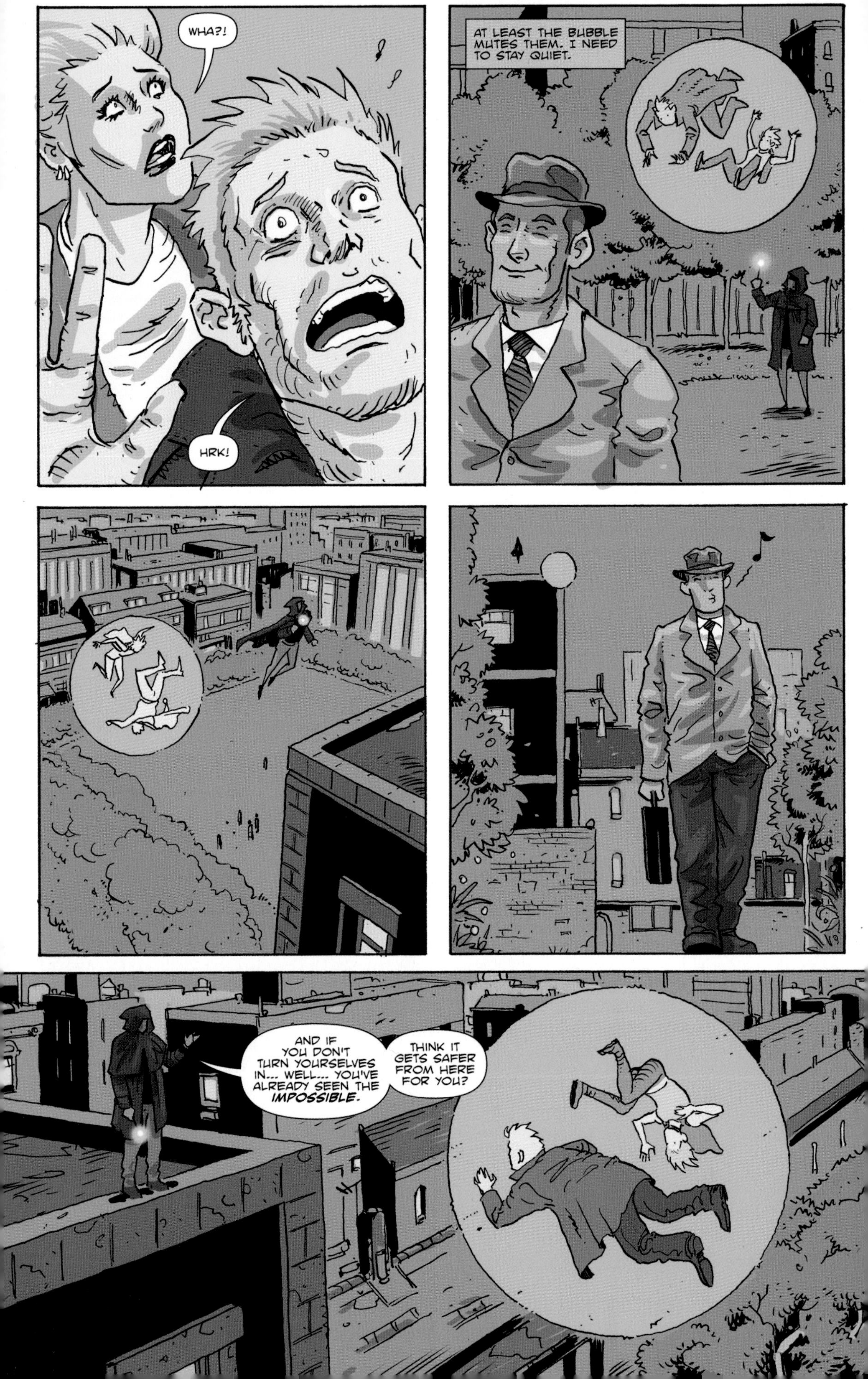
WHA?!
HRK!
AT LEAST THE BUBBLE MUTES THEM. I NEED TO STAY QUIET.
AND IF YOU DON'T TURN YOURSELVES IN... WELL... YOU'VE ALREADY SEEN THE IMPOSSIBLE.
THINK IT GETS SAFER FROM HERE FOR YOU?

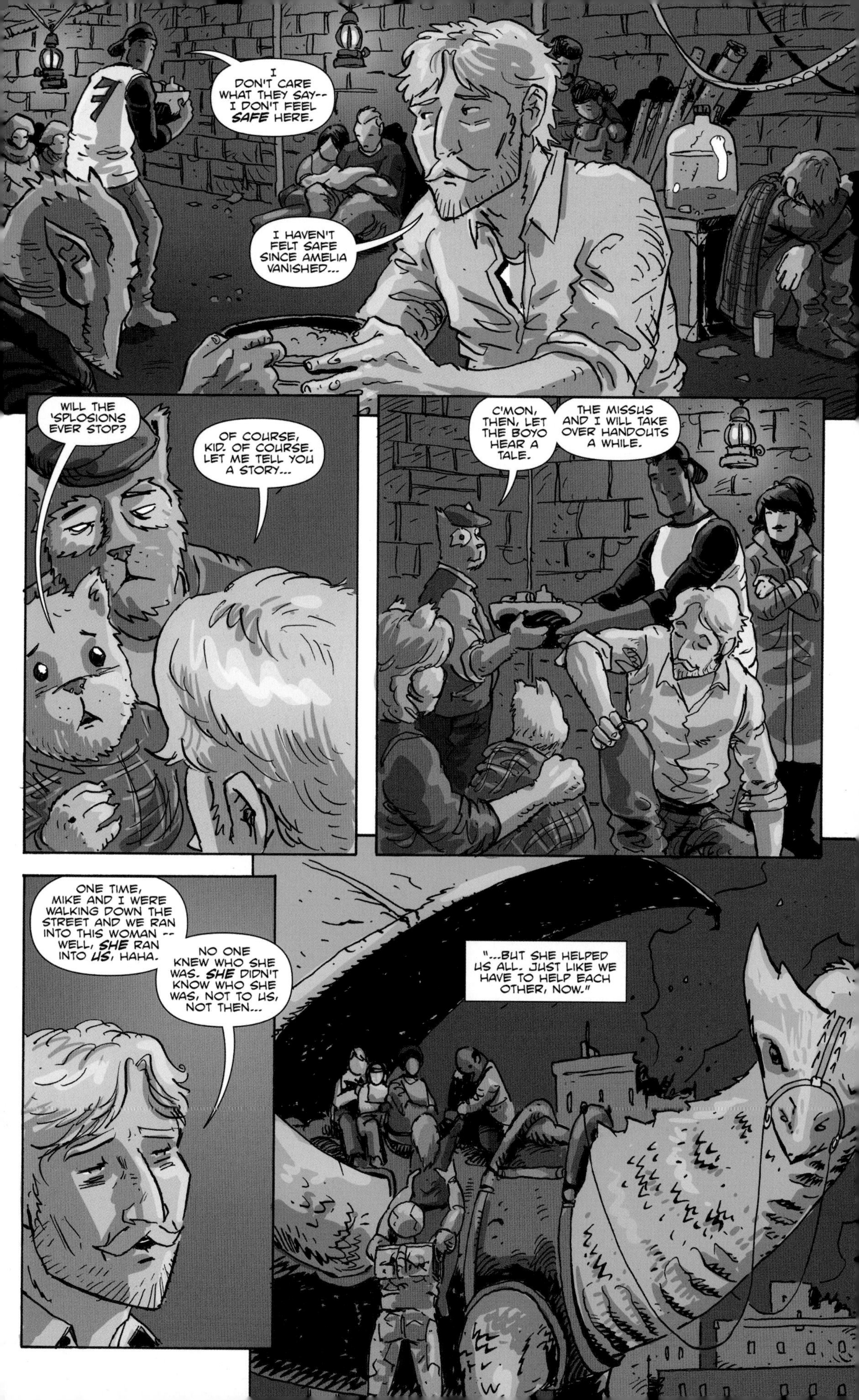
I DON'T CARE WHAT THEY SAY-- I DON'T FEEL SAFE HERE.
I HAVEN'T FELT SAFE SINCE AMELIA VANISHED...
WILL THE 'SPLOSIONS EVER STOP?
OF COURSE, KID. OF COURSE. LET ME TELL YOU A STORY...
C'MON, THEN, LET THE BOYO HEAR A TALE.
THE MISSUS AND I WILL TAKE OVER HANDOUTS A WHILE.
ONE TIME, MIKE AND I WERE WALKING DOWN THE STREET AND WE RAN INTO THIS WOMAN -- WELL, SHE RAN INTO US, HAHA.
NO ONE KNEW WHO SHE WAS. SHE DIDN'T KNOW WHO SHE WAS, NOT TO US, NOT THEN...
"...BUT SHE HELPED US ALL. JUST LIKE WE HAVE TO HELP EACH OTHER, NOW."

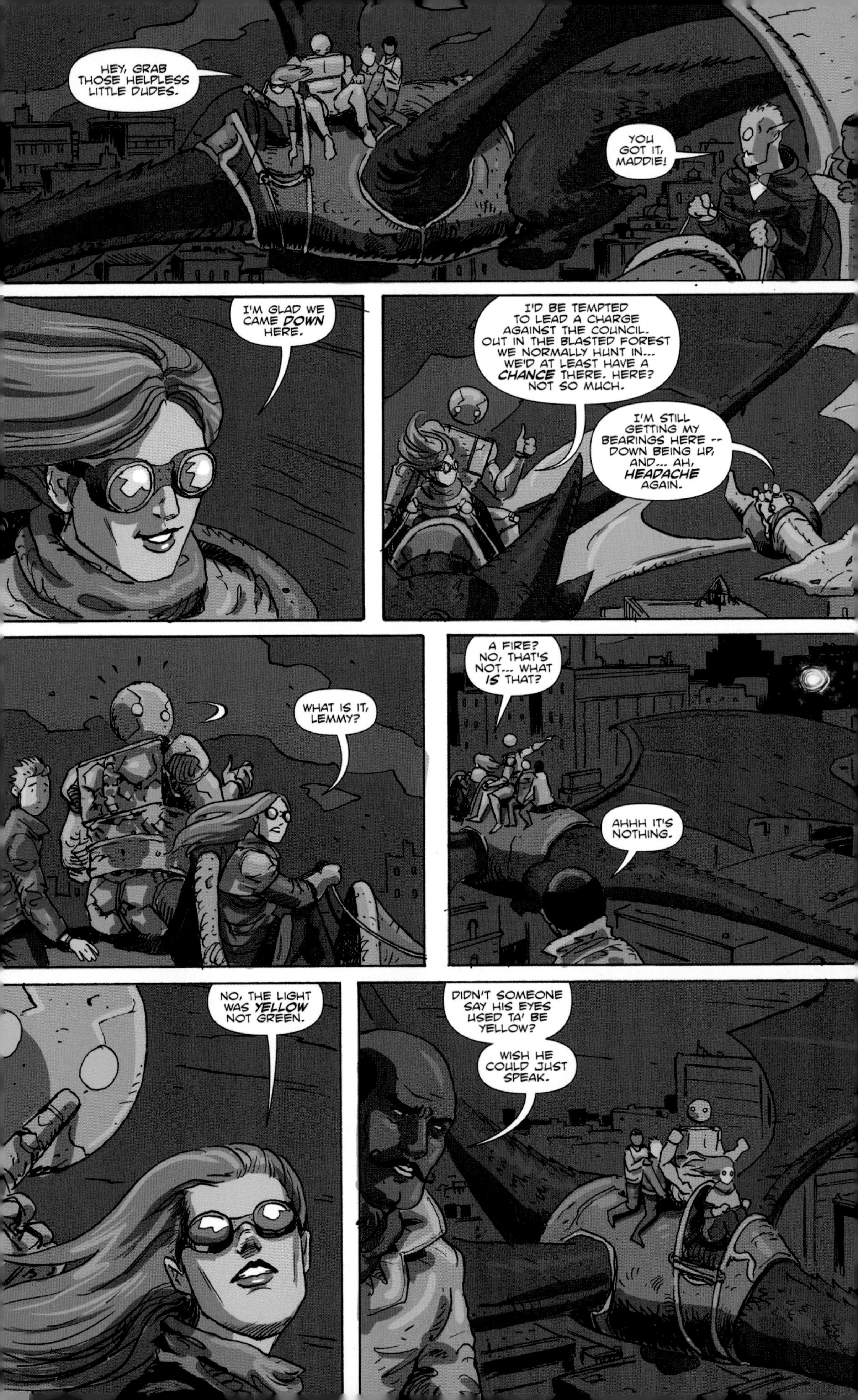
HEY, GRAB THOSE HELPLESS LITTLE DUDES.
YOU GOT IT, MADDIE!
I'M GLAD WE CAME DOWN HERE.
I'D BE TEMPTED TO LEAD A CHARGE AGAINST THE COUNCIL. OUT IN THE BLASTED FOREST WE NORMALLY HUNT IN... WE'D AT LEAST HAVE A CHANCE THERE. HERE? NOT SO MUCH.
I'M STILL GETTING MY BEARINGS HERE -- DOWN BEING UP, AND... AH, HEADACHE AGAIN.
WHAT IS IT, LEMMY?
A FIRE? NO, THAT'S NOT... WHAT IS THAT?
AHHH IT'S NOTHING.
NO, THE LIGHT WAS YELLOW NOT GREEN.
DIDN'T SOMEONE SAY HIS EYES USED TA' BE YELLOW?
WISH HE COULD JUST SPEAK.

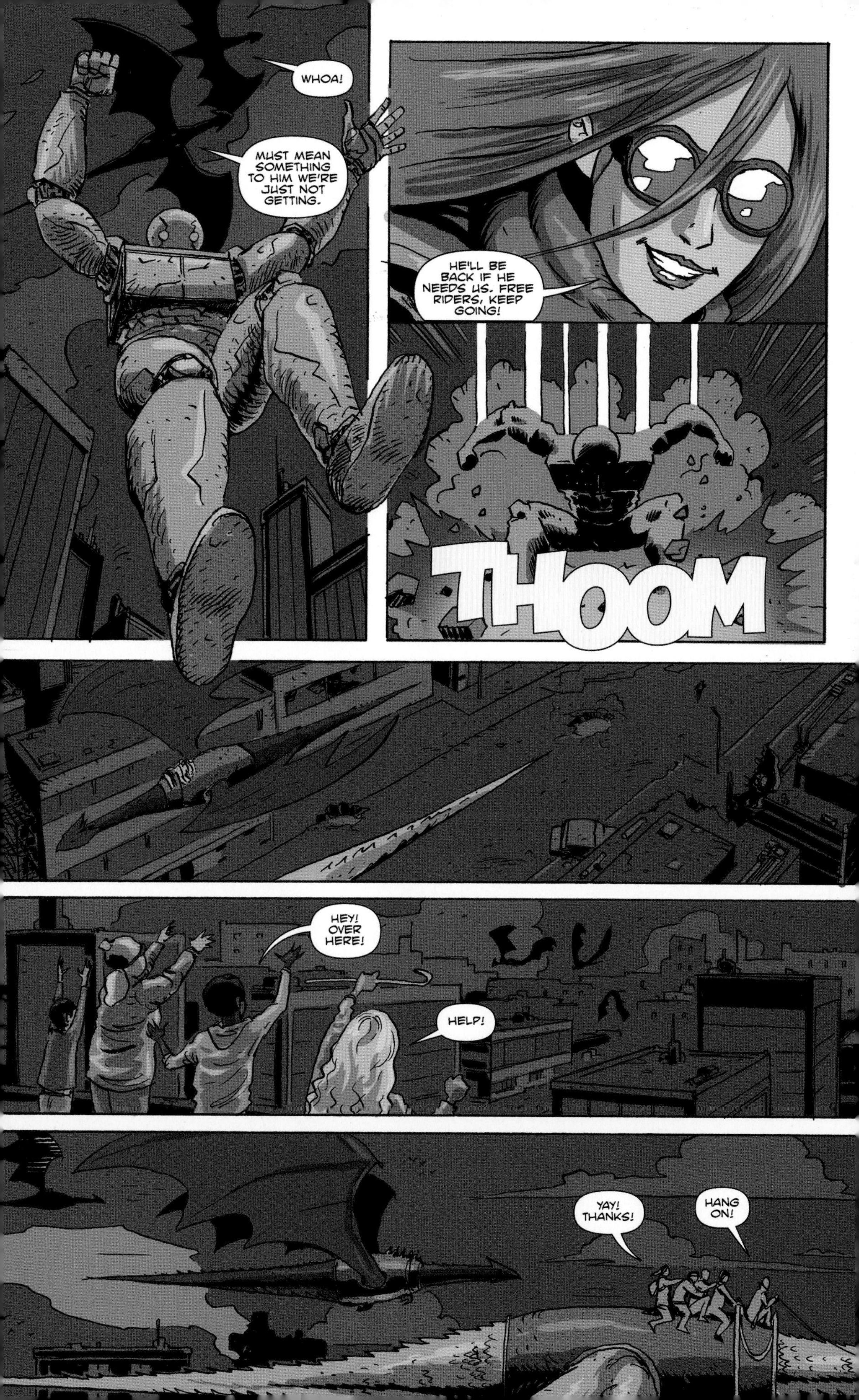
WHOA!
MUST MEAN SOMETHING TO HIM WE'RE JUST NOT GETTING.
HE'LL BE BACK IF HE NEEDS US. FREE RIDERS, KEEP GOING!
THOOM
HEY! OVER HERE!
HELP!
YAY! THANKS!
HANG ON!

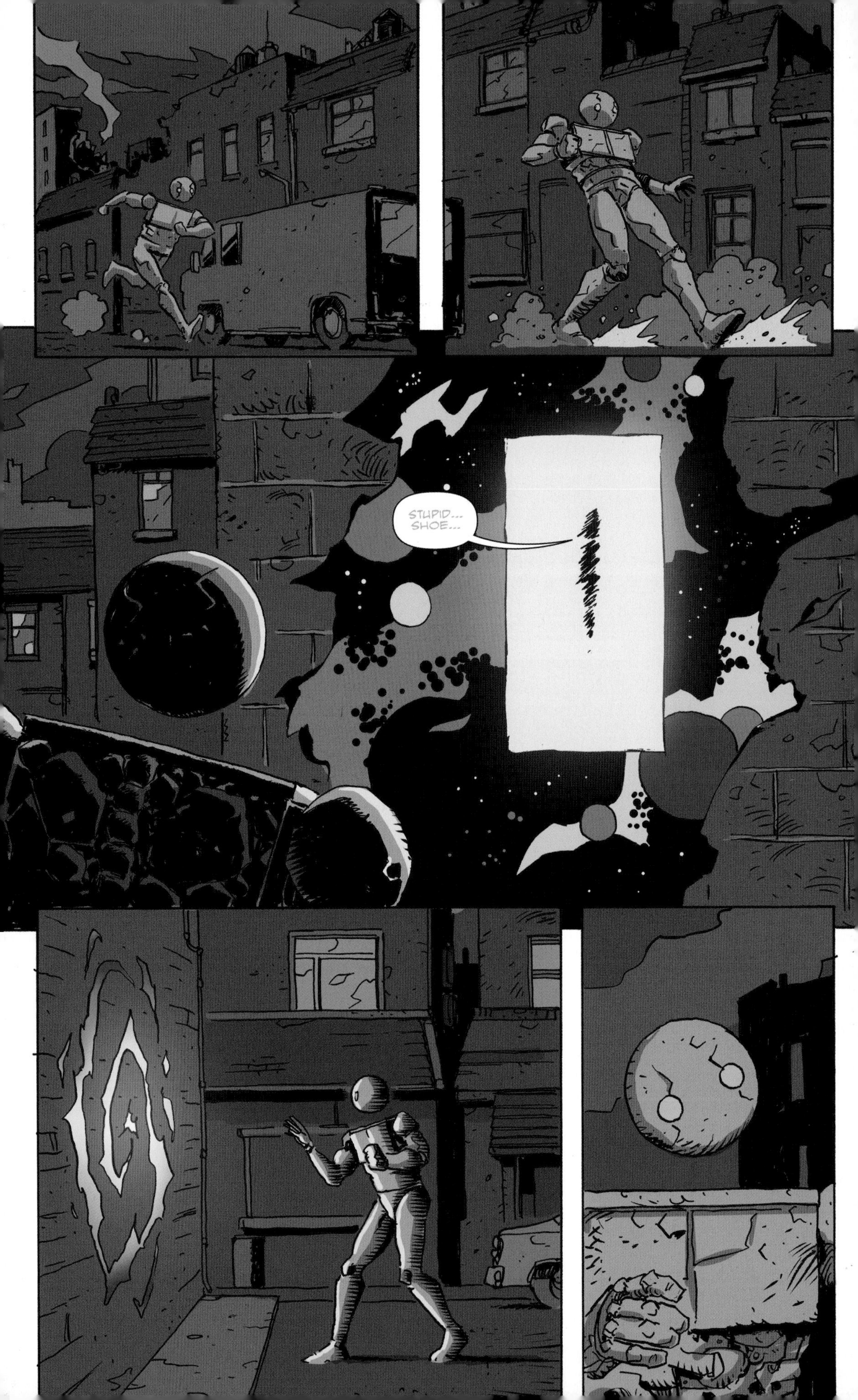
STUPID...
SHOE...

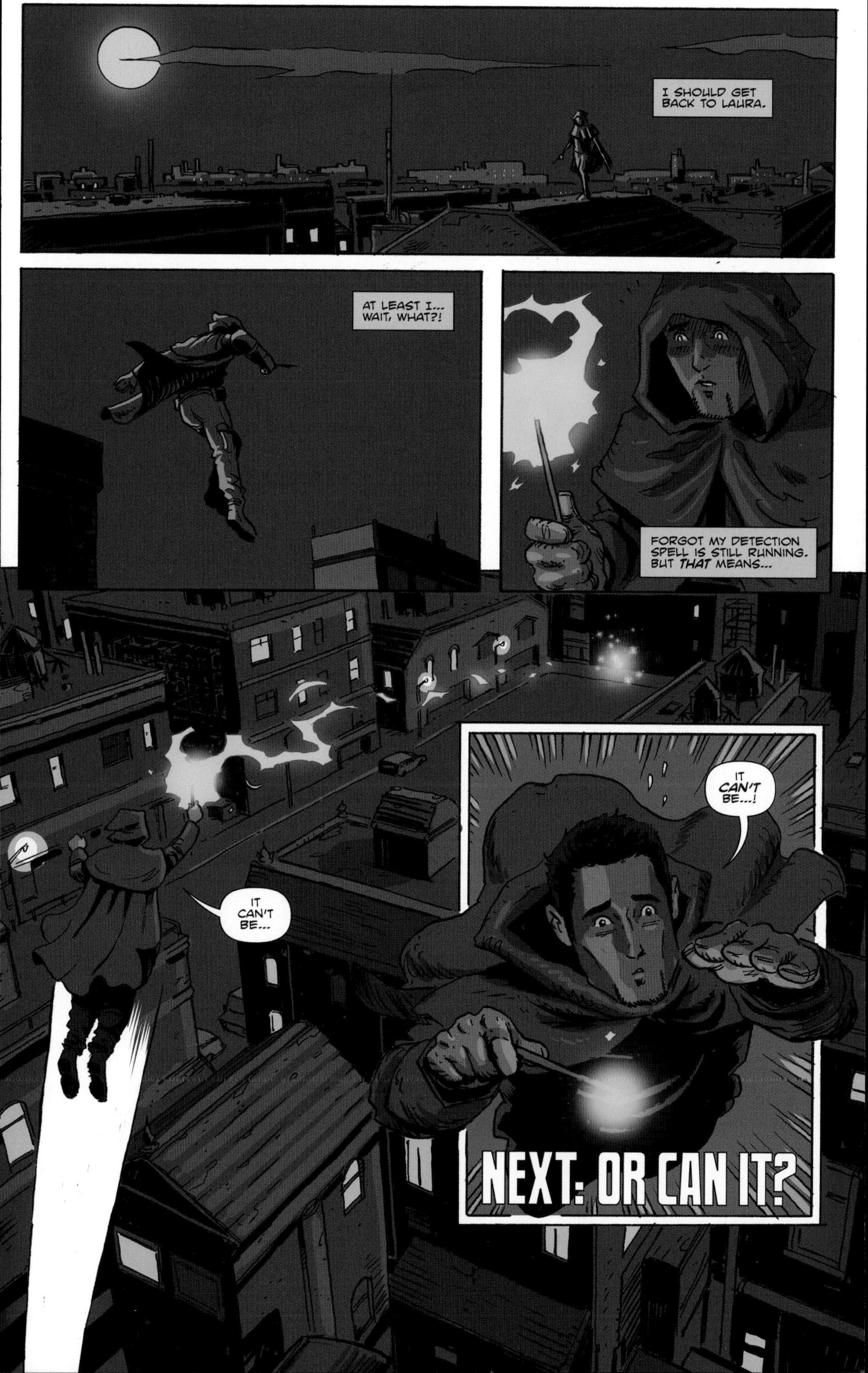
I SHOULD GET BACK TO LAURA.
AT LEAST I... WAIT, WHAT?!
FORGOT MY DETECTION SPELL IS STILL RUNNING. BUT THAT MEANS...
IT CAN'T BE...
IT CAN'T BE...!
NEXT: OR CAN IT?

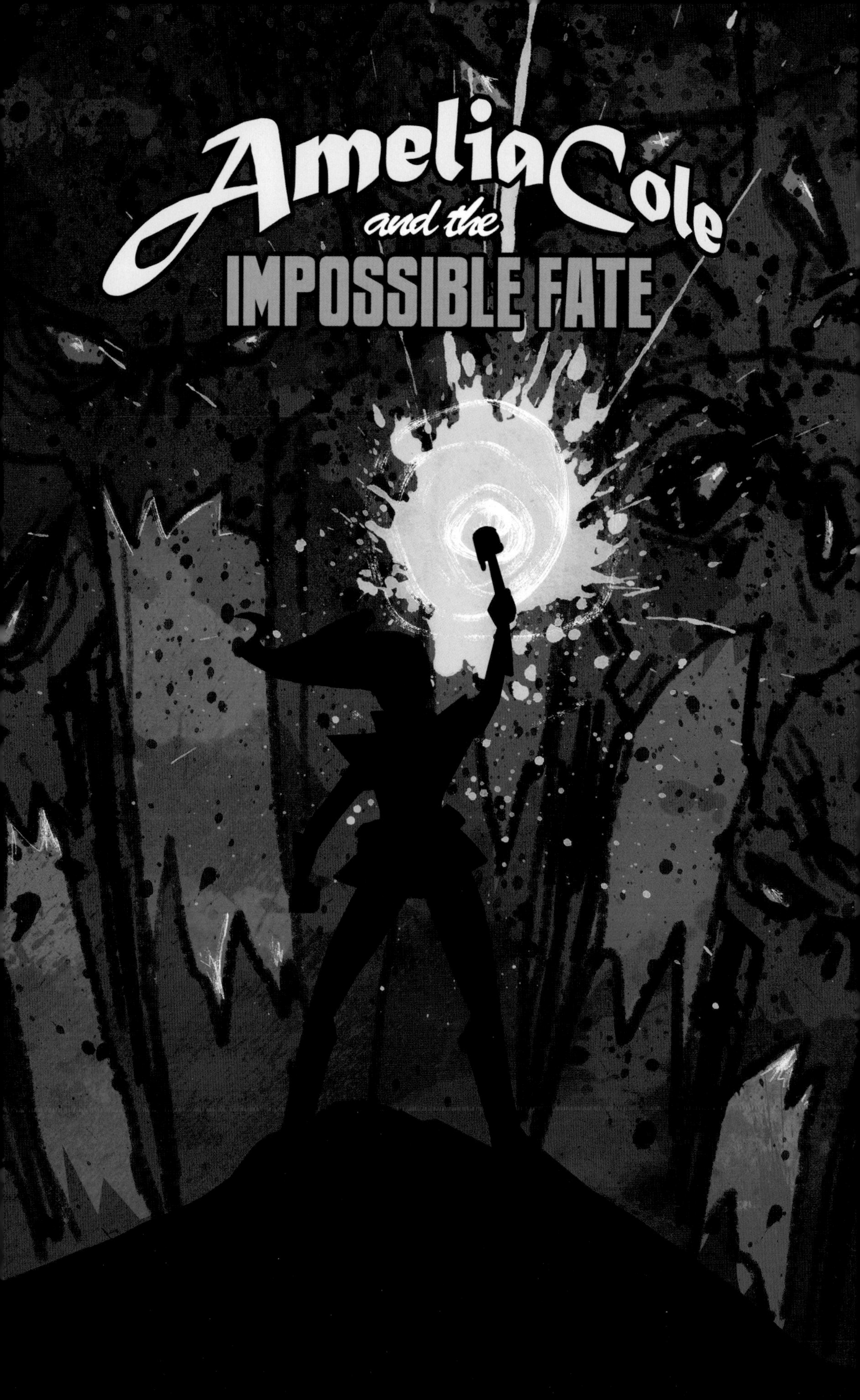
Amelia Cole
and the
IMPOSSIBLE FATE

CHAPTER 6

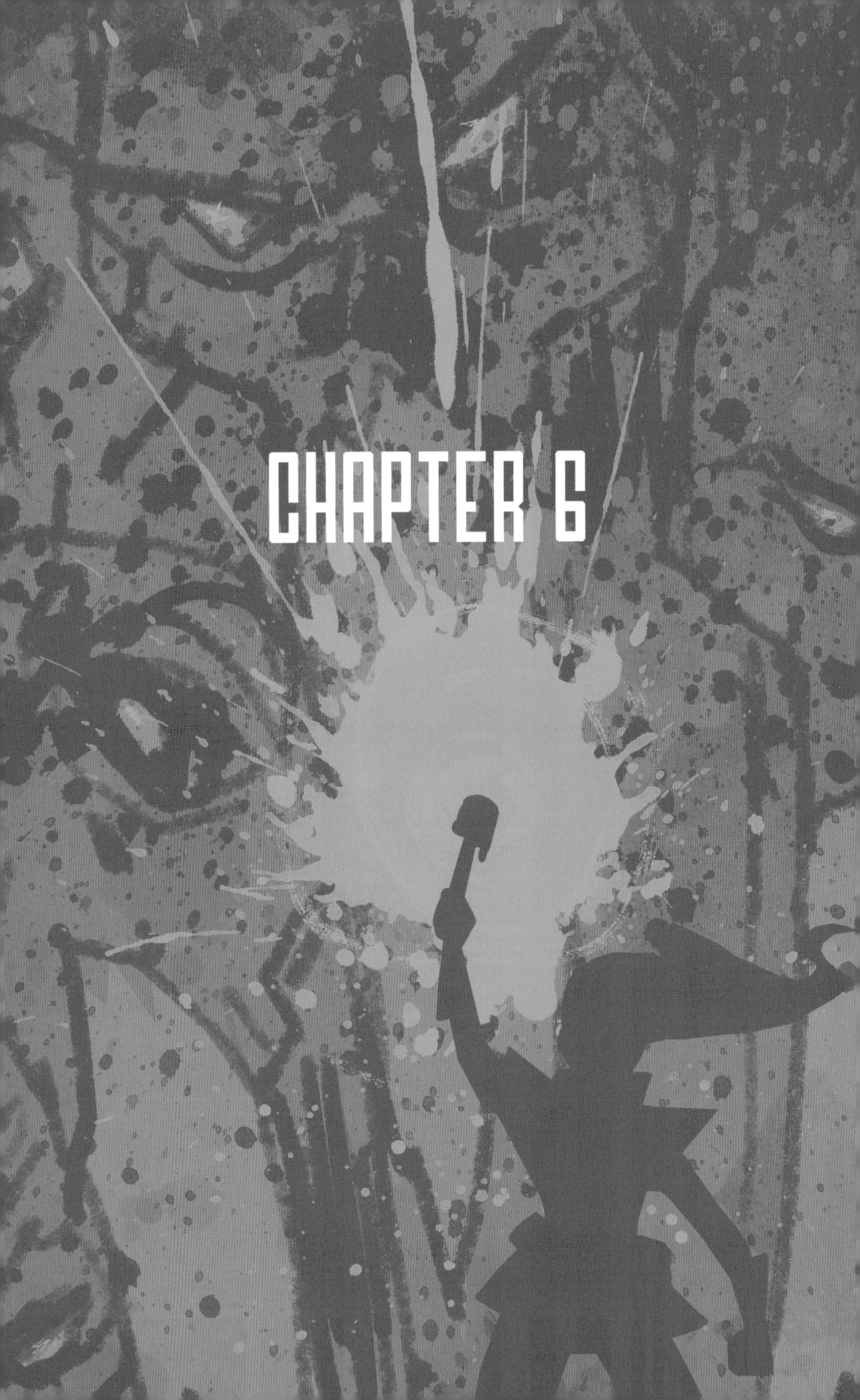

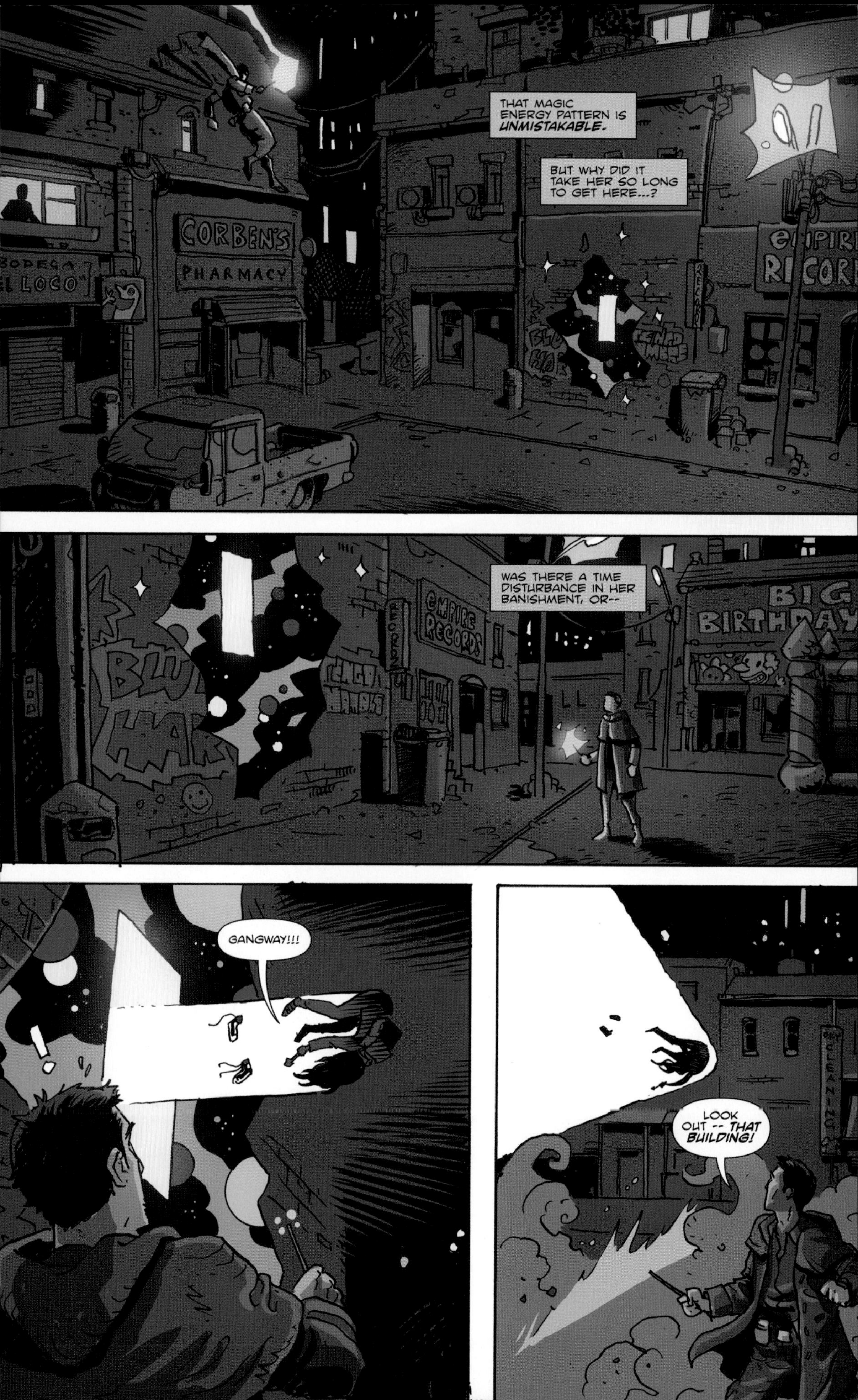
THAT MAGIC ENERGY PATTERN IS UNMISTAKABLE.
BUT WHY DID IT TAKE HER SO LONG TO GET HERE...?
CORBEN'S PHARMACY
BODEGA "EL LOCO"
EMPIRE RECORDS
WAS THERE A TIME DISTURBANCE IN HER BANISHMENT, OR--
EMPIRE RECORDS
BIG BIRTHDAY
GANGWAY!!!
LOOK OUT -- THAT BUILDING!
DRY CLEANING

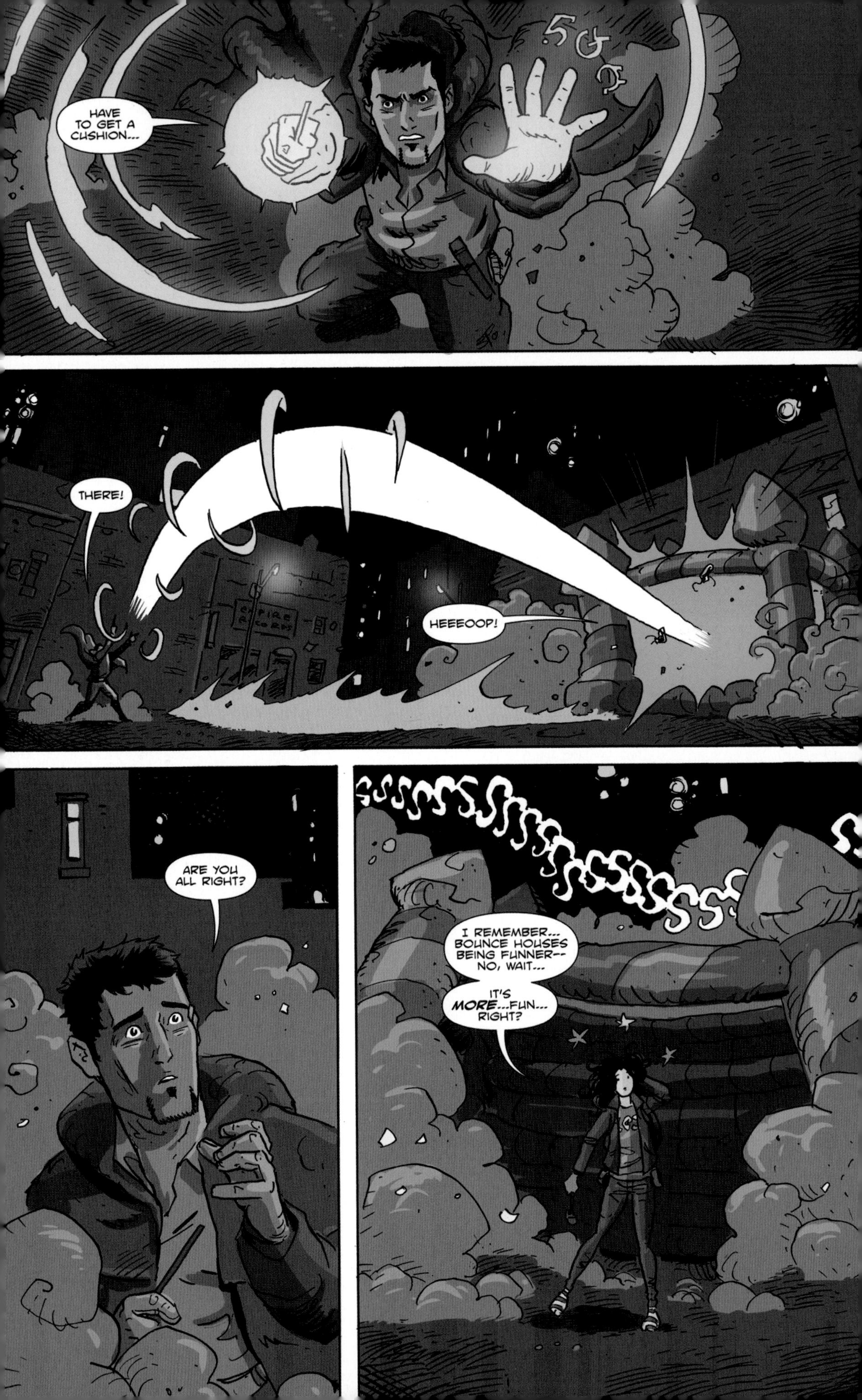
HAVE TO GET A CUSHION...
THERE!
EMPIRE RECORDS
HEEEOOP!
ARE YOU ALL RIGHT?
SSSSSSSSSSSSSSSSSSSS
I REMEMBER... BOUNCE HOUSES BEING FUNNER-- NO, WAIT...
IT'S MORE...FUN... RIGHT?

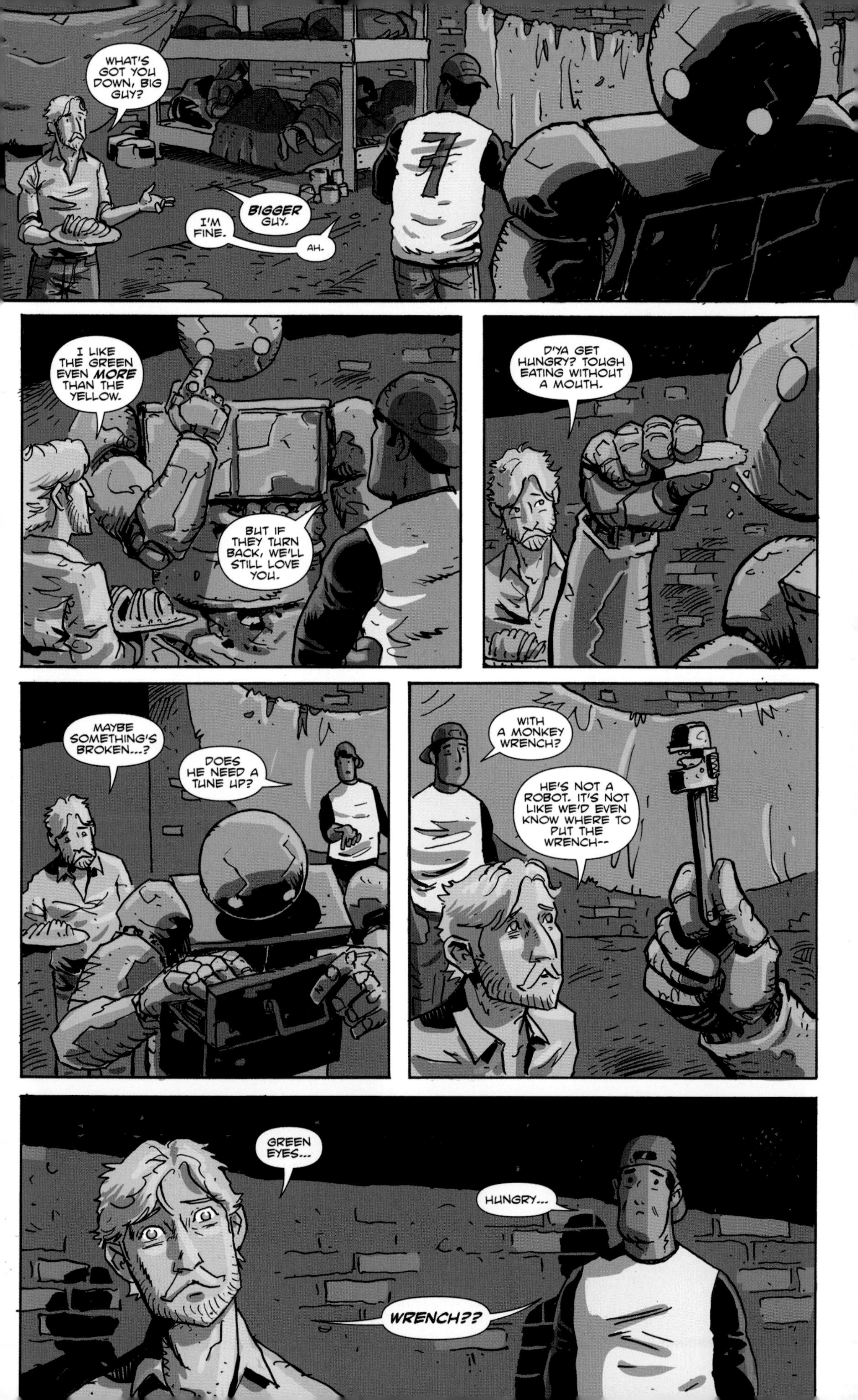
WHAT'S GOT YOU DOWN, BIG GUY?
BIGGER GUY.
I'M FINE.
AH.
I LIKE THE GREEN EVEN MORE THAN THE YELLOW.
BUT IF THEY TURN BACK, WE'LL STILL LOVE YOU.
D'YA GET HUNGRY? TOUGH EATING WITHOUT A MOUTH.
MAYBE SOMETHING'S BROKEN...?
DOES HE NEED A TUNE UP?
WITH A MONKEY WRENCH?
HE'S NOT A ROBOT. IT'S NOT LIKE WE'D EVEN KNOW WHERE TO PUT THE WRENCH--
GREEN EYES...
HUNGRY...
WRENCH??

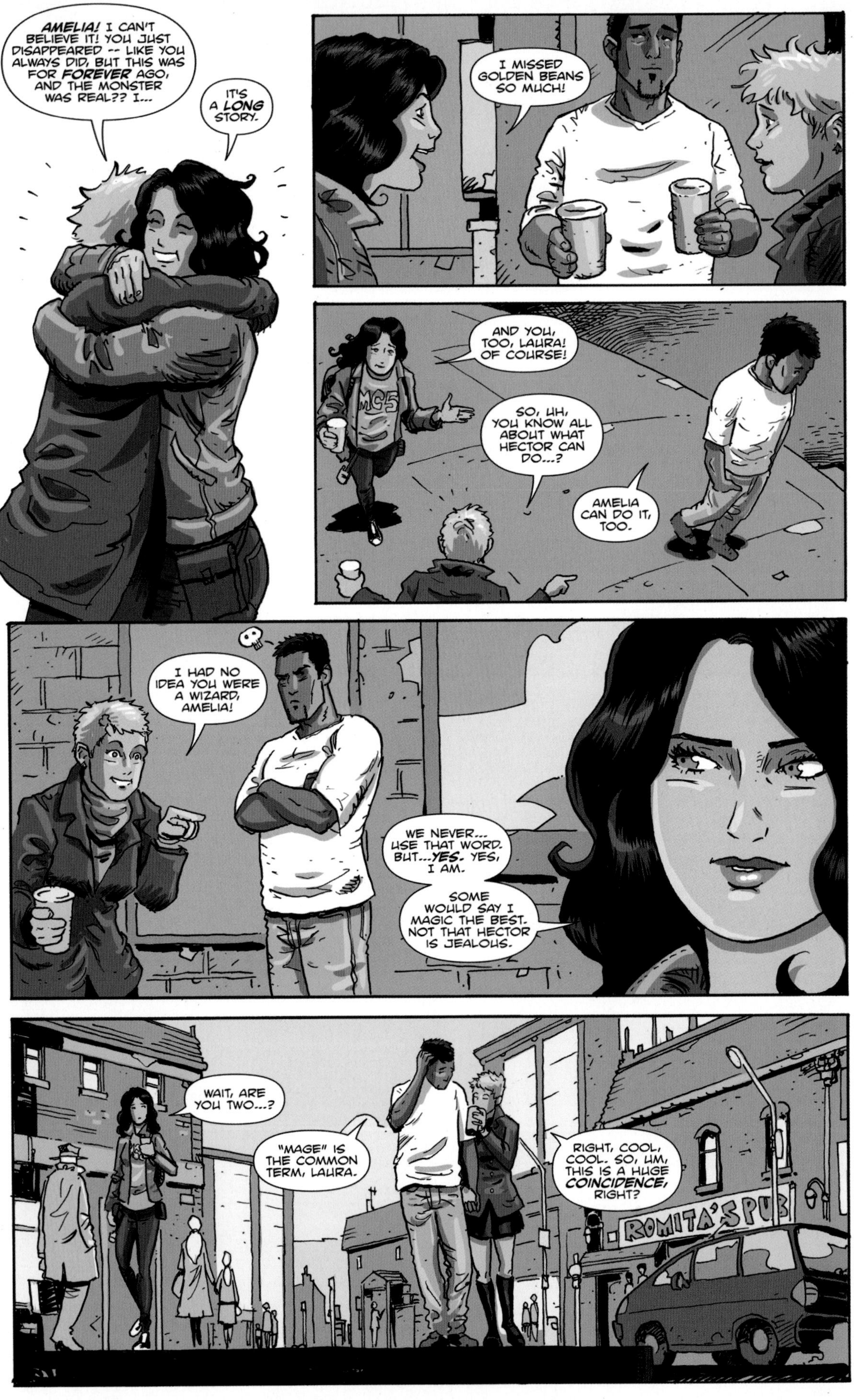
AMELIA! I CAN'T BELIEVE IT! YOU JUST DISAPPEARED -- LIKE YOU ALWAYS DID, BUT THIS WAS FOR FOREVER AGO, AND THE MONSTER WAS REAL?? I...
IT'S A LONG STORY.
I MISSED GOLDEN BEANS SO MUCH!
AND YOU, TOO, LAURA! OF COURSE!
SO, UH, YOU KNOW ALL ABOUT WHAT HECTOR CAN DO...?
AMELIA CAN DO IT, TOO.
I HAD NO IDEA YOU WERE A WIZARD, AMELIA!
WE NEVER... USE THAT WORD. BUT...YES. YES, I AM.
SOME WOULD SAY I MAGIC THE BEST. NOT THAT HECTOR IS JEALOUS.
WAIT, ARE YOU TWO...?
"MAGE" IS THE COMMON TERM, LAURA.
RIGHT, COOL, COOL. SO, UM, THIS IS A HUGE COINCIDENCE, RIGHT?
ROMITA'S PUB

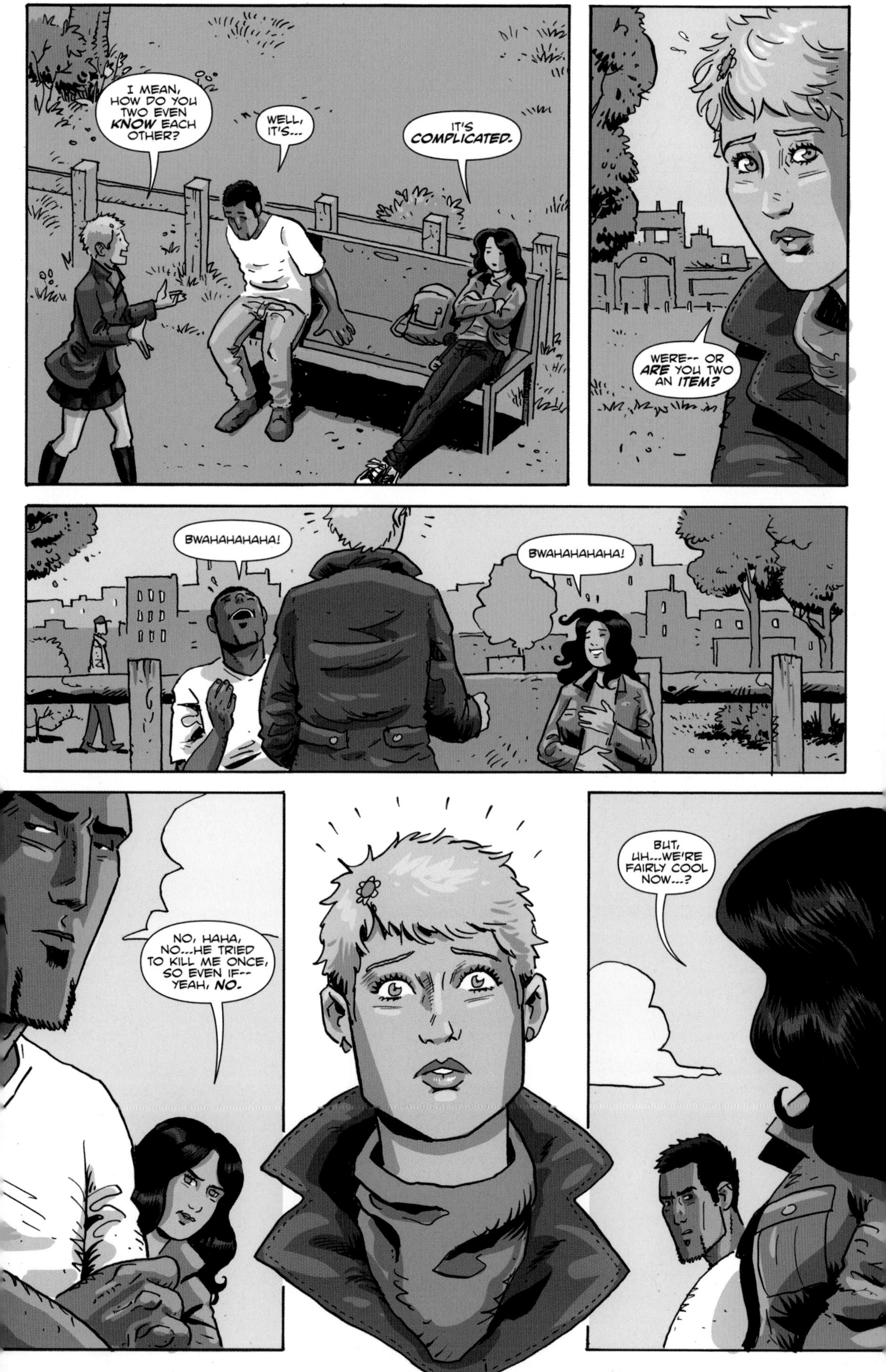
I MEAN, HOW DO YOU TWO EVEN KNOW EACH OTHER?
WELL, IT'S...
IT'S COMPLICATED.
WERE-- OR ARE YOU TWO AN ITEM?
BWAHAHAHAHA!
BWAHAHAHAHA!
NO, HAHA, NO...HE TRIED TO KILL ME ONCE, SO EVEN IF-- YEAH, NO.
BUT, UH...WE'RE FAIRLY COOL NOW...?

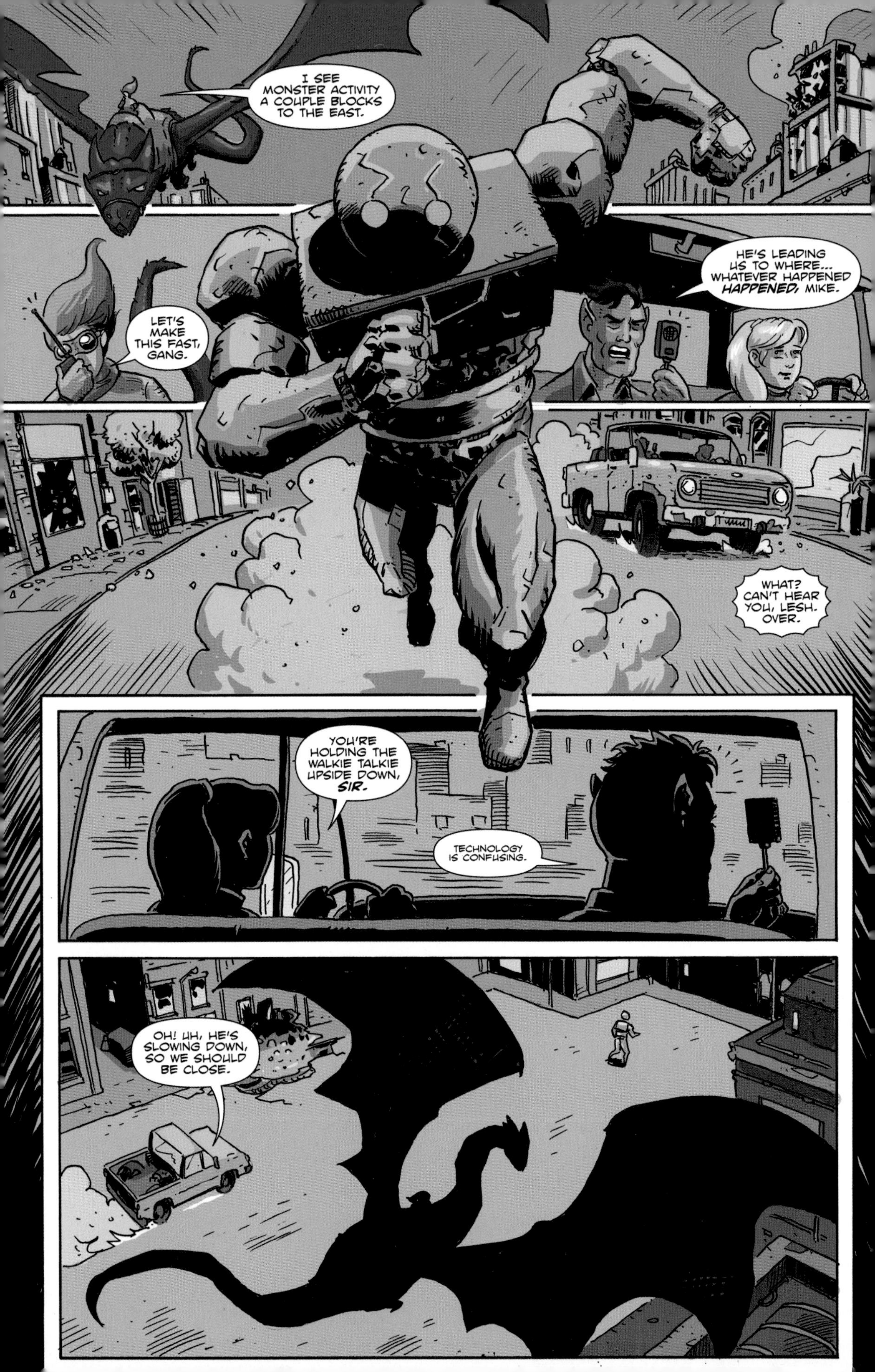
I SEE MONSTER ACTIVITY A COUPLE BLOCKS TO THE EAST.
LET'S MAKE THIS FAST, GANG.
HE'S LEADING US TO WHERE... WHATEVER HAPPENED *HAPPENED,* MIKE.
WHAT? CAN'T HEAR YOU, LESH. OVER.
YOU'RE HOLDING THE WALKIE TALKIE UPSIDE DOWN, *SIR.*
TECHNOLOGY IS CONFUSING.
OH! UH, HE'S SLOWING DOWN, SO WE SHOULD BE CLOSE.

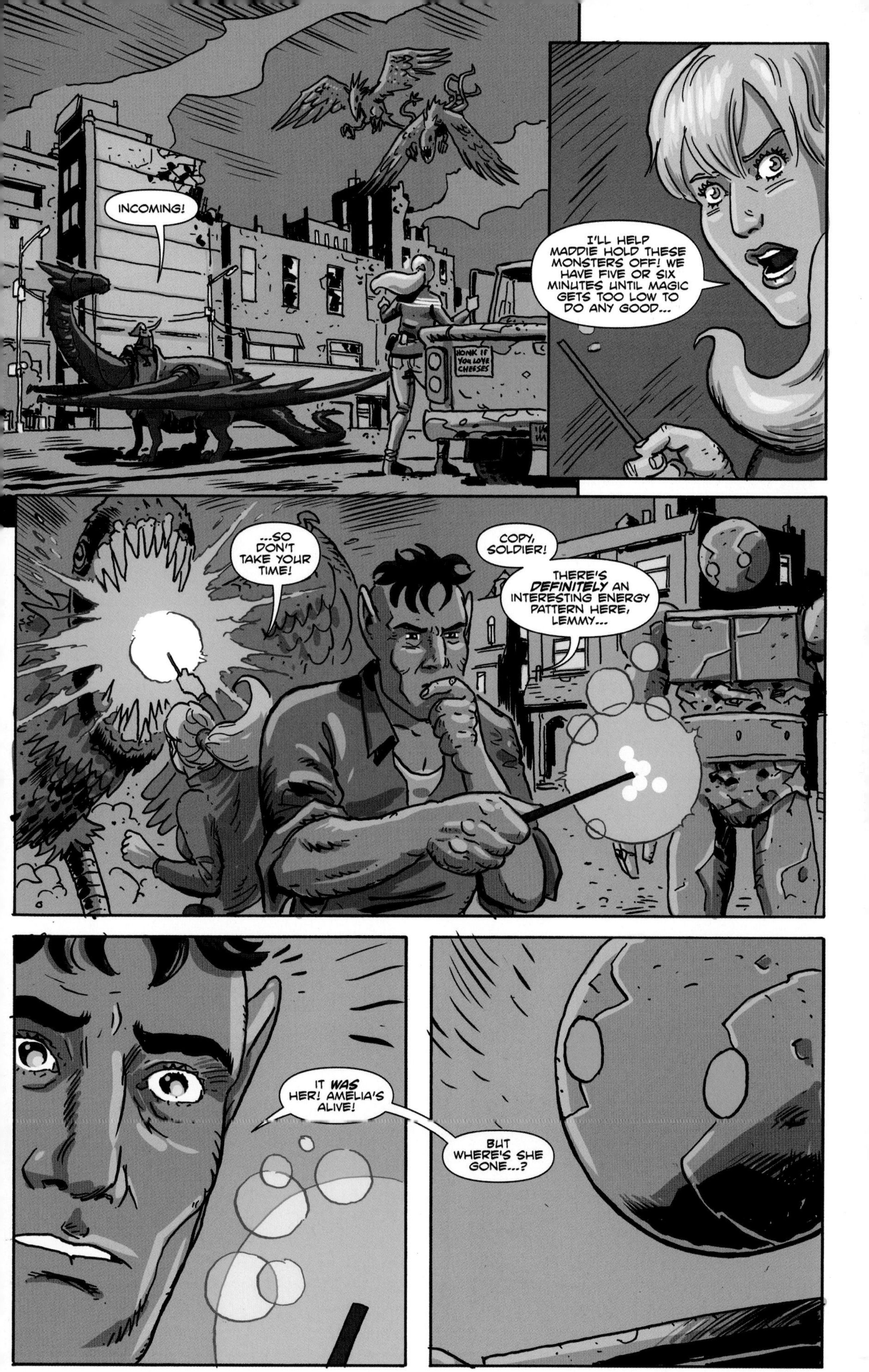
INCOMING!
HONK IF YOU LOVE CHEESES
I'LL HELP MADDIE HOLD THESE MONSTERS OFF! WE HAVE FIVE OR SIX MINUTES UNTIL MAGIC GETS TOO LOW TO DO ANY GOOD...
...SO DON'T TAKE YOUR TIME!
COPY, SOLDIER!
THERE'S DEFINITELY AN INTERESTING ENERGY PATTERN HERE, LEMMY...
IT WAS HER! AMELIA'S ALIVE!
BUT WHERE'S SHE GONE...?

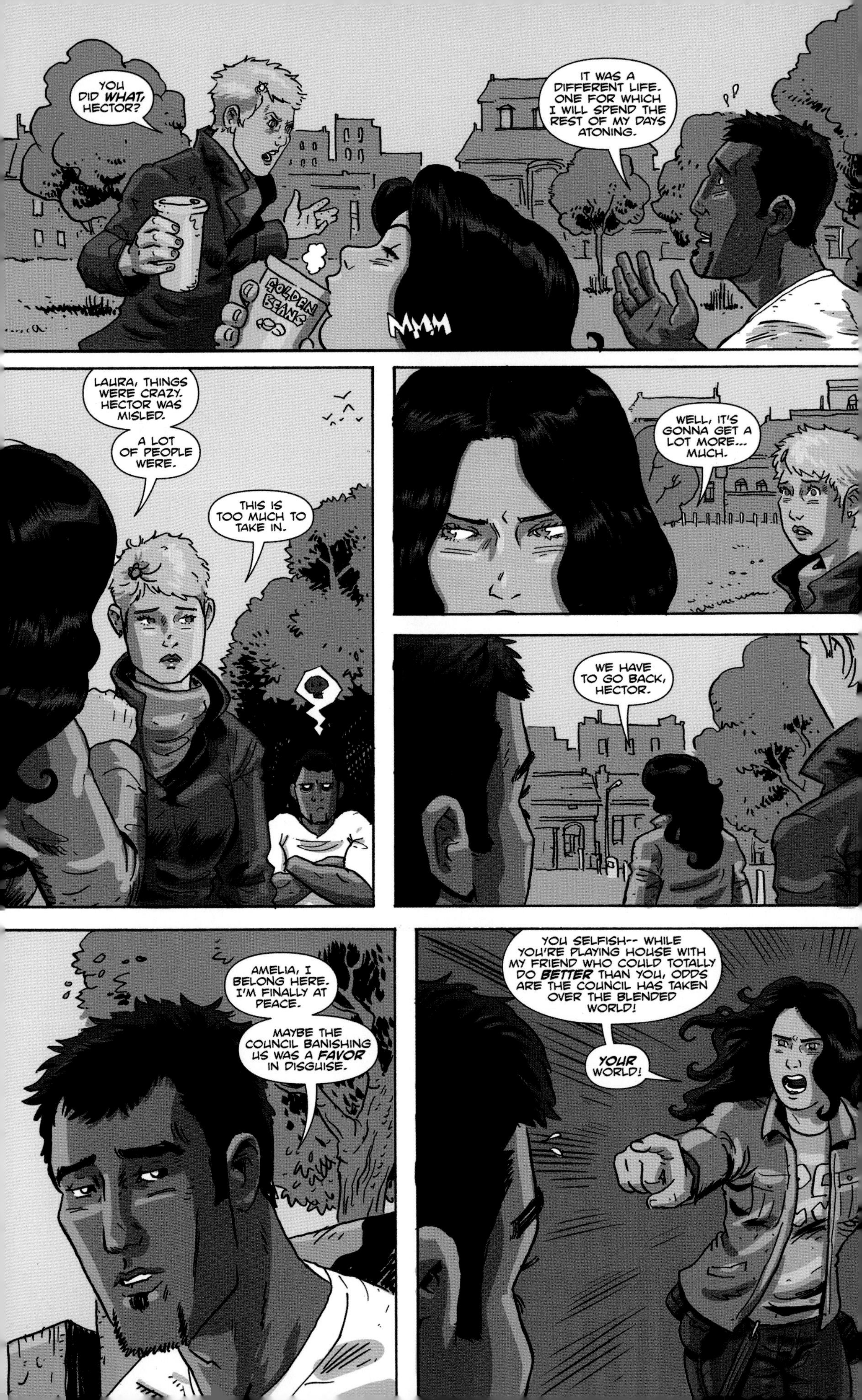
YOU DID WHAT, HECTOR?
IT WAS A DIFFERENT LIFE. ONE FOR WHICH I WILL SPEND THE REST OF MY DAYS ATONING.
GOLDEN BEANS
MMM
LAURA, THINGS WERE CRAZY. HECTOR WAS MISLED.
A LOT OF PEOPLE WERE.
THIS IS TOO MUCH TO TAKE IN.
WELL, IT'S GONNA GET A LOT MORE... MUCH.
WE HAVE TO GO BACK, HECTOR.
AMELIA, I BELONG HERE. I'M FINALLY AT PEACE.
MAYBE THE COUNCIL BANISHING US WAS A FAVOR IN DISGUISE.
YOU SELFISH-- WHILE YOU'RE PLAYING HOUSE WITH MY FRIEND WHO COULD TOTALLY DO BETTER THAN YOU, ODDS ARE THE COUNCIL HAS TAKEN OVER THE BLENDED WORLD!
YOUR WORLD!

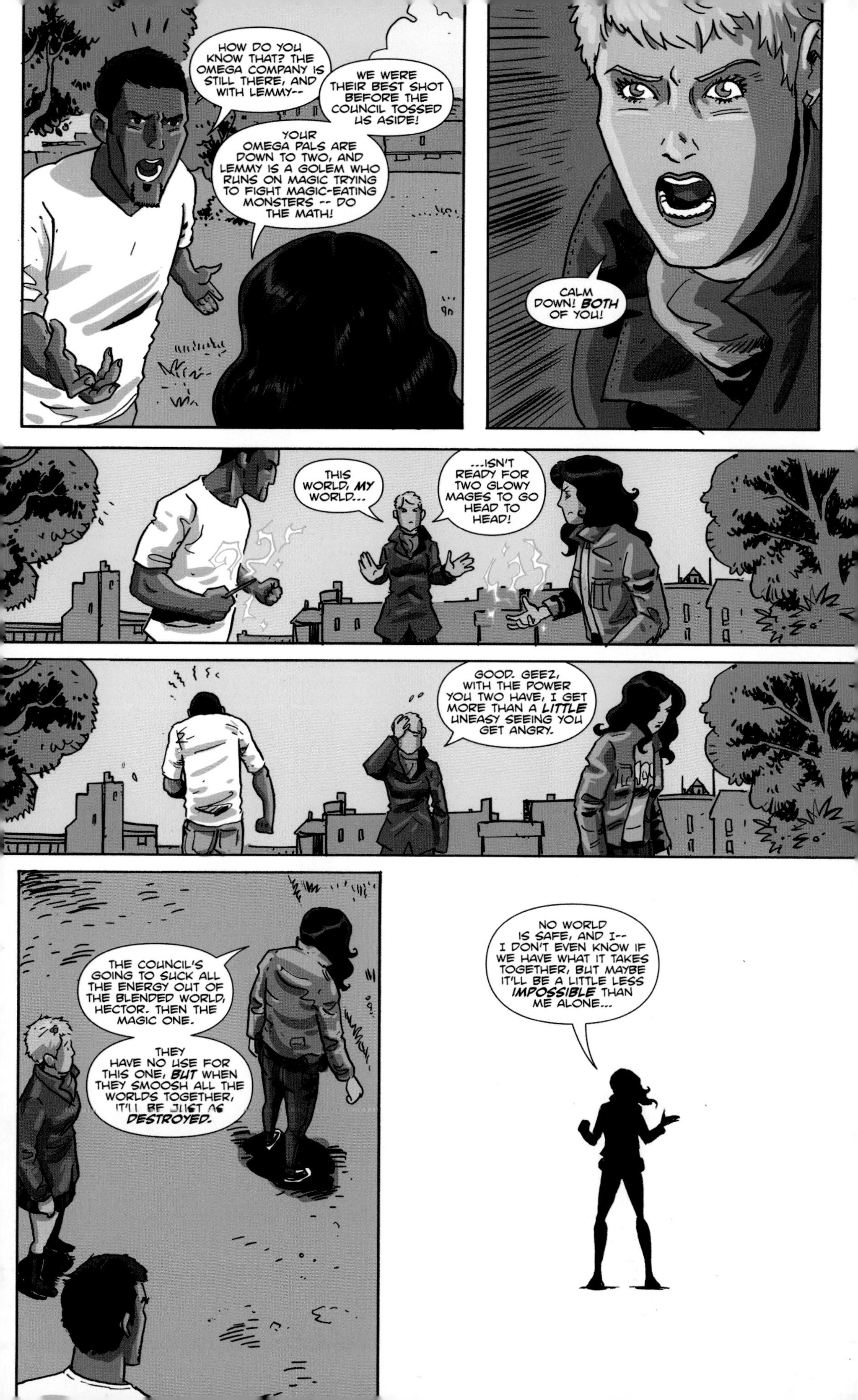
HOW DO YOU KNOW THAT? THE OMEGA COMPANY IS STILL THERE, AND WITH LEMMY--
WE WERE THEIR BEST SHOT BEFORE THE COUNCIL TOSSED US ASIDE!
YOUR OMEGA PALS ARE DOWN TO TWO, AND LEMMY IS A GOLEM WHO RUNS ON MAGIC TRYING TO FIGHT MAGIC-EATING MONSTERS -- DO THE MATH!
CALM DOWN! BOTH OF YOU!
THIS WORLD, MY WORLD...
...ISN'T READY FOR TWO GLOWY MAGES TO GO HEAD TO HEAD!
GOOD. GEEZ, WITH THE POWER YOU TWO HAVE, I GET MORE THAN A LITTLE UNEASY SEEING YOU GET ANGRY.
THE COUNCIL'S GOING TO SUCK ALL THE ENERGY OUT OF THE BLENDED WORLD, HECTOR. THEN THE MAGIC ONE.
THEY HAVE NO USE FOR THIS ONE, BUT WHEN THEY SMOOSH ALL THE WORLDS TOGETHER, IT'LL BE JUST AS DESTROYED.
NO WORLD IS SAFE, AND I-- I DON'T EVEN KNOW IF WE HAVE WHAT IT TAKES TOGETHER, BUT MAYBE IT'LL BE A LITTLE LESS IMPOSSIBLE THAN ME ALONE...

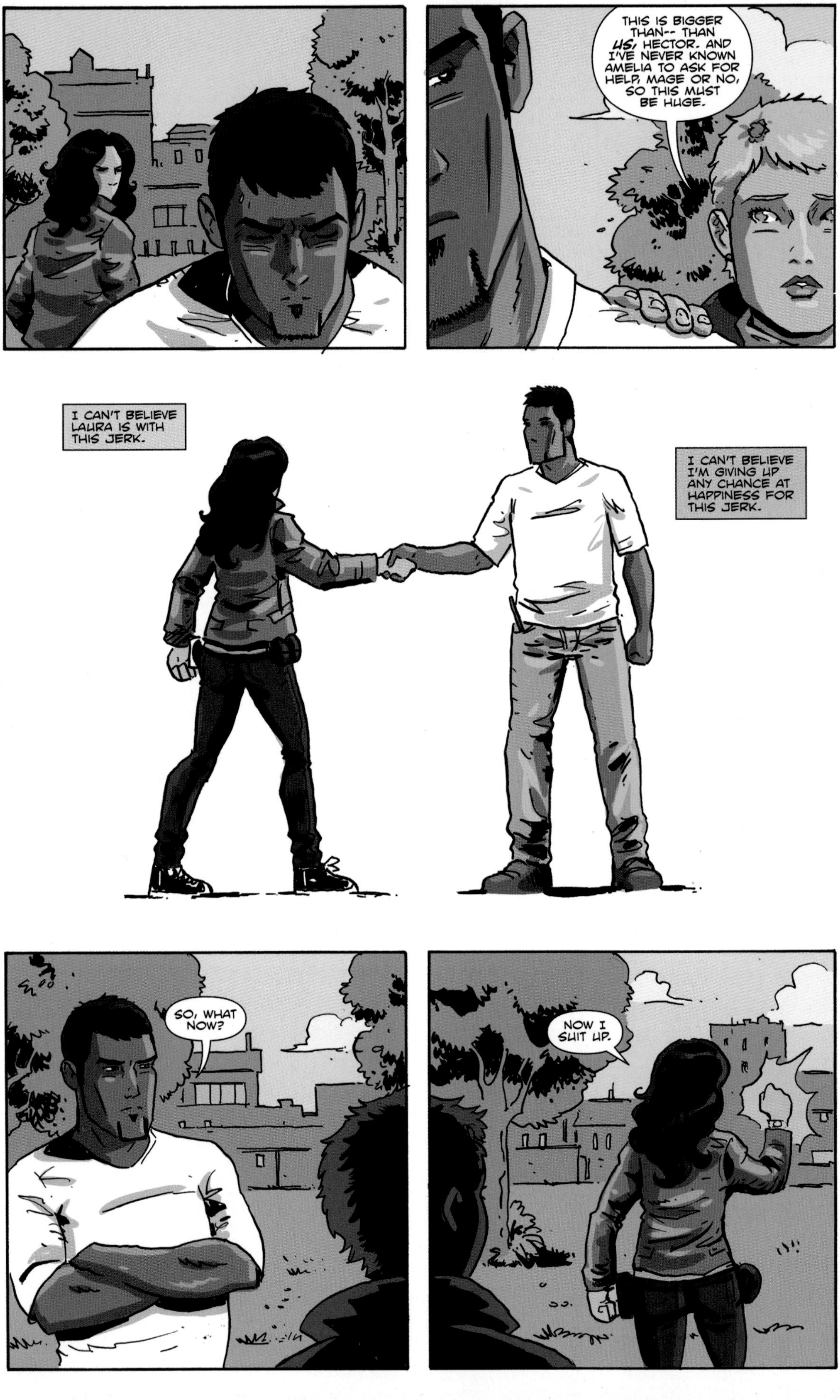
THIS IS BIGGER THAN-- THAN US, HECTOR. AND I'VE NEVER KNOWN AMELIA TO ASK FOR HELP, MAGE OR NO, SO THIS MUST BE HUGE.
I CAN'T BELIEVE LAURA IS WITH THIS JERK.
I CAN'T BELIEVE I'M GIVING UP ANY CHANCE AT HAPPINESS FOR THIS JERK.
SO, WHAT NOW?
NOW I SUIT UP.

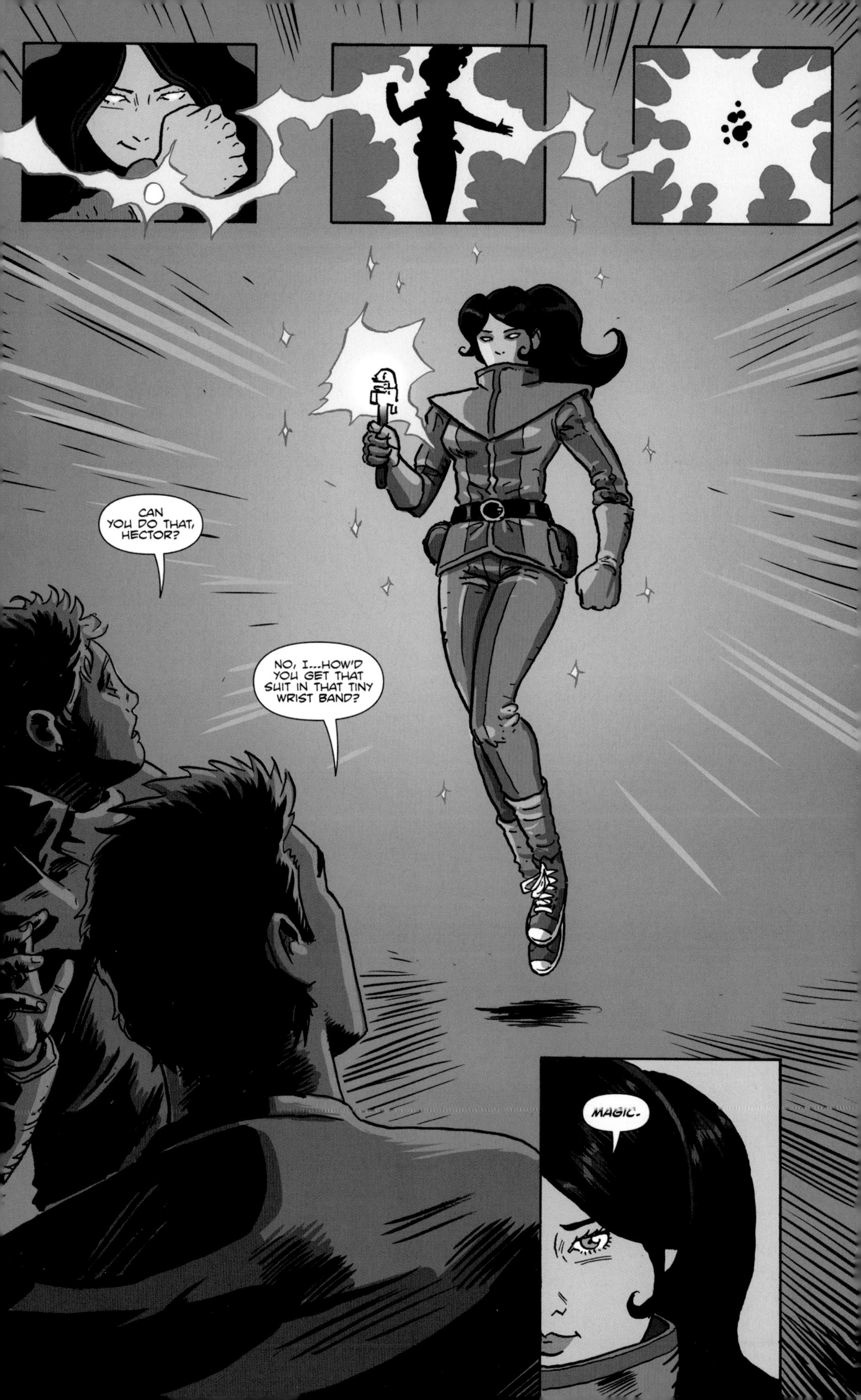
CAN YOU DO THAT, HECTOR?
NO, I...HOW'D YOU GET THAT SUIT IN THAT TINY WRIST BAND?
MAGIC.

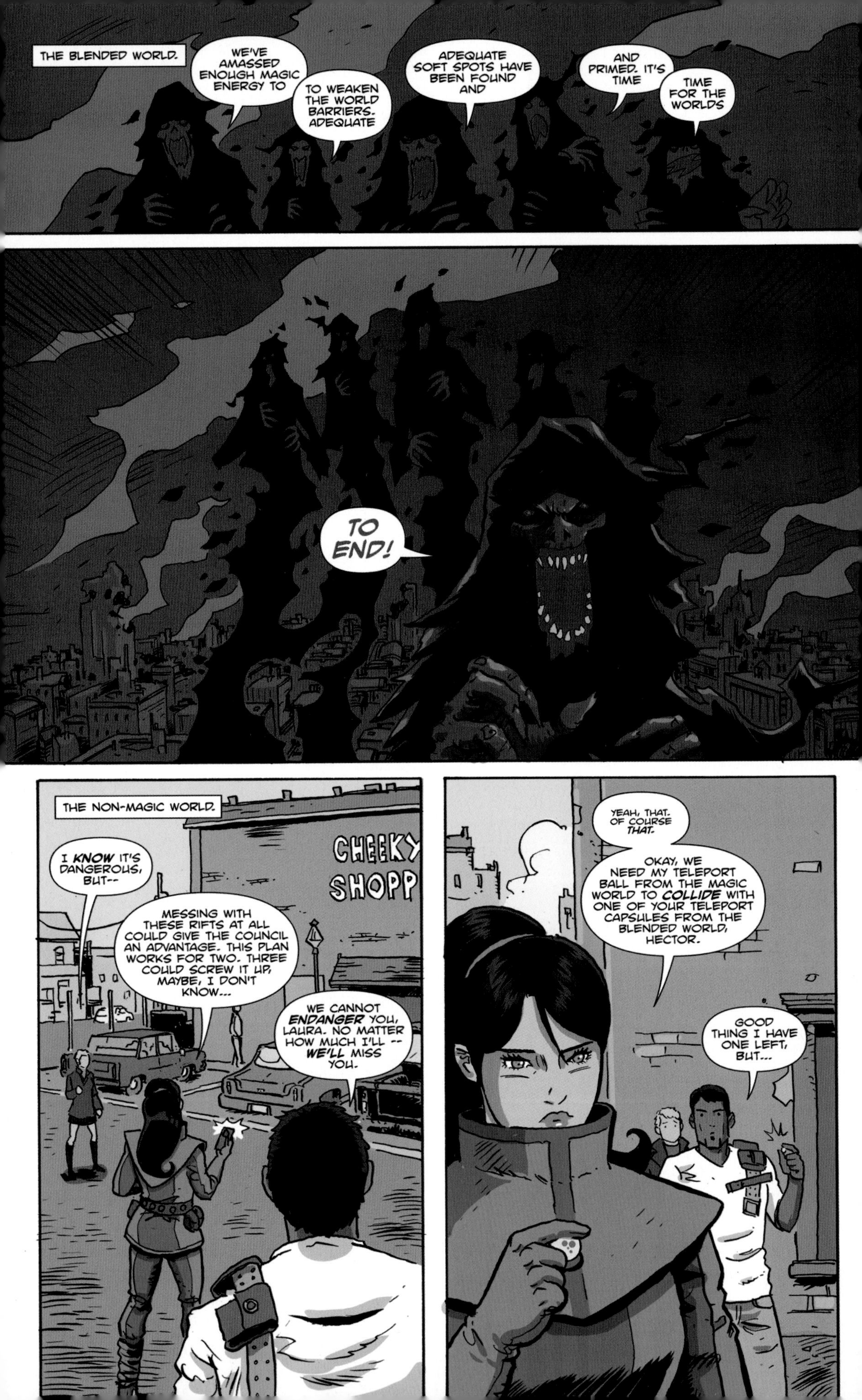
THE BLENDED WORLD.
WE'VE AMASSED ENOUGH MAGIC ENERGY TO
TO WEAKEN THE WORLD BARRIERS. ADEQUATE
ADEQUATE SOFT SPOTS HAVE BEEN FOUND AND
AND PRIMED. IT'S TIME
TIME FOR THE WORLDS
TO END!
THE NON-MAGIC WORLD.
CHEEKY
SHOPP
I KNOW IT'S DANGEROUS, BUT--
MESSING WITH THESE RIFTS AT ALL COULD GIVE THE COUNCIL AN ADVANTAGE. THIS PLAN WORKS FOR TWO. THREE COULD SCREW IT UP, MAYBE, I DON'T KNOW...
WE CANNOT ENDANGER YOU, LAURA. NO MATTER HOW MUCH I'LL -- WE'LL MISS YOU.
YEAH, THAT. OF COURSE THAT.
OKAY, WE NEED MY TELEPORT BALL FROM THE MAGIC WORLD TO COLLIDE WITH ONE OF YOUR TELEPORT CAPSULES FROM THE BLENDED WORLD, HECTOR.
GOOD THING I HAVE ONE LEFT, BUT...

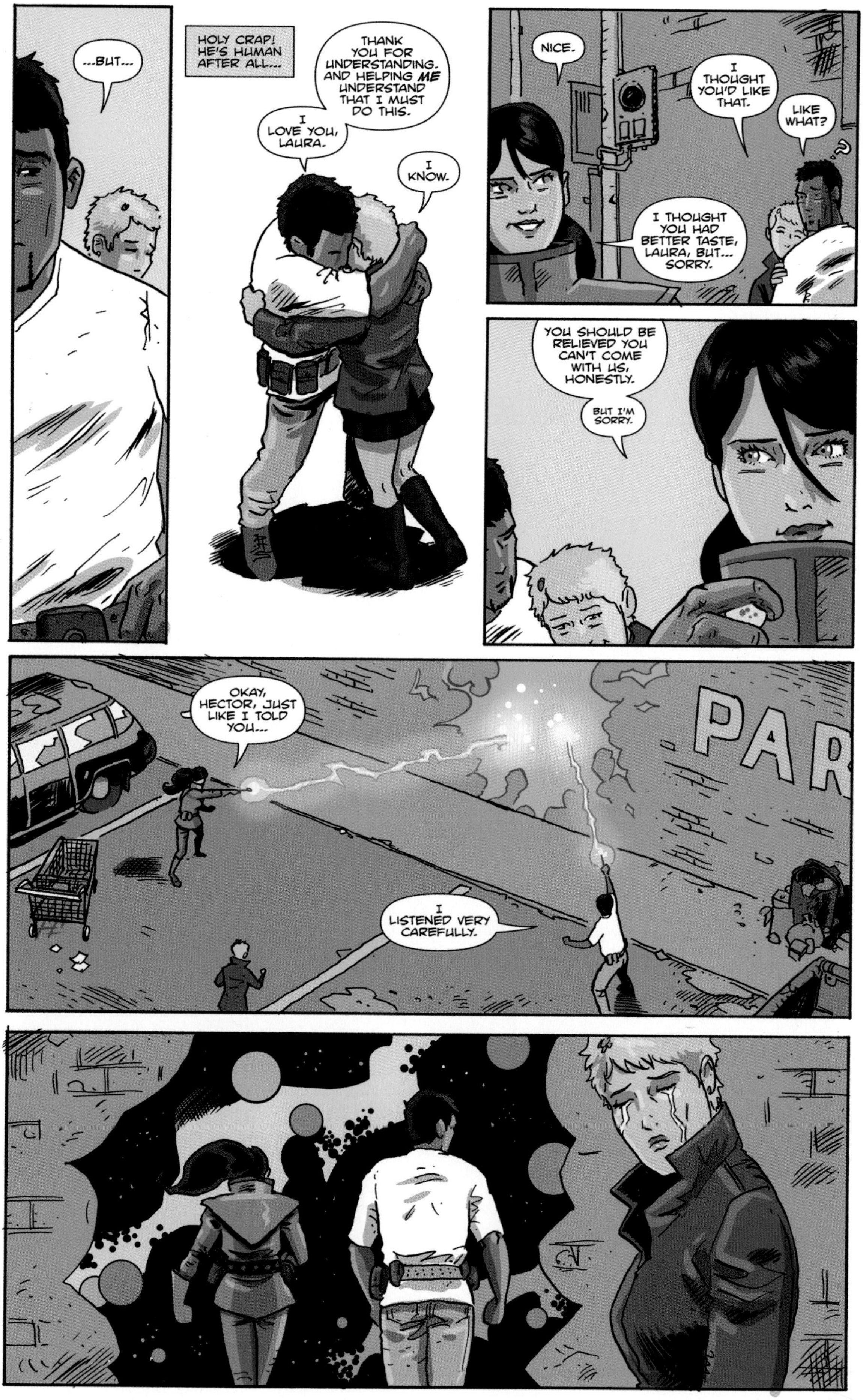
...BUT...
HOLY CRAP! HE'S HUMAN AFTER ALL...
THANK YOU FOR UNDERSTANDING. AND HELPING *ME* UNDERSTAND THAT I MUST DO THIS.
I LOVE YOU, LAURA.
I KNOW.
NICE.
I THOUGHT YOU'D LIKE THAT.
LIKE WHAT?
I THOUGHT YOU HAD BETTER TASTE, LAURA, BUT... SORRY.
YOU SHOULD BE RELIEVED YOU CAN'T COME WITH US, HONESTLY.
BUT I'M SORRY.
OKAY, HECTOR, JUST LIKE I TOLD YOU...
PAR
I LISTENED VERY CAREFULLY.

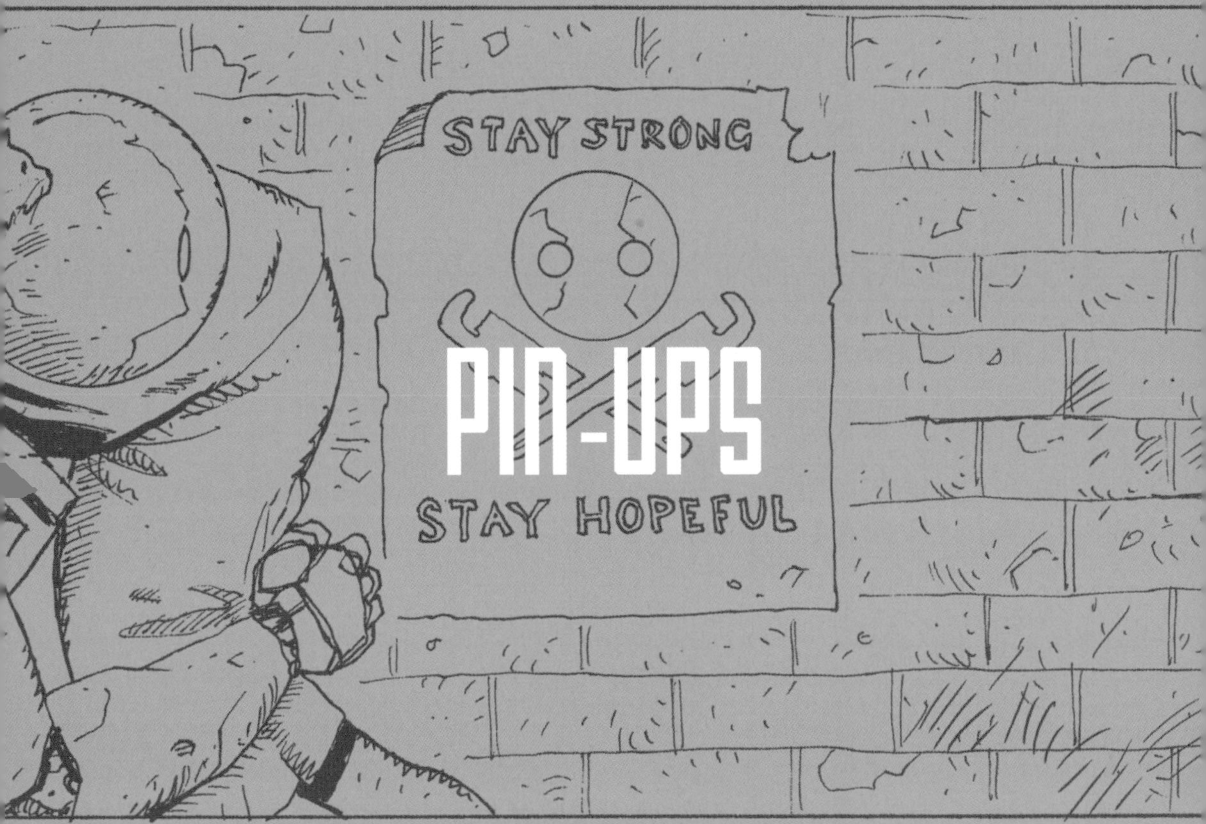
STAY STRONG
STAY HOPEFUL

PIN-UPS

ART BY

DARIEL FILOMENO

LEILA DEL DUCA

TANYA BJORK

VALENTINE BARKER

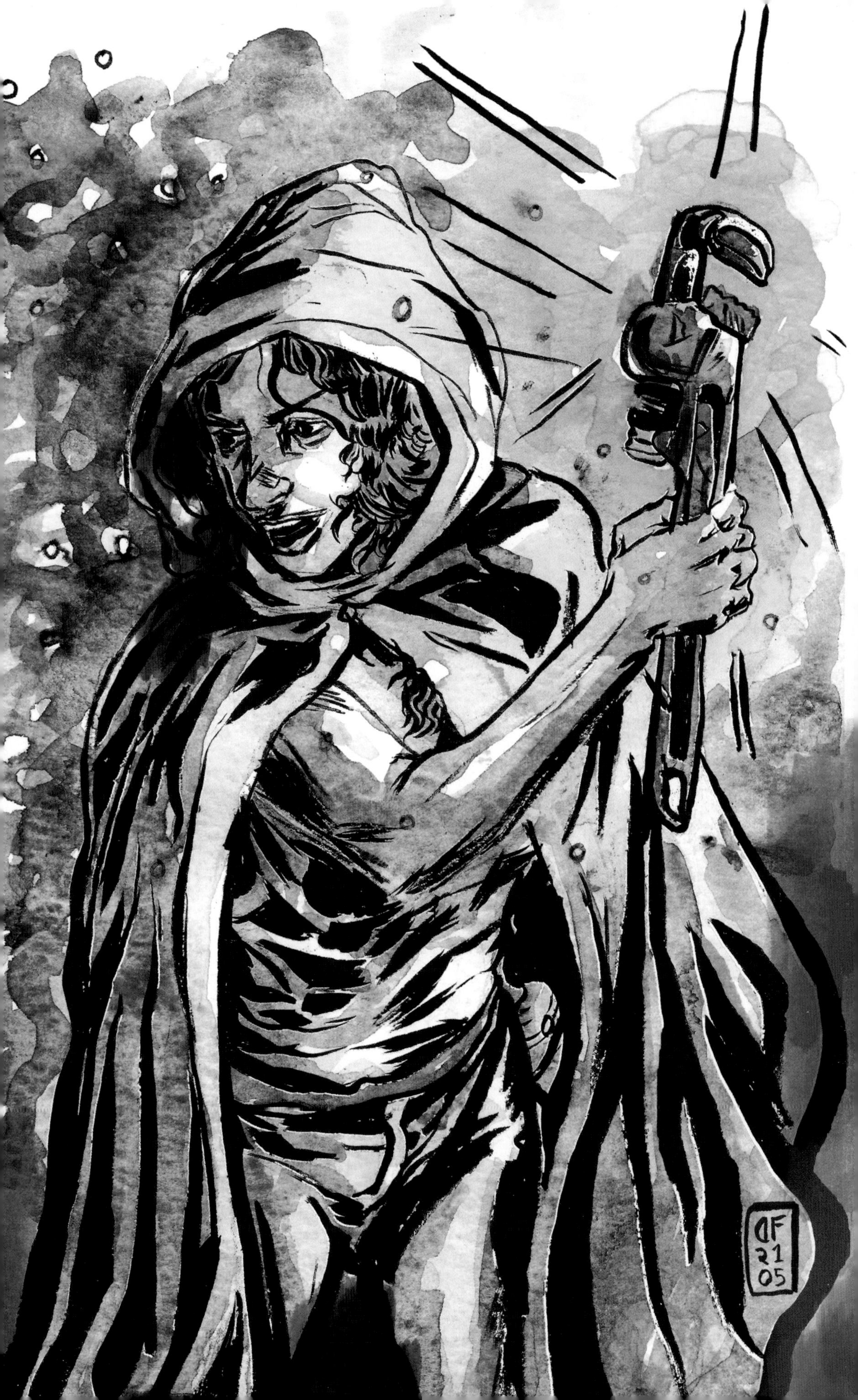

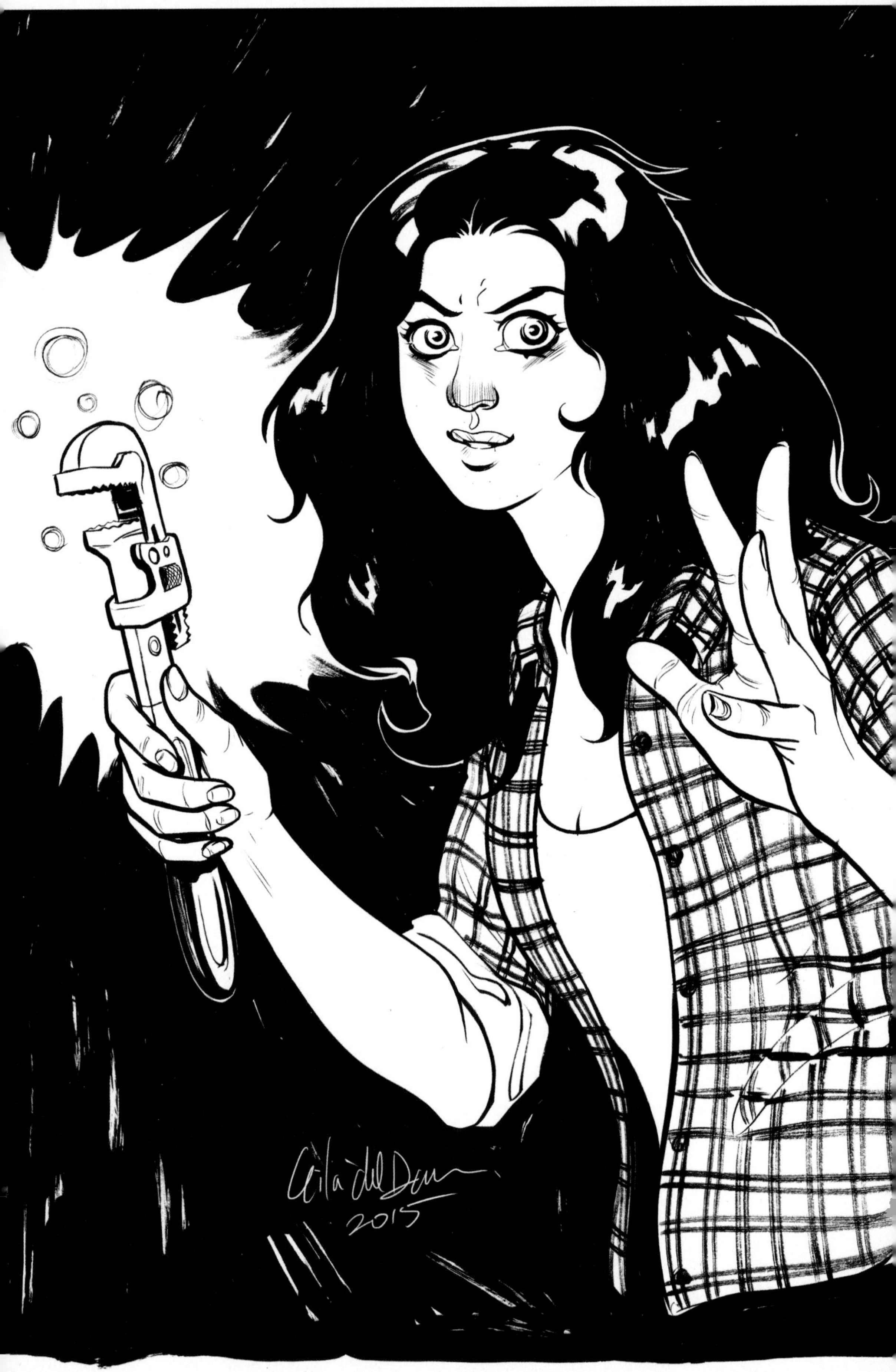

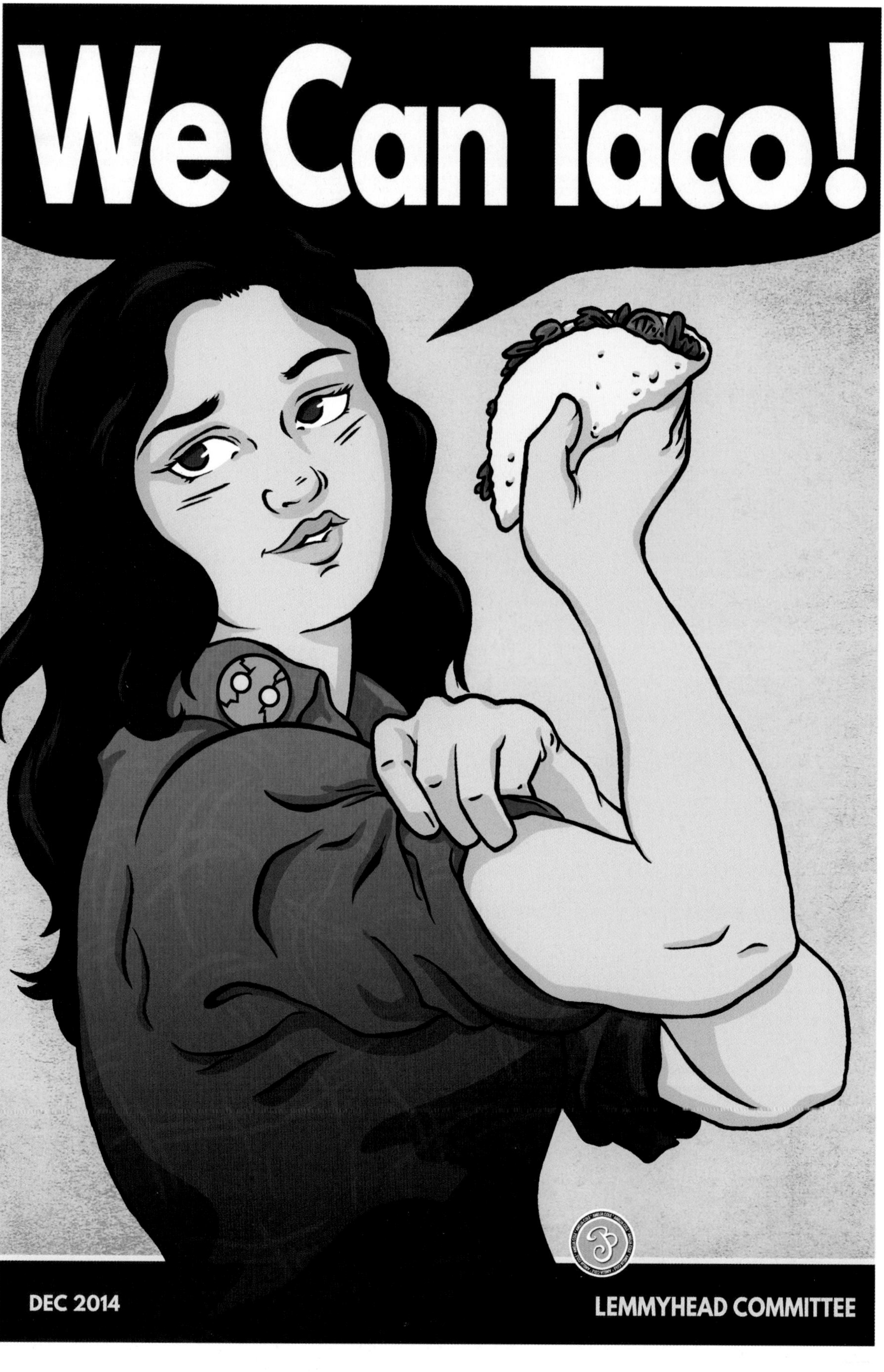
We Can Taco!
DEC 2014
LEMMYHEAD COMMITTEE

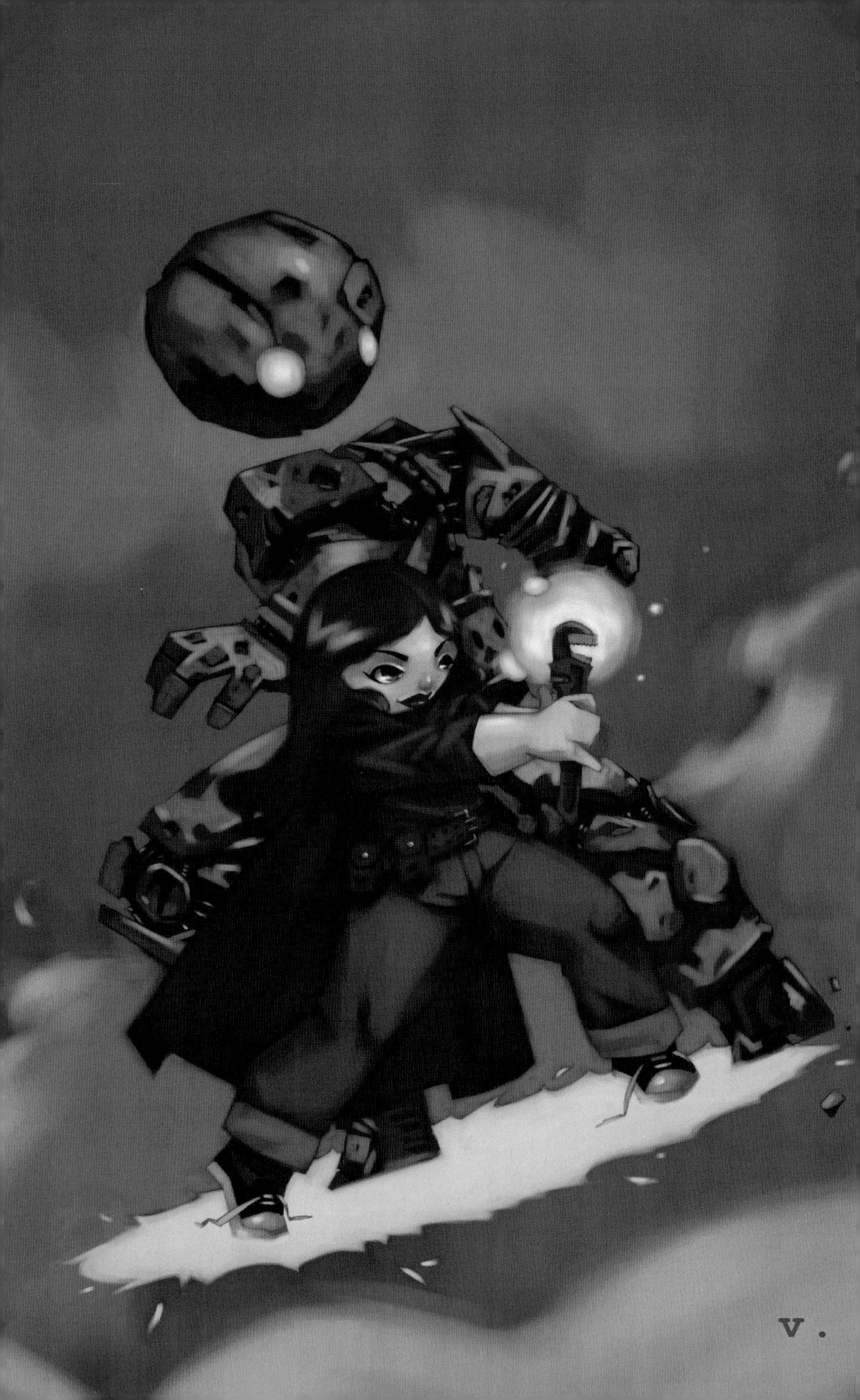
V.

SKETCHES + EXTRAS

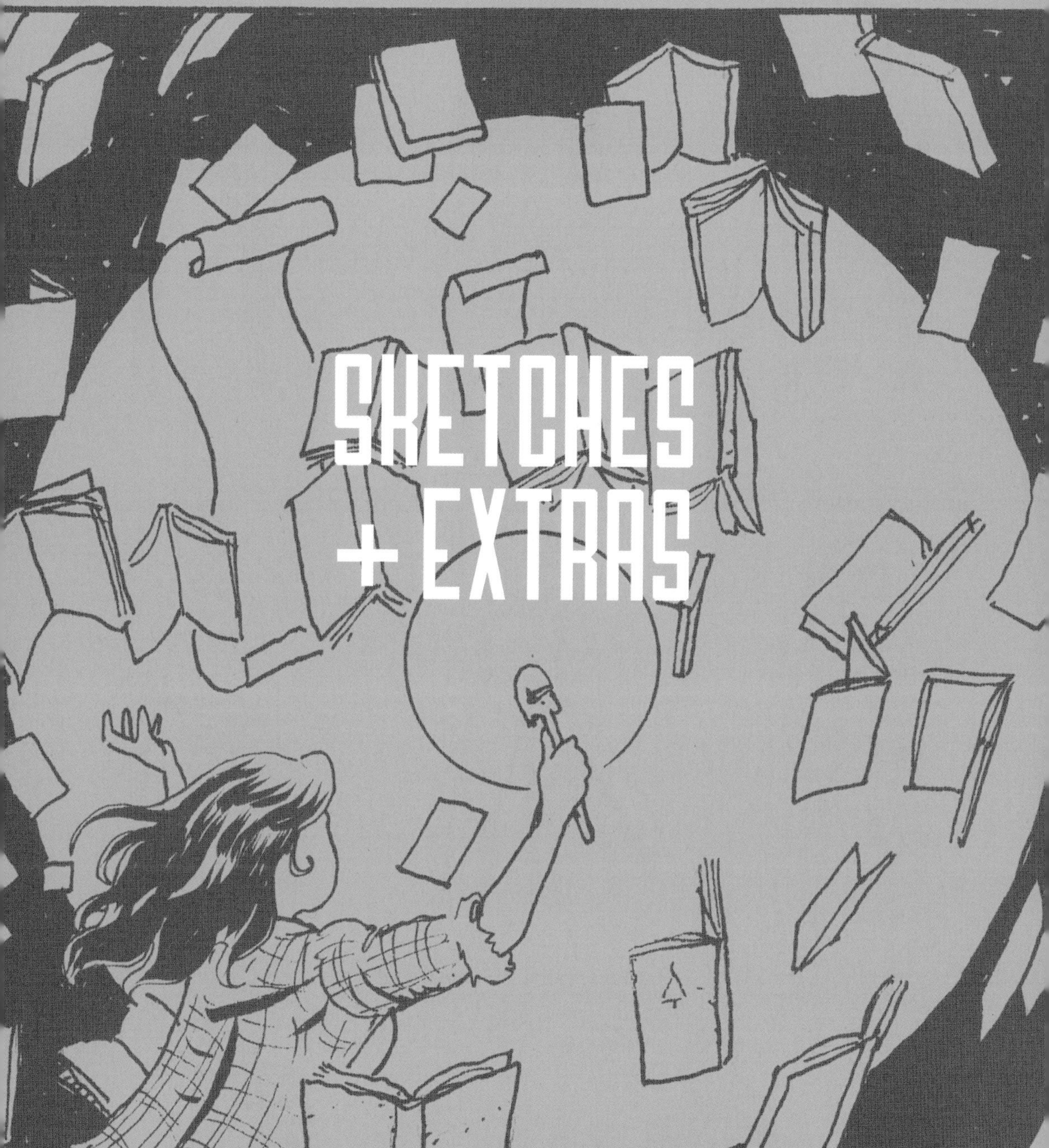

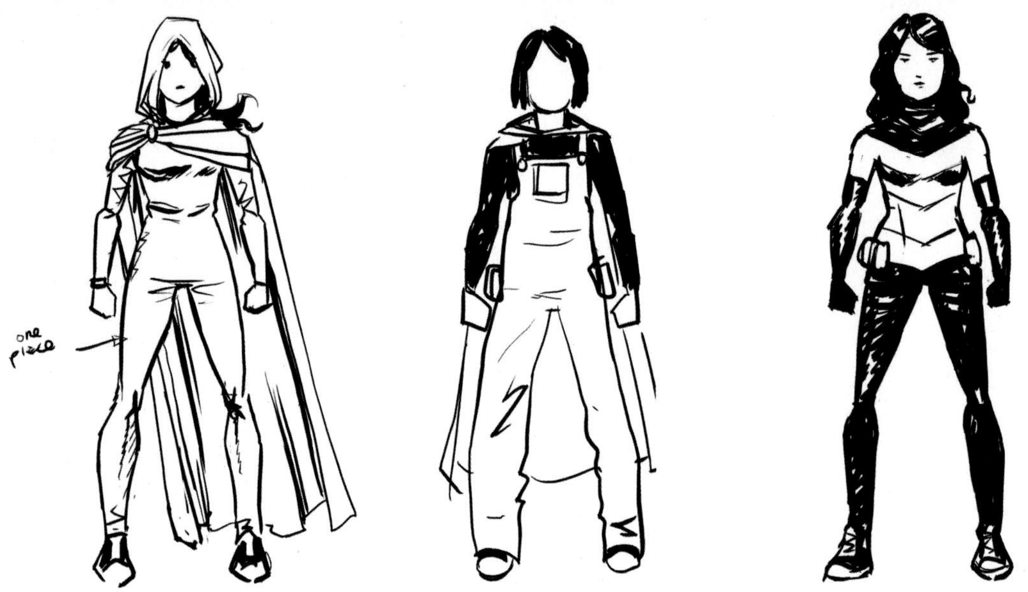
one piece

NICK'S ALTERNATE COSTUME DESIGNS FOR AMELIA

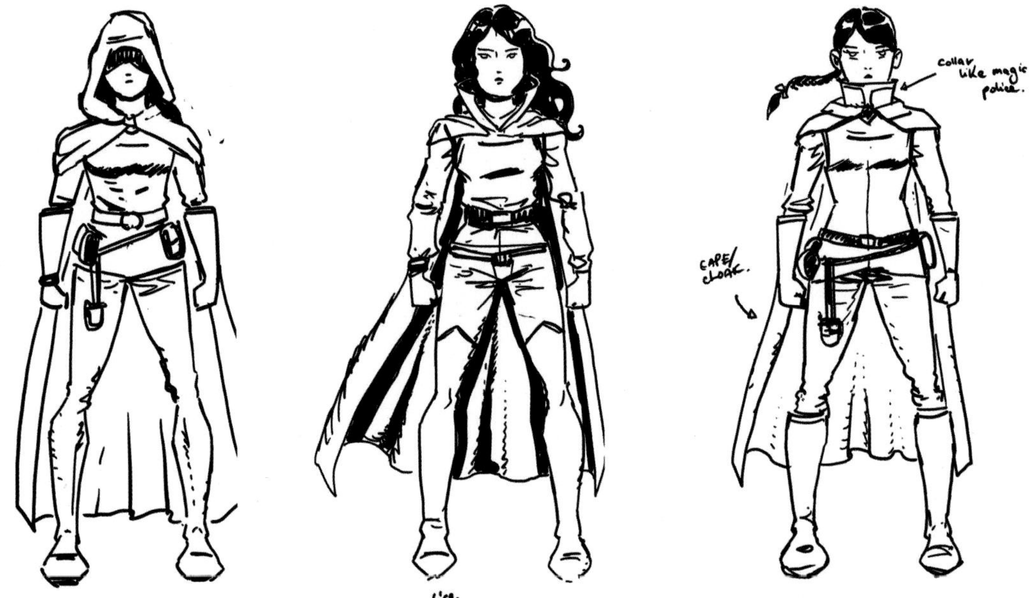
collar like magic police.
cape/cloak.

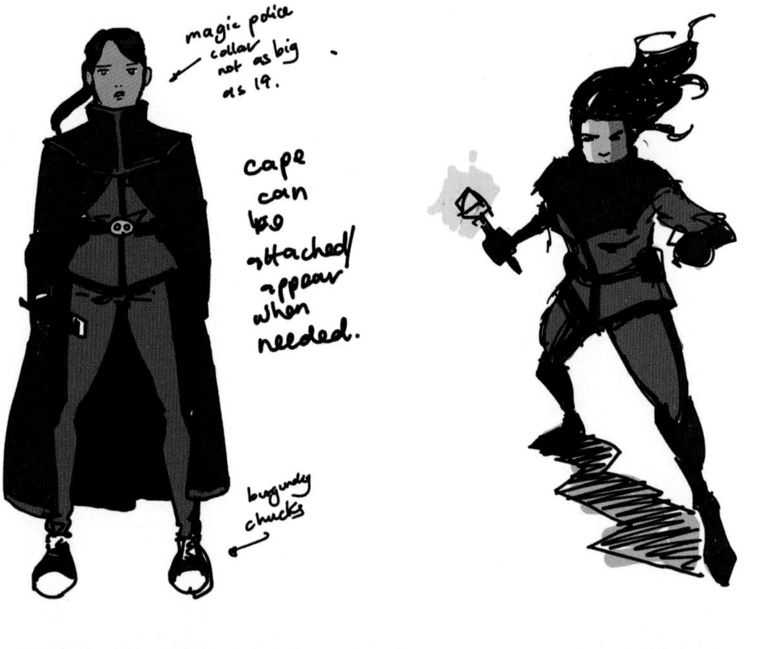
magic police collar not as big as 19.
cape can be attached/appear when needed.
burgundy chucks

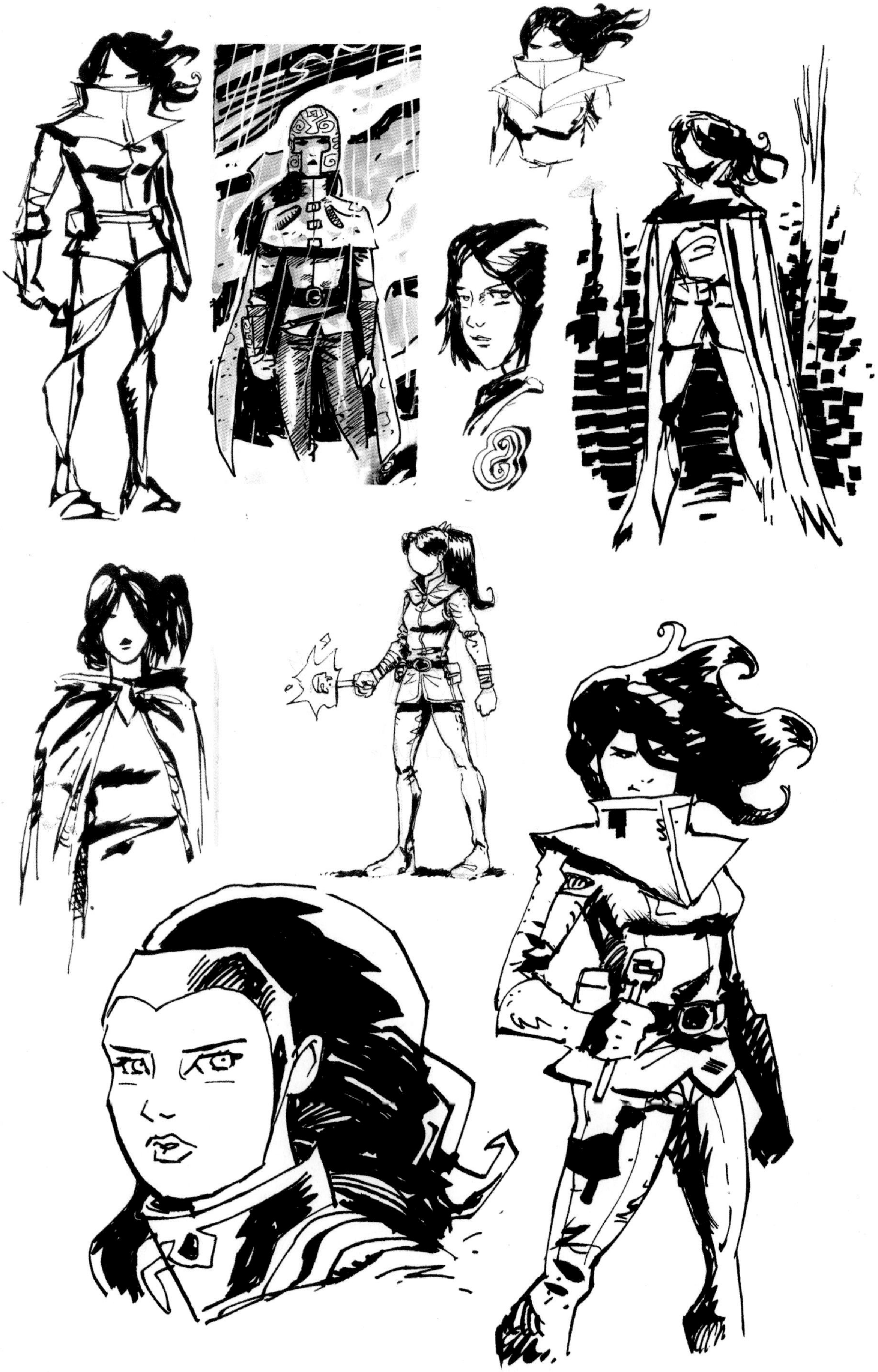

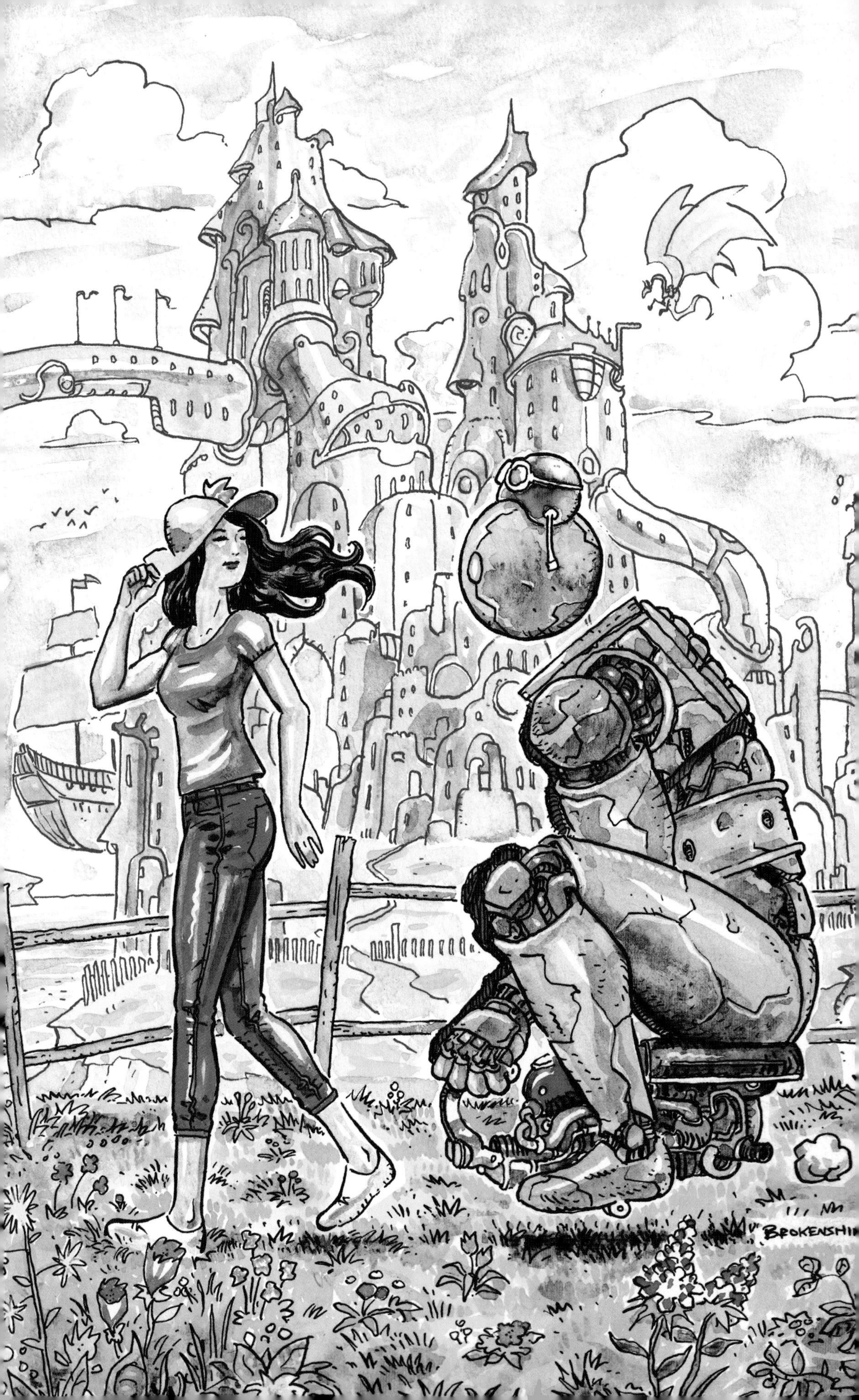
BROKENSHI

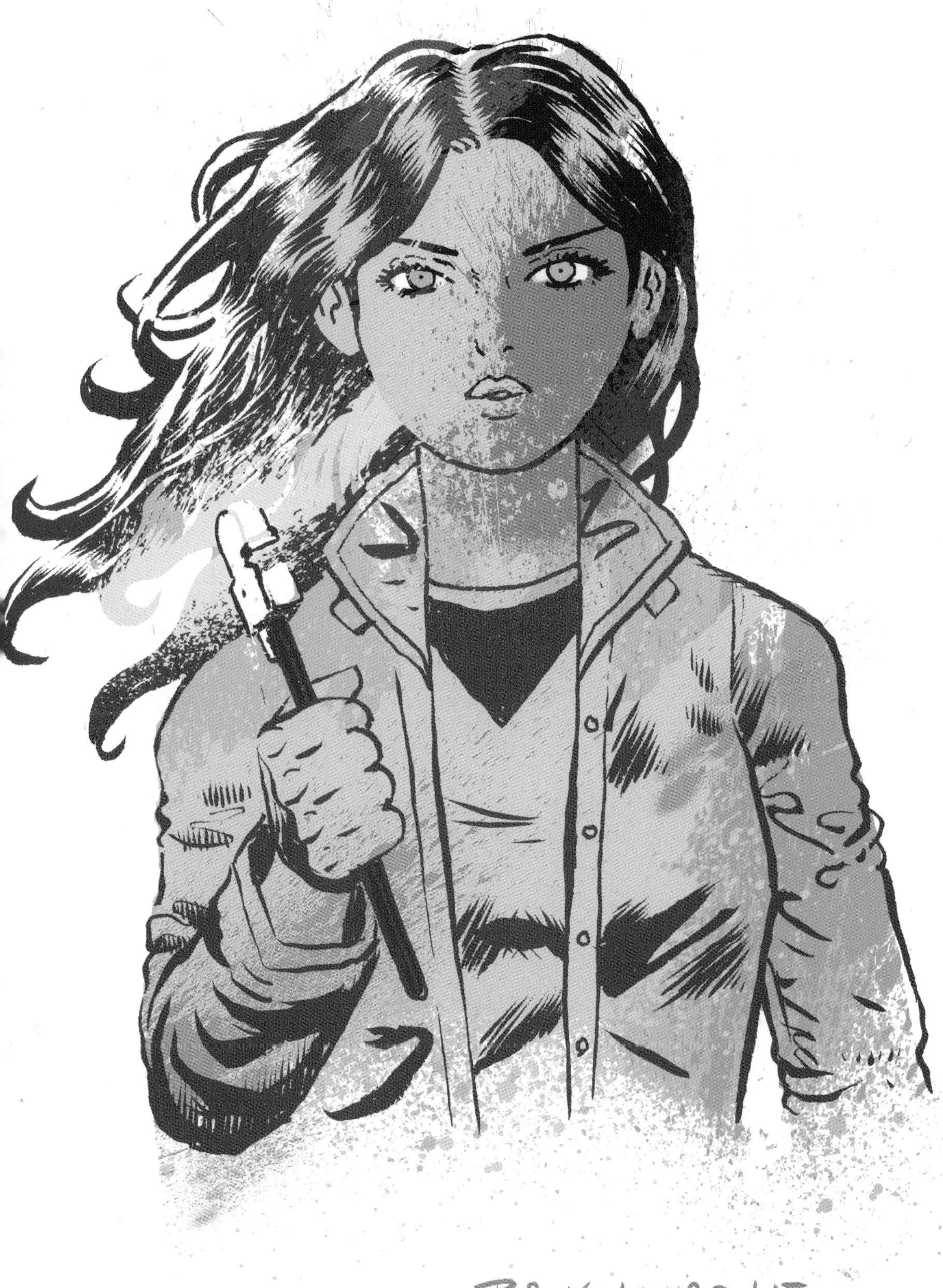
BROKENSHIRE '15

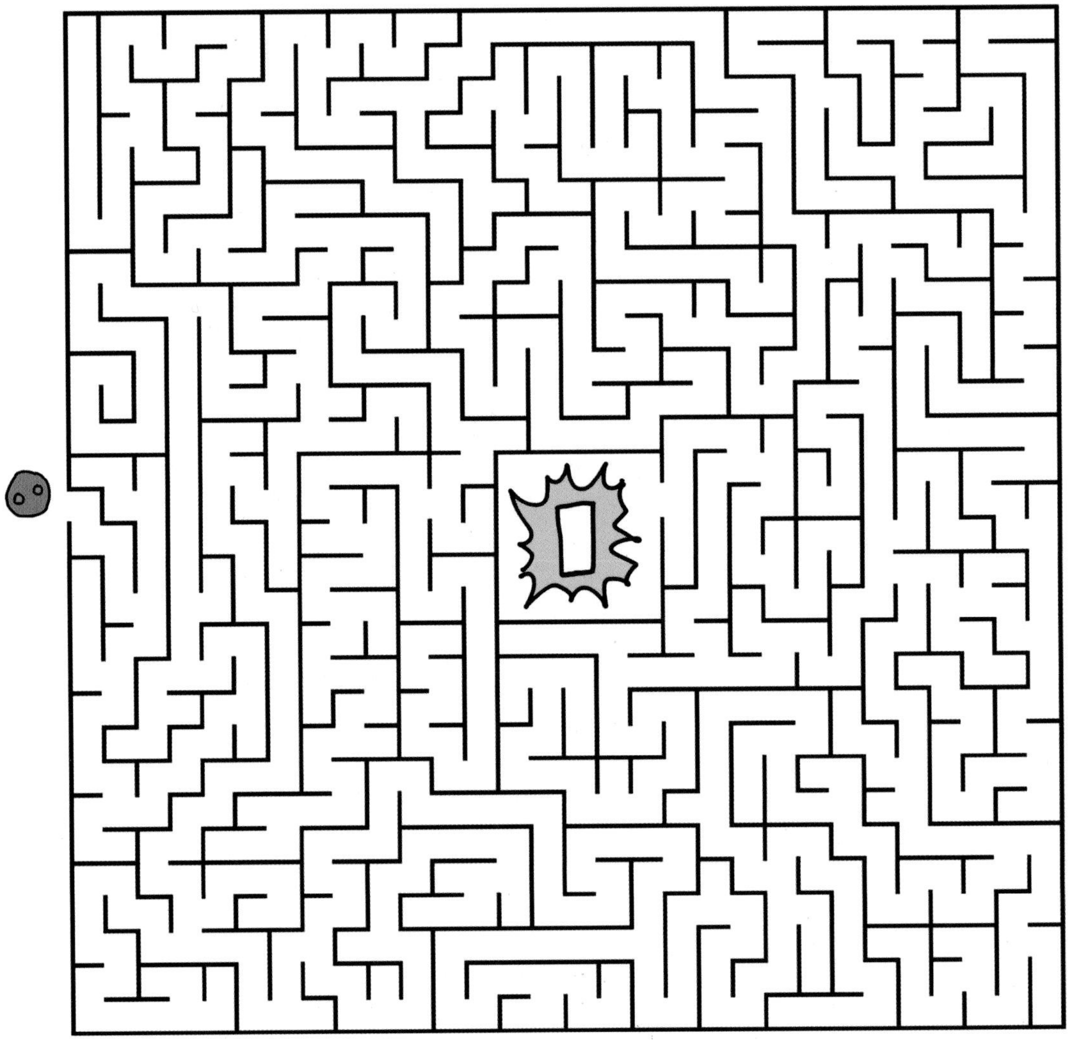

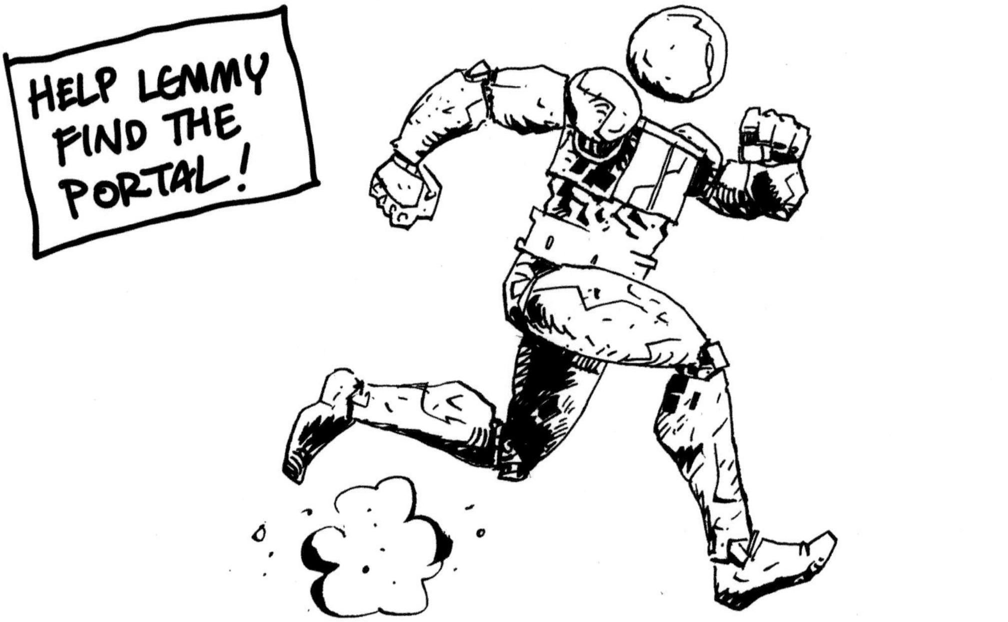
HELP LEMMY FIND THE PORTAL!

WORDSEARCH

```
K G V Q L L W A Z L Q R J E Y
A R U A L P E I A H T R G Y J
R J P K F E T L H J Q R M E S
H S E L Y O A E W N O M D J J
J S M V X O R M S E E B U Y N
A J A M O W T A G L N L D S Q
X G O O T E S U M D R R B L M
K B P C C W I R M I A B R J E
E U C T H E G F H H K I A W O
K Y B Z A Z A Q R E Y E I I M
R T B E P B M A G Z C C D N A
R E J A R A B S Y N F T S A L
P X N P Q T V A W Q R Q O D O
W K C E Z G J N F Q I H I R N
M A D D I E W Z C T A B C M E
```

AMELIA
BARHARDY
DANI
GEORGE
HECTOR
KUBERT
LAURA
LEMMY
LESH
MADDIE
MAGISTRATE
MALONE
MIKE
SANZ

Brok'15

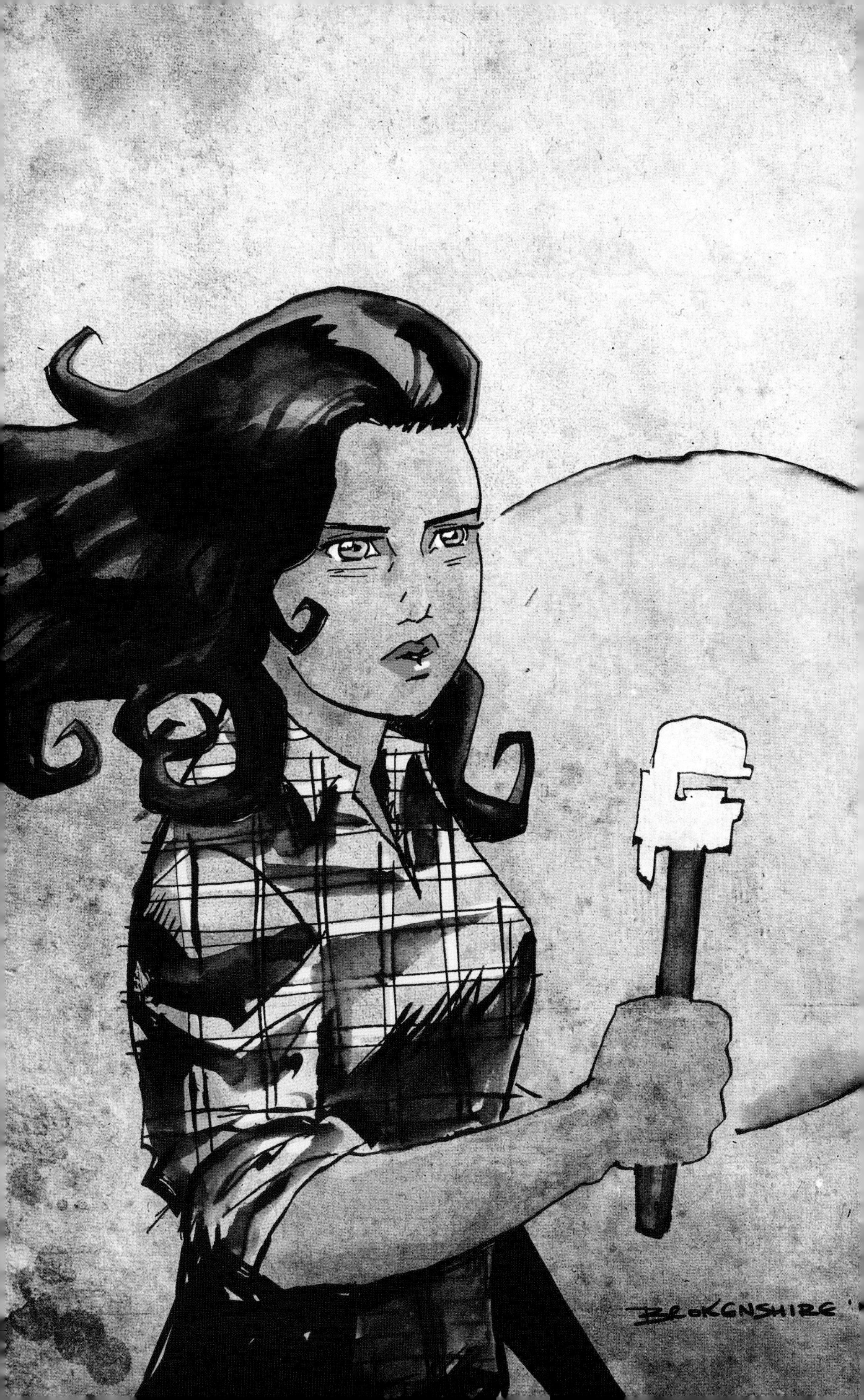
BROKENSHIRE

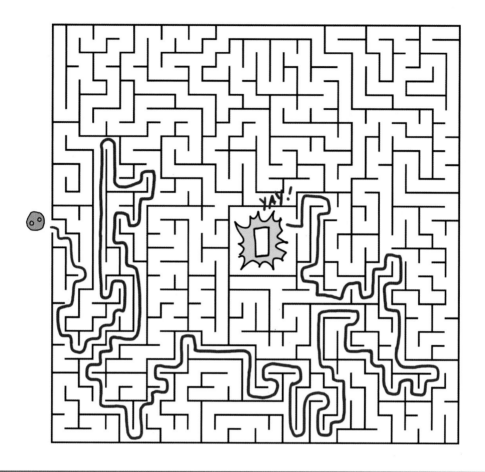

AMELIA
BARHARDY
DANI
GEORGE
HECTOR
KUBERT
LAURA
LEMMY
LESH
MADDIE
MAGISTRATE
MALONE
MIKE
SANZ

K G V Q L L W A Z L Q R J E Y
A R U A L P E I A H T R G Y J
R J P K F E T L H J Q R M E S
H S E L Y O A E W N O M D J J
J S M V X O R M S E E B U Y N
A J A M O W T A G L N L D S Q
X G O O T E S U M D R R B L M
K B P C C W I R M I A B R J E
E U C T H E G F H H K I A W O
K Y B Z A Z A Q R E Y E I I M
R T B E P B M A G Z C C D N A
R E J A R A B S Y N F T S A L
P X N P Q T V A W Q R Q O D O
W K C E Z G J N F Q I H I R N
M A D D I E W Z C T A B C M E

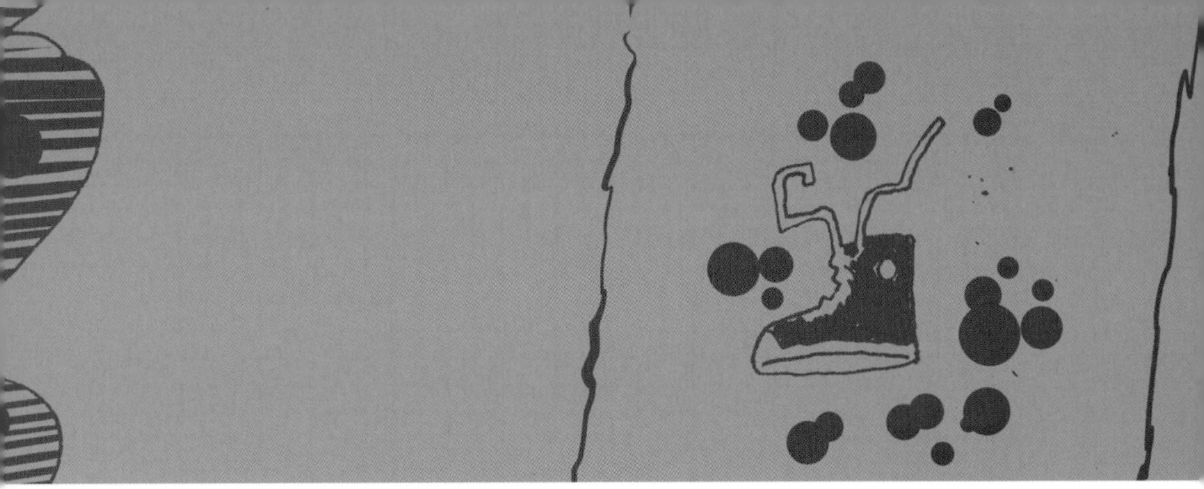

Adam P. Knave is an Eisner and Harvey award-winning editor and writer who co-writes *Amelia Cole, Artful Daggers* (with Sean E. Williams) and *Never Ending* (with D.J. again, those two, man, inseparable). He edits Jamal Igle's *Molly Danger*, Sam Read's *Exit Generation*, and was one of the editors on Image's *Popgun* anthology series. He also writes prose, short comics, and edits all sorts of things. He recently moved to Portland, OR after spending his first 38 years in NYC.

Follow him on Twitter **@AdamPKnave**

D.J. Kirkbride

In addition to *Amelia Cole*, D.J. Kirkbride co-wrote the Dark Horse Comics superhero mini-series *Never Ending* and wrote *The Bigger Bang*, a cosmic space opera from IDW Publishing. He won an Eisner and a Harvey as an editor and a contributing writer for the *Popgun* anthologies from Image Comics. He's also co-written stories for *Titmouse Mook* volume 2, *Fireside Magazine* issue 1, and *Outlaw Territory* volume 3. He lives in a land of great weather and terrible traffic with his wife and their two gray cats.

Follow him on Twitter **@DJKirkbride**

Nick Brokenshire is a freelance artist who grew up in Scotland and now lives in the North of England with his wife, Victoria. In addition to the *Amelia Cole* series, Nick is working on *Power Trio* with writer Alex Paknadel. He can be heard chatting about geek-related nonsense with some pals on the international smash hit podcast Droppings Science, as well as playing in his two bands: Los Vencidos and Blues Harvest.

Follow him on Twitter **@NickBrokenshire** and *Nick Brokenshire Comics & Illustration* on Facebook.

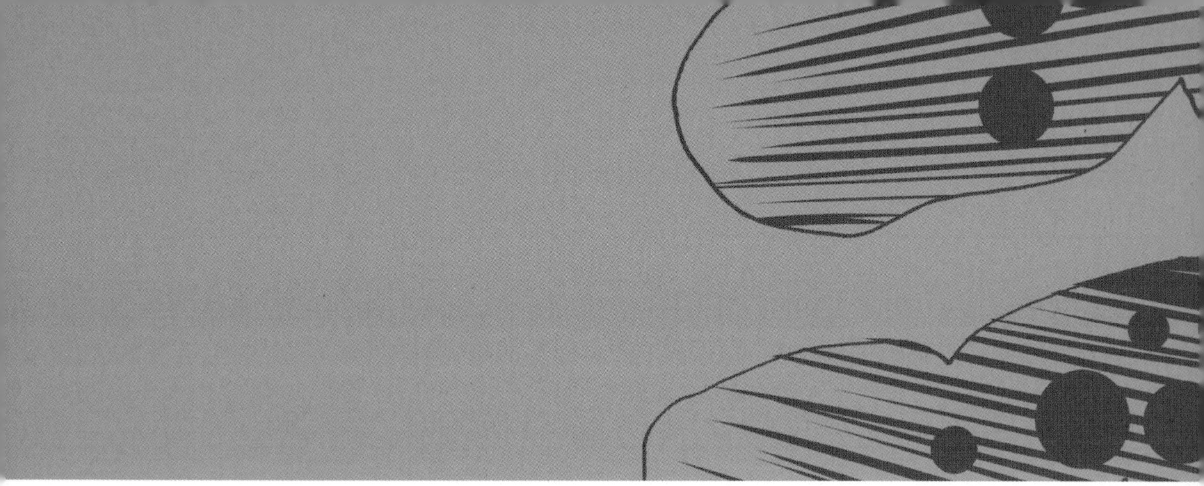

Rachel Deering is a vampire. No! A werewolf! She's a vampire-werewolf-witch who lives in a creepy old house... castle on the edge of town. Of all towns. She spends her days conjuring letters and weaving spells to try and make herself rich and famous. She does not enjoy windsurfing or long walks on the beach.

Follow her on Twitter **@RachelDeering**

Frank Cvetkovic is a comic book letterer whose work has appeared in *Artful Daggers*, *DRIVE*, Jamal Igle's *Molly Danger*, and *The Bigger Bang*. He currently lives in Cleveland, OH, where the home teams never win and the rivers occasionally catch fire.

Follow him on Twitter **@GoFrankGo**

Dylan Todd is a writer, art director, and graphic designer. When he's not reading comics, making comics, writing about comics or designing stuff for comics, he can probably be found thinking about comics. He likes *Star Wars*, mummies, D-Man, kaiju, and 1966 Batman. He's the editor of the *2299* sci-fi comics anthology and, alongside Mathew Digges, is the co-creator of *The Creep Crew*, a comic about undead teen detectives. You can find his pop culture and comics design portfolio at *bigredrobot.net*.

Follow him on Twitter **@BigRedRobot**

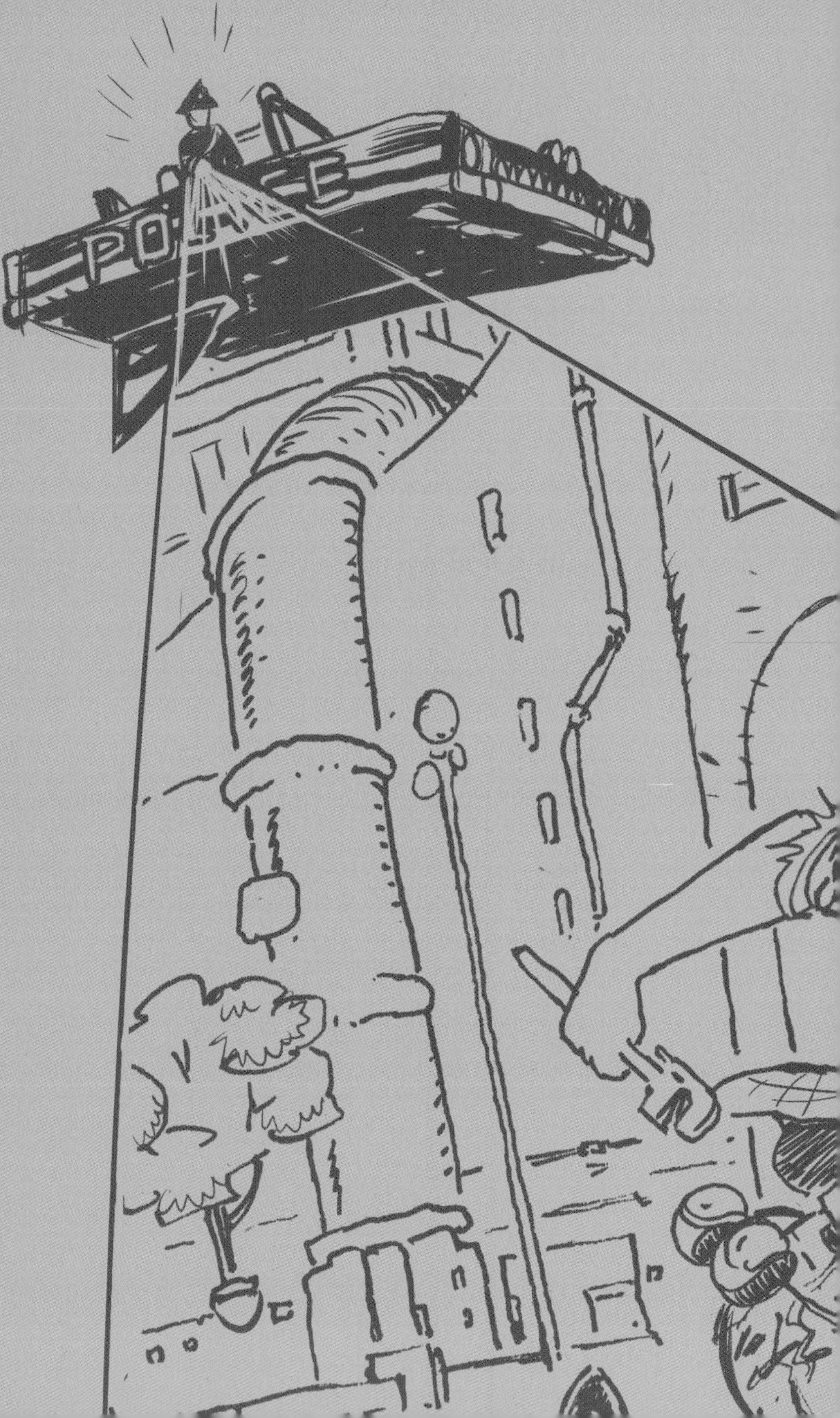

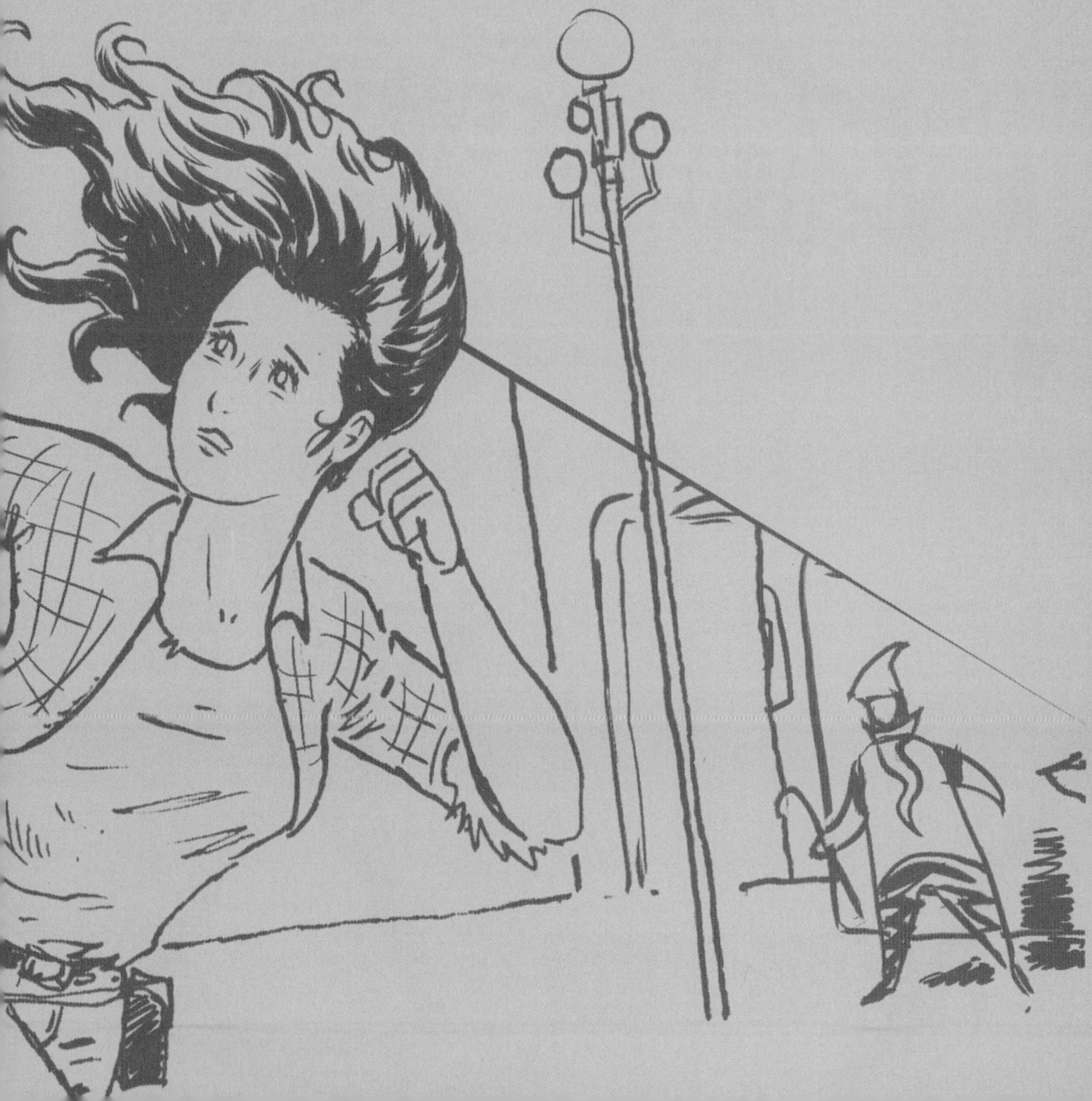

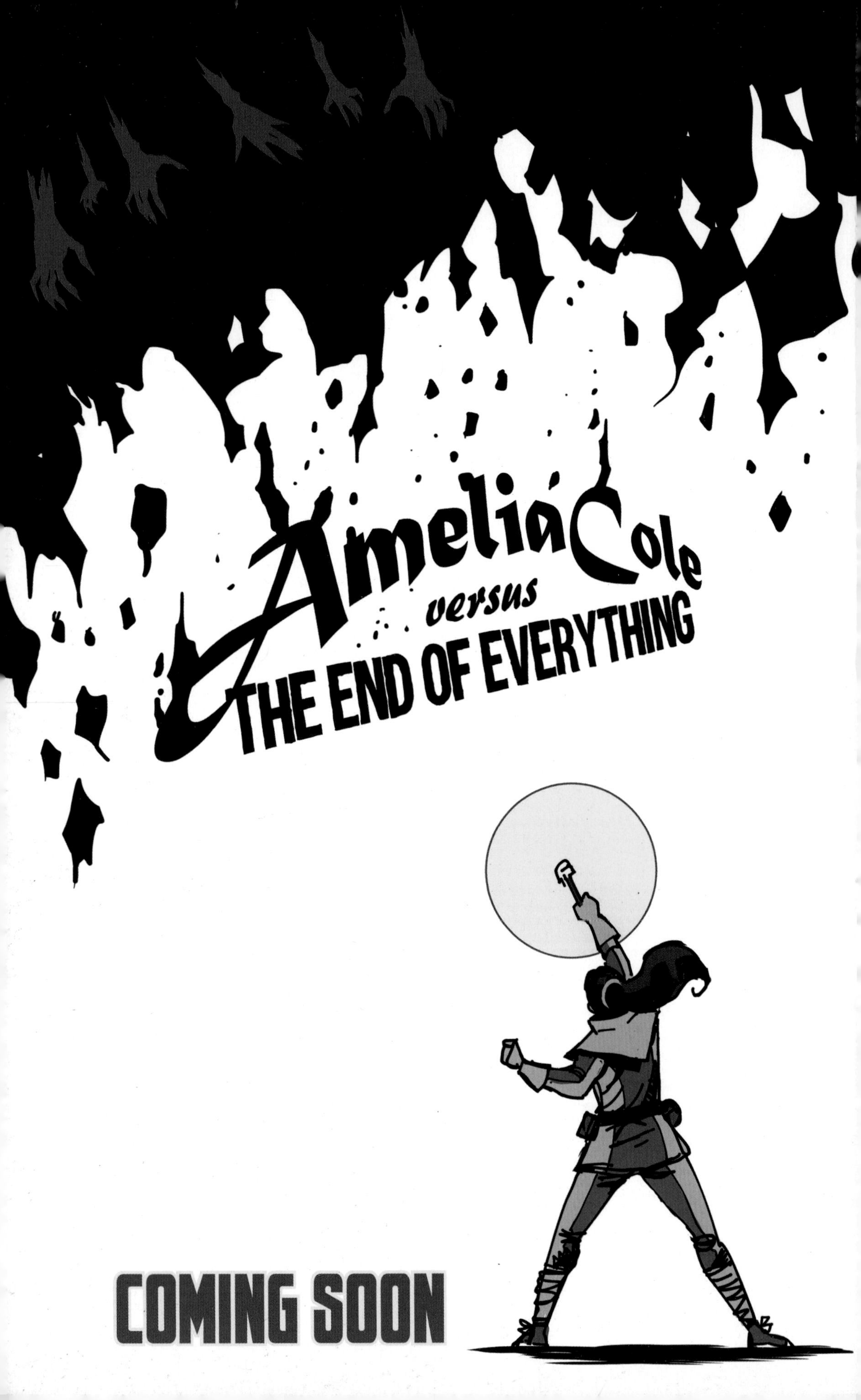
Amelia Cole
versus
THE END OF EVERYTHING
COMING SOON